MANUAL FOR YOUTH WORKSHOPS

ALTERNATIVES TO VIOLENCE PROJECT

Distributed Nationally By:
AVP Distribution Service
1050 Selby Ave
St. Paul, MN 55104
(888) 278-7820

MANUAL FOR YOUTH WORKSHOPS

ALTERNATIVES TO VIOLENCE PROJECT

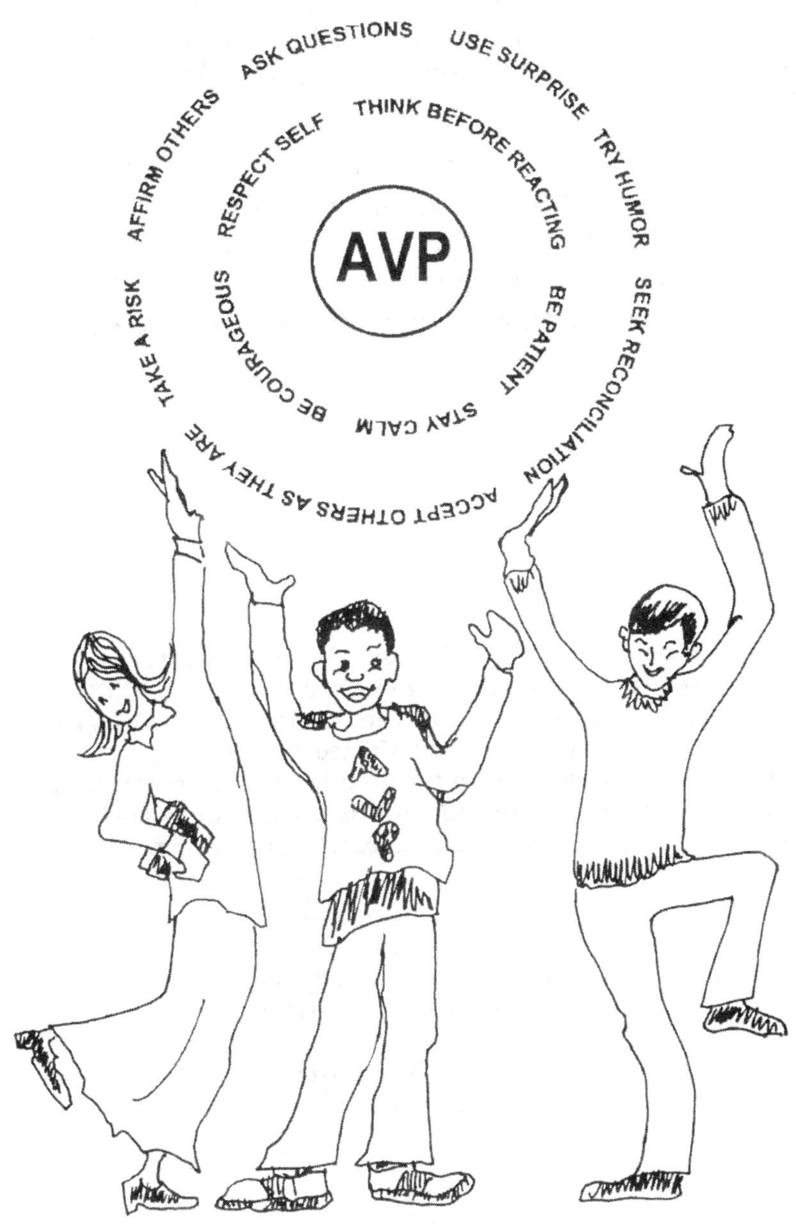

ACKNOWLEDGMENTS

This youth manual is the work of many dedicated, talented and generous AVP people who have created and contributed to the exercises and ideas that it contains, and to the others who have done the organizing, typesetting, formatting, copy reading and editorial work. Every one of their contributions counts, not only for its intrinsic value, but for their love of AVP and their desire to bring AVP to our young people. We wish to acknowledge them here with deepest gratitude.

- Material was adapted with permission from Friends' Journal.
- Exercises were adapted with permission from New Society Publishers for:
  Playing With Fire: Conflict Resolution for Young Adults by F. Macbeth and N. Fine.
  The Friendly Classroom for a Small Planet: A Handbook on Creative Approaches to Living and Problem Solving for Children by P. Prutzman, CCRC, L. Stern, M Burger, and G. Bodenhammer.
- We thank Joanne and Tom Truitt for many of the cartoons used throughout the manual.
- We thank Jennifer Snow Wolff for suggesting the layout of the section dividers. Cover artwork used with permission, © Copyright Jennifer Snow Wolff 1989.

Special gratitude is offered to the memory of Marge Zybas, who facilitated over 1000 AVP workshops in her lifetime, who was one of the first people to lead youth workshops, and whose spirit has been a model for all.

Distributed Nationally By:
AVP Distribution Service
1050 Selby Ave
St. Paul, MN 55104
(888) 278-7820

PREFACE

Few people today remain unaware of the rise of crime among our young people. Even the youngest of them are increasingly exposed to — if not directly involved in — unimaginable and unspeakable incidents. Those of us who believe there must be a way to alter the climate of violence that surrounds and engulfs our children have been hard at work creating and developing a variety of programs focusing on violence prevention. One of these programs is the Alternatives to Violence Project's (AVP) Youth Work.

The "work" has an interesting history. Borrowing from materials used in the Civil Rights movement of the 1960's, the *Children's Creative Response to Conflict* created an approach to conflict resolution for use in New York City schools — initially for elementary students. In the mid-seventies these materials and others were used to develop an AVP workshop for use in prisons. Now in the 1990's, largely at the urging of inmates who wished they had learned more skills and alternatives when they were younger, workshops have been developed and are being offered to young people in a variety of settings.

INTRODUCTION

Dear Reader,
Welcome to AVP youth work! This manual has been written for people who have done the three levels of AVP workshops (Basic, Advanced, and Training for Facilitators) and who wish to help facilitate AVP workshops for young people.

Usually workshops with a large proportion of young people are livelier than those involving only adults. Workshops that are set up with schools in "school time" often present challenges different from those offered in the general community. One thing is certain, workshops involving youth, as one facilitator put it, "aren't boring!"

This manual attempts to give you a taste of youth work. To appreciate the full flavor, as with any AVP endeavor, you must experience it! We hope these suggestions will be helpful as you prepare.

What follows may be read selectively. But if you read it all, the overall picture will be clearer.

So, Are Youth Workshops Unique?
Yes and no (or, no and yes)!

The structure, style and general content of the workshop is pretty much the same as an adult workshop. The fundamental approach is still:

EXPERIENCE FIRST; DISCUSSION SECOND!

But many youth have trouble handling lengthy discussions and long periods of sitting. Young people appreciate variety, movement and color (e.g., bright agendas and posters), and hands-on activities with physical "stuff." In this manual some re-styling has been done to both agendas and exercises to better meet the needs of youth.

Key Concepts
The following AVP concepts seem to be especially relevant to young people and those who work with them:

Affirmation, respect and communication, which provide a foundation.

Experiencing cooperation, which invites everyone to examine the emphasis on competition in our lives.

Sharing perceptions, which leads to better understanding.

Awareness of our ability to make choices, which can open up new horizons.

Distinguishing when we are and aren't responsible for situations, which can help us respond rather than react.

Being open, which can give us the power to transform a situation so that it ends with a Win/Win outcome.

Be Forewarned - AVP Is Not a Quick Fix
Establishing a long-term youth program and especially a school-based AVP program takes time. School personnel have super-full schedules. They may be able to help, but they can't be expected to take over the program. It is hoped that parents and other community people will see the value of AVP and be willing to carry on. This won't happen overnight. It will probably take from three to five years or more. A "long haul" strategy is definitely required.

Our Hopes - Our Vision
Working with young people has strengthened our faith in them and our commitment to their well-being. We are honored by the trust and respect they have shown us and we marvel at their energy, spontaneity and intelligence, all amidst a society that does too little to provide them with a safe and secure passage to adulthood.

Our hopes are challenging. We dream of communities in which everyone respects everyone else. We imagine schools as centers of empowerment.

Will it happen? Who knows? It will certainly take patience and persistence. But why not dream BIG!

Trust the Process
Much of what is included in this manual may be open to interpretation, variation and extension. Feel free to make it your own, while maintaining the integrity of the AVP experience.

And now, read on! Carry on! Enjoy!

TABLE OF CONTENTS

SECTION A

HOW TO USE THIS YOUTH MANUAL

General Information
AVP Terms and Ways
AKA List
(Exercises with more than one name)

How to Use this Youth Manual
How to Use this Youth Manual
How to Use this Youth Manual
How to Use this Youth Manual
How to Use this Youth Manual
How to Use this Youth Manual
How to Use this Youth Manual
How to Use this Youth Manual
How to Use this Youth Manual
How to Use this Youth Manual
How to Use this Youth Manual
How to Use this Youth Manual
How to Use this Youth Manual
How to Use this Youth Manual
How to Use this Youth Manual
How to Use this Youth Manual
How to Use this Youth Manual
How to Use this Youth Manual
How to Use this Youth Manual
How to Use this Youth Manual
How to Use this Youth Manual
How to Use this Youth Manual
How to Use this Youth Manual

GENERAL INFORMATION

This manual has been created for AVP facilitators interested in doing AVP Youth Workshops. It is divided into sections, as are other AVP manuals. The section letters precede the titles in the Table of Contents. The pages of each section are numbered.

Not as much detail has gone into the background material of AVP as is found in the Basic AVP Manual. It is hoped that facilitators using this manual already have a Basic Manual and hence have access to its introductory information, which is rich in content, particularly about the philosophy and process of AVP.

To start, you may wish to leaf through the entire manual to get a general idea of what each section and subsection contains. Section B gives some general suggestions for setting up youth programs, particularly in schools, and a rough idea of how a variety of youth programs are set up. The first subsection of section C is for all facilitators, and the following four subsections of section C are for facilitators who plan to set up a Youth Program.

Section D has sample agendas for different workshop Levels I or II, (or Basic and Advanced as they're referred to in this manual.) Section E has sample agendas for mini programs for elementary and middle schools.

Many of the sections and subsections have some introductory material which explains the contents of its particular section or subsection. For example, **D. Workshop Agendas** starts with Introduction to Workshop Agendas. In **F. Agenda Fundamentals with Their Exercises**, each of the subsections has its own introduction. Each of the subsections in section F contains exercises. If an exercise is in one of the sample agendas and you don't find it in the section **G. Exercises**, look in one of the subsections of section F.

Most accompanying material pertaining to particular exercises is found immediately after the particular exercise. In section F, some accompanying material may pertain to several exercises in their subsection and are placed at the end of their subsection.

Almost all of the activities mentioned in the sample agendas are described in an exercise format. It is hoped that this consistency will make it easier for new facilitators and facilitators who do not facilitate very often. (This is often the case with school staff and student facilitators.) The evaluations and gatherings are the only activities which are not formatted as exercises, except for some special "named" gatherings, such as Mirror Circle.

Sections F and G contain exercises other than those listed in the sample agendas. Section H contains L&L's other than those listed in the sample agendas. It is expected that people will be setting up their own programs and planning their own agendas. People can pick and choose which exercises they wish to use.

Section I deals with standard agenda items, and Section J contains resources.

AVP TERMS AND WAYS

Most of the AVP terms and ways used in this manual will probably be familiar to most AVP facilitators. Below are brief explanations of some special ones.

TERMS:

"clinic" — This is a term called when facilitators have a brief question to discuss. When the term is called, facilitators may gather/huddle in the middle of the circle to decide (or discuss openly from their seats) what to do about what ever has come up. (e.g., it might be a matter of time getting short.)

"fillers" — These are exercises to keep in mind in case you end up with excess time.

"go-around" — This is the process of going around a circle giving each person in the circle a chance to speak about a particular subject. (This has been called a "whip" but the term "whip" seems less user-friendly than "go-around.")

"hurricane" — When someone calls "hurricane", everyone gets up and changes seats. This is a good energizer. It's also a way of mixing people up. (*Note: If you wish to have friends who are sitting together in the circle end up in different smaller groups, don't call a "hurricane." Counting off will separate them more effectively.)*

"self talk" — This is consists of encouraging words or phrases one might say to oneself, e.g., "easy does it" or "I can handle this." Sometimes the phrase is repeated over and over.

WAYS:

"forgot sign" — Draw the side of the index finger of either hand across the forehead. This is the sign language sign for "forgot." It can be used to remind someone that they forgot to identify themselves with their adjective name before speaking.

"popcorn style" — This refers to a process where people respond to a question randomly, rather than going in turn as in a "go-around."

"silent sign" — A facilitator raises an arm. When people see this, they will raise their arm and complete the sentence they're saying. Eventually all do this and silence prevails.

"twinkling" or "thumbs up" — To show that you agree with what someone has said, you can make a ditto sign in the air with two fingers of both hands or you can raise both thumbs in the air. Both give a silent affirmation which doesn't disturb the speaker.

AKA LIST
(AS KNOWN AS)

Many of the exercises in this manual are variations of older versions. Names have been changed with a purpose in mind. Sometimes the wording is more appealing, e.g., ***Wacky Wishes*** for ***Goal Wish Problem Solving.***

Sometimes the wording is changed to open an exercise to more possibilities. ***Lots of Dots,*** for instance, has evolved from ***Colored Dots*** or ***Choosing Groups.*** Using the words "Colored" or "Groups" tend to lead people toward forming groups depending on color. Stating the purpose as "Arrange yourselves as you think best," as is done in ***Lots of Dots,*** leaves the process open to Transforming Power.

The names on the left are the first name given in the exercise format. If a name on the right is mentioned in a sample agenda, its AKA name is given beside it.

New Name	**Original Name**
EXERCISES	
Adjective Name Game Modified	Jack in the Box, What's in a Name
Buttons	Triggers
Concentric Circles	Talking Circles
Co-op Posters	Tool Box
Focusing on V/NV	Brainstorm on V/NV
Mind Bag	Baggage
Paper Bags	Bag Exercise
Power Trip	Power Grab
Territory	Crossing the Line
Two Chairs	Chair Exercise
Wacky Wishes	Goal Wish Problem Solving
Possibilities	Role Plays
L&L's	
Ball Toss	Pattern Ball
Crocodile and Frogs	Alligator and Frogs
Hot and Cold	Listen to the Universe
Sing Fling	Sing and Toss
Vegetable Cart	Ethnic Food Cart, Fruit Cart, Greengrocer, Pizza Pizza, Sneakers or Footlocker
Whass'up Whass'up?	Howdy, Howdy
CLOSINGS	
(High School Name) Crunch	Texas Hug

Developing Youth Workshops
Developing Youth Workshops
Developing Youth Workshops
Developing Youth Workshops
Developing Youth Workshops
Developing Youth Workshops
Developing Youth Workshops
Developing Youth Workshops
Developing Youth Workshops
Developing Youth Workshops
Developing Youth Workshops
Developing Youth Workshops
Developing Youth Workshops
Developing Youth Workshops
Developing Youth Workshops
Developing Youth Workshops
Developing Youth Workshops
Developing Youth Workshops
Developing Youth Workshops
Developing Youth Workshops
Developing Youth Workshops
Developing Youth Workshops
Developing Youth Workshops

SECTION B

DEVELOPING YOUTH WORKSHOPS

Youth Programs in General

Introduction to Youth Programs

Setting the Stage

Arrangements with the School

General Arrangements

Orientation of Participants

Some Specific Youth Program Models

The AViS Program
Audrey Mang and Rae Rosen, AVP Niagara Frontier Council, NY

An AVP/HIP Program
Terry Kayser, AVP Minnesota

AVP in the Classroom
Trace Ocampo-Gaskin, AVP New York City

Community Workshops for Youth and Adults
Tom Truitt
HIP/RAVE, New Jersey

The Portland, Oregon School Program
Jim Williams
AVP Portland, Oregon

Project Planet Peace
Meredith Egan, Marc Forget and Chris Hitchcock, AVP Canada

The Walton Experience
Florence McNeil and Kate Ryan, AVP Catskill Area Council, NY

YOUTH PROGRAMS IN GENERAL

Introduction to Youth Programs

The programs referred to in this manual have been developed in widely varying circumstances. This variety comes about because of many factors and each program has had to adapt to such realities as:

- Is it an urban or rural setting? There is a difference between a large city and a small town in terms of who is acquainted with whom and how well. This might influence how much flexibility the school has to support the program or who in the school is approached first and even what constitutes a "successful" program. For example, the bureaucracy in Buffalo, New York, with 48,000 students in 75 schools, requires a very different approach from that in Walton, New York, with fewer than one thousand students in one central school.
- Large vs. small schools. When students in a big city high school are in an unfamiliar setting, they may be reluctant even to take off their jackets (too many things can "disappear") until some trust is established.
- Timing. Days that can be made available for students to take workshops (3 consecutive days, 3 alternating days, Thursday/Friday/Saturday, etc.).

Decisions will vary on such points as:

- Total number of hours of workshop. Many programs offer workshops limited to three consecutive school days (3 x 6 hours), some offer workshops spread out on a weekly basis, while some provide overnight accommodations for a weekend workshop.
- Certificates and their wording. For example, AViS does not give certificates.
- Orientation. Generally an adult facilitator, sometimes along with student facilitators, does face-to-face orientation with high school student groups; no orientation is done for teacher workshops but background material is supplied.
- Mixing teachers and students. Some programs keep adults to a minimum in high school workshops—only the necessary teacher chaperones (one or two by school regulation). Occasionally AViS has invited three or four parents to an overnight high school workshop with good results. Other programs, like the HIP/RAVE program in New Jersey, encourage a mix of adults and students as workshop participants.

Setting the Stage

In line with the AVP tradition of going where we are invited, it is more useful to express concern and offer help rather than imply, or say, "Boy, do you need AVP!" Some suggestions:

- Going slowly during planning will make things easier later on. It is important to resist moving too quickly, which can be a temptation if we operate in an urgent "crisis" mode. A lot of time may be needed to talk with various groups within the school who may need, or want, to know what's going on. This can include the administration, guidance staff, school board, parents association, health and social workers, probation officers, security, etc.
- Stress to administrators that AVP takes a period of time to effect a change of atmosphere in the school community. It is not a "quick fix," therapy or a list of techniques for breaking up fights but a process of establishing a different environment — one that fosters an attitude of understanding and respect across age and role lines.
- Involvement in AVP doesn't mean we will never "spill the milk" again. We won't suddenly become perfect, but maybe we will spill the milk less often and be able to clean up the mess more quickly.

- Diversity among participants adds to the richness of the experience. A workshop peopled exclusively with needy or "at-risk" students usually doesn't work well. Having students of various ages, backgrounds, genders and cliques interacting with adults such as school staff, parents and general community members begins to break down barriers and broaden everyone's perspective. The process of building respect and acceptance among everyone present really helps build community both within the school and in the surrounding community.
- In mixed workshops a proportion of about fifteen students to five adults works well.
- Participation in AVP is voluntary. People may be encouraged to attend, but mandatory attendance is usually counterproductive, if not outright disastrous. Typically, after one workshop is held in a school, many hesitant students will choose to attend at the urging of their peers.
- However, some models offer a workshop or a shorter program across an entire grade, for example, five different classes in the same grade doing five simultaneous workshops.
- Having three consecutive days for the workshop is best, but sometimes bureaucratically this is not possible. And sometimes more needy participants may find such an intense experience overwhelming.
- It can be very helpful if some school-based person such as a guidance counselor or a caseworker can take an AVP workshop before beginning to make plans for introducing AVP into that person's school. Such a knowledgeable "inside advocate" for the program can be a contact person or liaison (see Arrangements with the School below) and can help set up the program.
- Be sure, as well, to invite other support staff members to every workshop. They can make significant contributions to the group and may gain valuable insights.

Arrangements with the School

A school-based liaison (guidance counselor, physical education teacher, etc.) is needed to take care of arrangements such as:

Scheduling (Time, Place, and Back-up Personnel)

- Different groups have experimented with a variety of time "models."
- Workshops conducted off-site insure confidentiality and avoid interruptions. Suggested locations are a church, fire hall, Mason hall, retreat house, camp. If this is impossible, it is essential that the in-school location be private, quiet and without distractions.
- Some have found it extremely beneficial to schedule the workshop overnight, especially with high school students. This allows time for participants to interact personally in a safe setting without the typical "demands and distractions" of the school day, but **it does require through-the-night supervision.**
- Schools usually must have some faculty or staff member present during the entire time period students are off the premises for a school function.
- An immediate contact for emergency situations (health, extreme discipline, etc.) should be prearranged. A counselor should also be "on-call" for backup. Both of these individuals should be familiar with AVP. Means for contacting them should also be planned.

Lining up participants:

- "Inviting" participants, both older and younger, is a good way to ensure diversity. Some parents may need some direct contact in order for them to understand and accept the purpose and value of the workshop. It is valuable for people to have the right to turn down the invitation. However, in some school systems workshops are offered across an entire grade and students are expected to attend.

- The age span for students probably shouldn't be too wide. For instance, two groups, one composed of grades six through eight and the other composed of grades nine through twelve, will work better than one group covering grades six through twelve.
- You will want a list of all participants who have signed up, which may be surprisingly different from the group which will eventually show up! (You'll learn to deal with this.) Find out who will be responsible for taking attendance.

Informing participants of their responsibilities:

- General school regulations need to be discussed (e.g., hats, smoking). Do regulations pertain to off-campus activities? Students attending workshops at another school need to know and agree to the host school's regulations.
- Students will be required to make up any school work they miss. The students and their parents need to be informed of this. It is important to alleviate teachers' concerns about missed classes.
- Teachers and parents need to know that the school administration supports what the students are doing. The administration might write and distribute a letter to participants' parents and teachers.
- Teachers might be asked to have assignments for participants available before the workshop starts.
- Teachers or others might volunteer to act as mentors for a few students in each workshop to check to see if the students need help catching up with school work.
- Tutoring and "make-up" time might also be pre-arranged.

Setting up orientation time:

- It is helpful to have an orientation time (about fifteen minutes) for students and adults separately. This way you can tune into their different energy and concerns more appropriately. (See "Orientation of Participants," following) Showing a short video of an AVP Workshop might be effective here.

Providing supplies:

- Ask the school to furnish snacks, meals and workshop supplies, such as easel, markers, access to the copy machine and possibly transportation (if the workshop is conducted off-site).

Requesting donations:

- We suggest that you request a donation from the school to cover additional materials (broken squares, tinker toys) and facilitators' expenses (telephone, transportation). Some area councils suggest something in the area of $100 per workshop. Many schools need a written request for such "donations."

General Arrangements:

- Arranging for a team of four or five, with one or two student facilitators, works well. Student participants definitely appreciate student facilitators. Having two young people on the team gives them important peer support. With a team this size, one (adult) member can give extra time to anyone who may need it. (See "Notes for Lead Facilitators," Sect. C)
- Gather materials the school isn't able to supply according to the exercises you decide to use. Using the accompanying, "Packing for a Workshop," (Sect. C) might help.

Orientation of Participants:

It has worked well having separate orientation times for students and teachers/others, several days before the workshop. Most of the information that needs to be covered is the same. "Responsibilities" is about the only area that differs (see below). Points to cover are

Opening:

Welcome them and tell them that you're pleased that they're coming to the workshop. Let them see your enthusiasm.

Introduce yourself, using your full name. Explain that we use first names during the workshop. Afterward, students will have to go back to the more formal way of addressing their teachers and other adults. (Though some adults are a little concerned about this, it doesn't seem to create subsequent problems.)

Participation:

- Say something about everyone being on equal footing during the workshop. We all hope to relate to everyone as a person, not as "teacher" or "student," or "youngster" or "adult." We depend on everyone's contributions to make the workshop "work."
- Explain that they may be interacting with people they don't know well. We hope to establish a safe place where we can get to know ourselves and others better. They might want to imagine, in the time before the workshop, what a "safe place" would be like.

Activities:

- Talk a bit about "experiential." We don't teach classroom-style; we learn together from exercises, games, projects, and discussions. You may want to do the "Paper Bags" exercise as an sample of "experiential."
- Mention casual dress. Workshops are active; comfortable clothes and sneakers are perfect.

Schedule:

- Make sure everyone knows the dates, times, location of the workshop and the need to attend all sessions. Also clarify plans for food and transportation.

Responsibilities:

- **Students:** They should have been informed of the need to make up school work, but it's good to say it again. Smoking regulations are very important to clarify. Making sure all are willing to comply with the regulations avoids complications later.
- **Adults:** Ask teachers to relax while in the workshop and leave the driving to the facilitators, who will maintain safety. This will be done in an AVP fashion, which is different from what's required in a classroom. If they are uncomfortable with something in the workshop, ask them to express their feelings as a "concerned person" rather than as a "teacher," "parent," etc. Explain that you have a back-up person you can contact in an emergency.

Conclusion:

- If they have no questions, thank them for their time and say that you look forward to seeing them in the workshop!

SOME SPECIFIC YOUTH PROGRAM MODELS

The Alternatives to Violence in Schools (AViS) Program, Buffalo, NY

AViS began in 1989 as one response of the Western New York Peace Center (a community-based social change organization) to the increasing level of violence in our community. Our initial goals were to offer Basic workshops to staff members of elementary Buffalo Public Schools (BPS) that had supportive principals and to provide follow-up curriculum strategies for teachers interested in implementing conflict resolution in their classrooms.

About the same time, we facilitated a weekend overnight Basic workshop for a group of 15 year-olds. It was student-initiated and supported by an outstanding teacher who assumed responsibility for all the logistics. We ultimately did two Advanced workshops and a Training for Facilitators with this same group and were able to assign a number of them to teams as we continued providing workshops at that school.

While we have been pleased with individual responses to both student and faculty workshops, it has been a struggle to make any real lasting change in general school climates. As with AVP youth work elsewhere, there were (and still are) many obstacles to long-term in-depth work in schools in Western New York: an already overcrowded time schedule, difficulty finding financial support and good curriculum material plus an emphasis on "standards" that further pressures teachers. Fortunately over the years, the availability of direct conflict resolution resources for teachers has improved tremendously.

We have continued to evolve into a successful, respected program in spite of early disappointments. At this juncture (summer 2000), the AViS program is composed of these elements:

- AVP Basic workshops for **staff members of elementary schools** in Western New York (primarily BPS), usually those with a grade 3-8 population (ages 8-13). We have occasionally done an Advanced workshop for interested faculty members.
- Follow-up work, in after-school sessions as well as individualized mentoring work, with teachers who voluntarily agree to implement a minimum of 20 conflict resolution lessons (45-60 minutes each) in their classrooms during the school year. Such mentoring involves developing lesson plans with a teacher, demonstrating those lessons in the class, and providing whatever backup and support are helpful until the teacher is ready to carry on the teaching alone. (See Elementary School Sample Lesson page E-3)
- AVP Basic/Advanced/T4F workshops for **high school students** (usually starting at age 15-16 **and staff members** who accompany them to an off-site location. Ideally a rural camp with over night accommodations adds a great deal to the experience, but this is difficult and costly to arrange. Usually we are in a local church. We have also done a workshop for **pregnant and new parents** still attending high school (with the same schedule as regular school workshops).
- AVP Basic workshops for **parents/guardians** of children who attend BPS schools, with one or more "reunion" days to continue building a supportive community in which parents can develop trust and increased respect for themselves and others.
- We are very fortunate to have several **bilingual** (Spanish) facilitators who have enabled us to provide workshops in Spanish for parents and high school students who naturally respond more openly and express themselves more eloquently when they have the opportunity to use their first language.

We have come a long way toward reaching our goal of changing school cultures so that everyone can grow and live in a nonviolent community. This could not have been accomplished without the support and resources of the Western New York Peace Center, the vision and enthusiasm of the principals, and the energy and commitment of the teachers involved.
Audrey Mang and Rae Rosen, AVP Niagara Frontier Area Council, NY

An AVP/HIP Program, St. Paul, Minnesota

Getting into a school and to the right (decision-making) person can be the biggest hurdle to establishing a school-based AVP/HIP program. A school contact can ease entry into a new school program — but it does not guarantee that it will be easy. Being a parent of a student helps, as does knowing a teacher, or better yet, an administrator. If you're just starting, it is best to focus on a single school or two rather than broadcasting widely. (You need to think of having enough facilitators if you get lots of requests. And, some facilitators prefer not to work with youth). Be prepared for many phone calls and one-way conversations with answering machines. One alternative might be a custom-made videotape (made by your local AVP group), no longer than 15 minutes, which highlights the program and introduces your youth facilitators. It has the advantage of being a consistent message and available to be shared with many decision makers at their convenience. A mini session would be a further option. One needs perseverance and tenacity in breaking into a school community.

Once you've developed a stable contact, communication is the critical process in moving toward actual workshops. Remember, your contact probably has a dozen or more similar projects s/he is handling — and you have a single purpose. Have patience and be flexible to meet with your contact or other school officials (including parent groups).

Part of that communication will focus around developing details of the workshops. In selecting a location (probably within the school building), inquire what other activities are taking place within the workshop time. In St. Paul, we were competing for space with Saturday tutoring and a local college's in-service program. This required shifting rooms and dealing with a noisy environment. Be conscious of the need for security of the building and participants. Participants from another school will be curious and may wander into areas off-limits during breaks or meals. Establish what school equipment is available (white boards, flip charts etc.) and what you need to provide. Arrange for food and especially snacks. Typical youth are growing rapidly and require frequent snack breaks beside regular meals. Plan for energy-producing foods, including fruit, and avoid junk food (if possible). During guidelines/introduction to the workshop, offer participants the flexibility to get up during a non-active time and get a snack, (if they don't disrupt the group) and can pay attention to what is going on.

Probably the most important and difficult task will be the determination of a schedule for the workshop. Weekends, evenings, one day, two days, three days: that depends on a lot of factors. In St. Paul, we settled on a two-day workshop — Friday and Saturday. Friday we started at 1:30 and went to 10 PM. On Saturday we went from 9 AM to 9 PM. The Friday sessions were short, and each session had a break and at least two L&L's.

Each workshop was a different experience, although other than being aware of the participants' needs for frequent breaks, food/snacks, small talk among participants, very little of the standard AVP workshop was changed for youth. We found that a certain level of distraction had to be tolerated and, when close attention was required, just our mention was enough to put everyone on track. We had adolescent students ages 14-17 from various schools in the workshop, but we also had a staff person participate from each school.
Terry Kayser, St. Paul, Minnesota

AVP in the Classroom, New York City, New York

In the spring of 1994, a group of teachers in a middle school (ages 12-14) in New York City put together the Study Center for Law And Peace which combined a law-related education program with conflict resolution. It was the first time that this was ever put together in this fashion; in many ways it was a response to incidents of violence in the school when the children were harming each other and their teachers.

The program is part of the regular curriculum and the students meet with the teacher three times a week for 40 minutes. The format is similar to an AVP workshop, although, because it is a regular classroom, the model is different in that the material is taught rather than facilitated. Each class begins with an Agenda Preview (listing all the exercises related to the day's lesson), and a Gathering (sometimes writing a paragraph, or just going around the room). Each class ends with an Evaluation, and homework. (Homework might be, "Find a situation at home to apply the specific tools we learned today").

Typically a lesson includes an exercise, for example, on Anger Management such as Triggers (called "Buttons" in this manual) or Sharing a Conflict I Resolved Nonviolently. We include most of the Affirmation Exercises to build self-esteem.

Using Light and Livelies for behavior modification and to reinforce the concepts of Cooperation, Communication, Community Building, Conflict Resolution and Affirmation has been an effective way to teach and to drive home the message that each individual has something to offer the group.

Each person is expected to contribute energy, attention and a willingness to at least hear everything out before rejecting an idea. The right to pass comes with the expectation that the person is participating but chooses to sit out of a particular exercise for whatever reason. The right to pass does not mean you can sit there and do nothing. Students use adjective names with one another, as well as with the teacher in the classroom setting.

AVP is used with 7th, 8th and 9th graders (12, 13 and 14 year-olds). The 7th graders are presented specific skills such as: Brainstorming, Win-Win, Affirming Self and Others, Stress Management, Anger Management, Trust Issues, I-Messages, Decision-Making and Problem Solving Techniques. The plan for the 8th Graders teaches the concept of Consensus and more advanced levels of Communication and Cooperation. The 9th graders get the opportunity to review what was taught in the 7th and 8th grades and then learn about international conflict resolution as they participate in the Model United Nations program. Here they learn the deeper roots of racism and stereotypes and learn to appreciate diversity. At all levels, we work on developing empathy and especially use scenarios where students role play their parents or other authority figures. Meanwhile ALL the students are taught to mediate conflicts. As a result, they are more than capable of training other students to be mediators. They become skilled facilitators.

How has AVP helped? It has helped students to bond with one another. It has given them some options to consider when they are angry, as well as creative ways to deal with the violence in their environments. The students are more articulate, more willing to take a risk to keep the peace and they are achieving their goals. There have been many potentially violent incidents in the school (sometimes involving other teachers or administrative policy) that the students have successfully resolved.

Trace Ocampo-Gaskin, New York City

Community Workshops for Youth and Adults - Burlington, New Jersey

An AVP youth program was started in 1995-6 in a Trenton high school and middle school. To overcome difficulties experienced in scheduling classroom space and staff, and in order to reach a broader and more diverse population from the public and private schools in New Jersey and Philadelphia, a change in format was instituted in 1997. The Burlington NJ Meeting House Youth Conference Center, equipped with eighty-eight bunk beds, large kitchen and large meeting rooms is used on alternate months to house three 18-hour workshops concurrently for a residential community from 30 to 70 teenagers and adults. Any combinations of Basic, Advanced and T4F Workshops are possible on a particular weekend. The workshops are led by volunteers from a pool of youth and adults, which at one point numbered 30 AVP facilitators. Modest stipends are given to facilitators (to help ensure the return of youth facilitators). Workshop agendas and procedures follow the guidelines of AVP and of the HIP Project. The workshops are known as HIP/RAVE workshops: "Help Increase the Peace/Real Alternatives to Violence for Everyone."

The residential feature of this arrangement makes it convenient for people traveling from a distance; thus the community can be very diverse, which always improves the experience for participants. Age diversity is also a goal, so that up to 30% of the participants may be adults (as old as 80!). The three workshop groups mingle at meals and during evening activities, and there are cooperative experiences as participants share the kitchen and clean-up duties. The experience of being away from home is a big factor for many young people. Like a summer camp experience, there are benefits as well as extra challenges for the staff. More activities outside the workshop format must be planned and volunteer monitors are needed at night.

Ideally, each workshop has a facilitator team of two adults, two youth, two females, two males, two minorities, and two Caucasians — in any combination, for a total of 4 or 5. A program oversight committee called Community Peace Trainers (an AFSC Program) provides planning and fund-raising for the program. Grants pay for scholarships for many participants and keep the participant fees as low as $70 per workshop. While networking in faith communities, local publicity and mail-out flyers are effective, paid staff has been needed to market the program to school principals, guidance counselors and teachers. The greatest success has been with community and school groups, who keep returning with more students and who then integrate the AVP guidelines into their own activities.
Tom Truitt, Chestertown, MD

The Portland, (Oregon) School Program

One of the most important ingredients in a school-based AVP program is the support of someone within the faculty or staff. Our most successful high school program (14 to 18 year-olds) is to the credit of the vice principal of the school. She was able to convince other teachers that it was better for their students to be released from class to do the workshop than to attend class. And she had a good enough relationship with the students that she was able to convince a wide range of students to attend the workshop. She became a facilitator herself and also knew that the workshop needed all kinds of students, not just those from the anger management program.

We have used a few variations on the usual weekend format for our school-based workshops: all day Saturday, Sunday and Monday; Sunday, Monday and Tuesday with students excused from class (but not from homework); Thursday evening, all day Saturday and Sunday; Monday, Tuesday and Wednesday. Students are given 1/4 to 1/2 credit for the workshop.

We have always attempted to train students as facilitators, but they do grow up and move on so fast that it has been hard to keep a core of student facilitators. We have found that all youth workshops work fine; but I do think that a few selected adults improve the quality of the workshops. These adults need to be selected; they have to be willing to sit on the floor with students and treat them as equals and to be in the workshop as coequal participants. They have to be willing to share their stories and not be judgmental when students share their own stories. If they are there to supervise or to see what happens or only for the benefit of the students, rather than for their own learning, they can be detrimental to the workshop.

The content differs from community-based workshops very little. We schedule more L&L's (at least one per hour) and more breaks; exercises go faster because students take less time to debrief; debriefing is difficult until later in the workshop. There are some exercises that really work in youth workshops that seem to have less relevance for adults. Two examples are Choices and Consequences and Life Beliefs, both of which are included in this manual.
Jim Williams, Portland, Oregon, AVP

Project Planet Peace, Mission, British Columbia, Canada

This project begins in September when, in order to establish a strong sense of community, we offer a one-day workshop to the entire school: students, teachers, parents, support and administration personnel. Generally there have been 20-30 people who have volunteered to take this one-day workshop. Since this is only one day, we do some explanatory work, as well as some experiential exercises. We generally end the day with an exercise combining "Imaging a New Community" and "Where Do We Go From Here?". As a result, by the end of the day, this community has created its image of an ideal school and determined its priorities for the school year. All decisions are arrived at with a consensus model of decision making, and the principles governing this workshop are the same as those used within student workshops.

In our area, there are many French and English speakers, but we choose not to have separate workshops for different languages. This workshop is offered with simultaneous translations into English and French, as an important part of the group developing a strong sense community, as well as a model for the entire school community.

This is followed the next week with a variety of workshops for the students:

Half day workshops provided for the different age levels with the following focus:
5 year-olds (kindergarten) - Affirmation and Encouragement
6-7 year-olds (first and second grades) - Diversity and Respect
7-8 year-olds (second and third grades) - Conflict and Communication

9-10 year-olds (fourth and fifth grades) - A three-day Basic workshop
Ideally we have 15-20 participants in the workshop, and we prefer to hold it off school grounds, at a local church or community center.

11-12 year-olds (sixth and seventh grades) - A three-day Advanced workshop
This is for those students who have participated in a Basic workshop. The group chooses one or two subjects to cover more fully. The number of participants is limited to 12-16. Again, an alternative setting to the school is preferred.

Follow-up possibilities have included: Monthly mini workshops (sometimes with as many as 80 participants!), a full workshop offered to the entire school community (with total number of participants limited to 20, preferably with some youth participants), a T4F workshop offered to those students who have completed the first two levels, and Advanced and T4F workshops offered to adults in the community.
Meredith Egan, Marc Forget and Chris Hitchcock, British Columbia, Canada, AVP

The Walton, (New York) Experience

In 1993, the first year of AVP at the Walton School, 2 Basic, 1 Advanced and 1 T4F workshops were offered each semester or half school year. Now, in 2000, one Basic and one Advanced workshop are held each semester. One T4F is offered each year.

Basic Workshops for students in grades eight through twelve (13 through 18 year-olds) initially were held on full school days, totaling 16-18 hours. The preferable days were Wednesday, Thursday and Friday; this gave everyone a chance to catch up on work and life before returning to the usual school setting.

Now the Walton school system has adopted a new schedule using ninety minute periods. It is more intense and one subject is covered in a shorter period of time. Missing three days in a row means a student would miss a great deal of work. In 1999 Basic Workshops were scheduled on 3 consecutive Fridays. Now in 2000, a schedule similar to that of the Advanced (see below) is being tried.

Advanced Workshops and T4F's are usually offered on Thursday (noon to 6 PM); Friday (full school day); and Saturday (9 AM - 4 PM).

Many older students, after completing a workshop, suggested that AVP be offered to younger students, 10-13 year-olds. Mini-programs were introduced toward the end of the second year of AVP in Walton, when enough facilitators were available. Having older students on the teams has been and is particularly helpful.

Fifth Grade: The first mini-program is done with 10 year-olds toward the end of the school year. It is an introductory session of about 1 hour, a prelude to the longer program that is offered to them the next year. The program is offered in the corner of a gym to one class at a time, the last period of the day. Doing the program in a location other than the class gives facilitators time to hang posters and set up a circle of chairs, etc.

Sixth Grade: This program for eleven year-olds is run over the course of four days, two periods per day - for a total of about 6 hours. It is scheduled at the beginning of the school year. The program is offered to the entire grade at the same time. It is done with "student advisor groups" which vary in number from 8 to 18 participants. Some staff also participate. Usually two or three facilitators (staff, older students, and community volunteers) work with each group. The first day uses Periods 7 and8; the second, Periods 5 and 6; the third, "advisor" time and Periods 3 and 4; and the fourth, Periods 1 and 2 and "advisor" time.

Seventh Grade: The program presented to twelve year-olds is done in three short sessions over the course of an entire day (about 6 hours). It is offered early in the year, to the entire grade at the same time, in groups of 15-20.

For agendas regarding these three mini programs, see Elementary and Middle School Program Agendas, Section E.
Florence McNeil and Kate Ryan, AVP Catskill Area Council, NY

Facilitator and Team Development
Facilitator and Team Development
Facilitator and Team Development
Facilitator and Team Development
Facilitator and Team Development
Facilitator and Team Development
Facilitator and Team Development
Facilitator and Team Development
Facilitator and Team Development
Facilitator and Team Development
Facilitator and Team Development
Facilitator and Team Development
Facilitator and Team Development
Facilitator and Team Development
Facilitator and Team Development
Facilitator and Team Development
Facilitator and Team Development
Facilitator and Team Development
Facilitator and Team Development
Facilitator and Team Development
Facilitator and Team Development
Facilitator and Team Development
Facilitator and Team Development
Facilitator and Team Development
Facilitator and Team Development
Facilitator and Team Development

SECTION C

FACILITATOR AND TEAM DEVELOPMENT

General Tips and Thumbnail Tips for Facilitators Doing Youth Workshops

Notes and Thumbnail Tips for "Lead" Facilitators

Suggested Agenda for First Team-Building/Planning Session

Suggestions for Giving and Receiving Feedback

Packing for a Workshop

GENERAL TIPS FOR FACILITATORS DOING YOUTH WORKSHOPS

The Aesop's fable of the elephant and the ant seems very applicable for facilitators working on teams for Youth Workshops. The fable tells of an elephant coming upon an ant who is lying on its back with all its feet up in the air. Puzzled, the elephant asks, "What are you doing, ant, lying there like that?" The ant answers, "Somebody told me that the sky was falling and I'm getting ready to hold it up." The elephant scoffs at the ant, "With your little feet, you can't hold up the sky." The ant replies, "One does what one can."

All of us facilitators basically try to "do what we can." Just as participants are voluntary, facilitators volunteer for exercises with which they feel comfortable. And fortunately, since we work as teams, we "do what we can" with others. We don't have to do it alone. We can rely on our team members for help and encouragement.

We do have the responsibility to prepare; just as the ant, we try to be "ready." Being present for team-building and planning is an essential part of "getting ready," particularly since AVP works by consensus, except in very rare circumstances. In fact, if a facilitator isn't able to be present for the team-building and planning, it's probably wiser that s/he not facilitate at that particular workshop.

Studying the procedure of any exercise for which we volunteer is also important. It's also wise to practice the delivery of instructions for exercises in front of a mirror or to another facilitator. Jotting down a few key points and questions on an index card can also bolster one's confidence.

The acronym KISS is particularly apt when working in Youth Workshops —Keep It Short and Simple. But this does require practicing.

In workshops for youth, at least two team members should be experienced. Two or three apprentice facilitators can complete the team. If a couple of these were students, it would be excellent. In evaluations, participants almost always comment favorably on having student facilitators. Having as diverse a team as possible shows that "all sorts" can work together in a positive way.

Working in teams is one of the joys of AVP; it is also one of the ways AVP models empowerment and shows that each of us has something to offer the rest of us. Seeing a team working together, supporting and affirming each other, illustrates this message better than words.

There are a few particular cautions facilitators in Youth Workshops might want to consider. We are not teachers but rather facilitators of an experiential process. The AVP process expects that the wisdom will come from the group. As facilitators we hope to help this wisdom come forth easily. Somehow, whenever young people are around, many of us adopt a teaching mode rather than a facilitating mode. Perhaps we forget that young people have an abundant supply of wisdom.

To help stay in the facilitating mode, remember to sit when giving directions or asking processing questions. Having specific questions in mind for processing is also a good idea. Asking how an exercise connects with real life often draws out hidden wisdom. Asking others to comment on what's been said can encourage discussion. And asking if there's any connection between one exercise and another can lead to an even deeper awareness of the AVP process.

It is important to mention that not all facilitators feel at ease working with young people. For some people, excessive energy can be a distraction. Being comfortable with chaos (the unlimited variety) is essential for those who volunteer to facilitate in youth workshops.

Facilitators may feel a little intimidated facilitating in workshops which include their peers. This may be true for either students or staff, whether the staff be teachers, custodians, secretaries or counselors. If it is made clear in the Opening Talk that facilitators are not there as teachers, that everyone is there as equals and that everyone is there to learn together, it can help alleviate this feeling of intimidation.

When one or more teachers are scheduled to attend an AVP workshop as participants, the lead facilitator might speak privately to them to ask that they take off their "teacher's hats" and enjoy the workshop as participants.

Visualize that ant! Remember, "One does what one can." Kick up your heels and have fun! Get together with other facilitators to share concerns, tips and triumphs or to practice new exercises. Monthly or bi-monthly facilitator support meetings can be a big plus!

Last, but definitely not least, **"Trust the Process."**

Thumbnail Tips

Being a Team Member

Support other team members.
Present a united front.
Clinic between sessions.
Be aware of time.
Be willing to give and receive feedback.

Leading Exercises

Volunteer only for exercises with which you feel comfortable.
Be prepared.
Practice what you'll say.
Be conscious of participants' needs.
Let participants have most of the "air-time."
Ask questions rather than making speeches.
Respect others' opinions.
Remember to ask, "Does the team have anything to add?"
Walk your talk.

NOTES FOR "LEAD" FACILITATORS

The role of a "lead" facilitator involves "chores" but more important is the mind-set—the commitment to AVP values in our lives and to being open to Transforming Power. It's not as much the polished skills that are important as the belief in the good in everyone and the eagerness to let that goodness shine. The spirit of AVP is more critical than the techniques. (Note: some groups chose not to adopt this terminology of a "lead" as it implies a hierarchy)

There are many chores involved in running a workshop. That's what's wonderful about a team. These chores can be shared. If several facilitators are experienced enough, the "job" of "lead facilitator" can be shared. This can lessen the responsibilities of any one person. Probably before setting up any youth workshop it would be wise to have at least two experienced facilitators planning the "set up" together. This being said, the following suggestions are directed toward a "lead" facilitator, simply for convenience sake.

The basic chores of a "lead" facilitator include the following:

Before the workshop:

1. Arranging the time and place of the workshop; publicizing the workshop; getting a list of the participants, or, if it is to be held in a school or for a youth club, working on these logistics with the school or club's coordinator.
2. Arranging for meals and snacks. Sometimes the sponsoring group does this but it's important to know time frames for same.
3 If you choose to do a brief orientation for participants before the workshop, the time and place will have to be arranged.
4. Setting a time and place for the team-building session; notifying the team members of same; leading the actual session. (see Suggested Agenda—Team-Building/ Planning First Session, Page C-7, — this considers chores that others can do, e.g., writing up the first agenda, being aware of time)
5. Preparing a tentative agenda and having copies of same and manual materials available for use during the team-building session and the workshop. (see Other Suggestions below)
6. Gathering materials for the workshop. (see Packing for a Workshop at the end of this section). The sponsoring group may supply some things, e.g., markers, newsprint, easels, etc.

During the workshop:

1. Arriving early, particularly on the first day to set up chairs, posters, easels, materials; checking the area at the end of each day too.
2. Checking with team members during the workshop to see if everyone is prepared and comfortable with the exercises they're setting up. Sometimes people have new ideas. Some may not be appropriate, others may be great.
3. Encouraging teammates, holding a "clinic" when you sense nervousness, etc.
4. Having team meetings during the course of the workshop for feedback and further planning. (See Suggestions for Giving and Receiving Feedback)
5. Checking with participants to see how they'd like their names to appear on their certificates and writing and signing the certificates.
6. Having a feedback period for facilitators at the end of the workshop, a short debriefing discussion with the full facilitator team to highlight:
   — What we did well.
   — What we might change next time.
   — Affirmation of all facilitators.

After the workshop:

1. Completing a Workshop Report Form if appropriate for local group.

Other Suggestions

1. When working with young and/or inexperienced facilitators, you may wish to make expanded agendas for each session.
2. If planning time is at a minimum, you may wish to form special loose-leaf folders for inexperienced facilitators and put all activities for a particular workshop in chronological order.
3. If you expect that the program you're planning will include both a Basic and an Advanced Workshop, you may wish to plan at the outset which L&L's you'd like to use in the Basic and which you'll save for the Advanced.

Thumbnail Tips for "Lead" Facilitators

Re the team:

- Encourage team members
- See that co-facilitators have needed exercises
- Be sure they have materials
- Ask if they have questions
- Give constructive feedback
- Share responsibilities
- Use a clinic if you think a teammate is unsure of something

Re the workshop:

- Plan a tentative agenda
- Gather materials (see "Packing for a Workshop" at the end of this section).
- Schedule a team planning meeting (see Suggested Agenda for First Team Building/Planning Session).
- Check on logistics, (participants, place, time, meals, transportation, etc.)
- Be aware of time.
- Use "Re-entries" or "Gatherings" to tie up loose ends from previous sessions.
- Reinforce the positive behavior you want from participants. Applause at the right time can be a powerful affirmation.

Re challenges:

- Clinic if problems arise.
- If an exercise is totally blown, let it go (though sometimes exercises with problems lead to the best learnings).
- If discussions get heated, call for a minute of silence. Or, try some deep breathing. First breath in deeply, then breath out the negatives, then breath in the positives, etc.
- Sometimes Fish Bowl Modified is helpful for a hot topic or for an Unanswered Question.
- Have a couple of exercises in mind for fillers in case you find time on your hands.

Suggested Agenda - Team-Building/Planning First Session

Gathering: (Choose one)

- Something going on in my life just now that might influence my performance in the workshop.
- What I'm looking forward to with this group in this workshop. OR
- My strengths/weaknesses as a facilitator.

Contract: Can we all agree on the following?

1. ***Time / Attendance:*** Is time a problem for any of us? When will we plan? Are we all going to be present for all sessions and available for planning? If an absence by one team member is unavoidable, do the rest of us consent to this?

2. ***Decision Making:*** Will all decisions be made by consensus? If no consensus is possible, does the lead facilitator have team approval for making a decision for the team? (Note: Some programs choose not to structure teams with a "lead facilitator")

3. ***Participation:*** Will we all let other team members know which exercises we feel comfortable doing and which exercises we'd prefer not to do?

4. ***Support:*** Do we all agree that no team disagreements will be expressed in the presence of participants?

5. ***Commitment:*** When leading exercises, do we agree not to deviate from the team's plan without first calling a clinic for consensus?

6. ***Additions:*** Do we mind someone adding to someone else's presentation? Will we try to remember to say, "Is there anything the team would like to add?"

7. ***Emergencies:*** If a crisis occurs, e.g., a participant becomes extremely emotional or a fight breaks out, might an experienced person volunteer to step out with a participant for a short while or go to contact someone for assistance?

8. ***Feedback:*** Are we all willing to both give and receive feedback, including suggestions for change?

9. ***Challenge:*** Is there something we would like to challenge ourselves to do during this workshop on which we'd particularly like feedback?

Logistics:

a) Who will sit where, when?
b) How will we handle transitions from one activity to another?
c) What will we do when another is "on?"
d) Who will keep track of time?
e) What signals shall we use, e.g., pointing to our watch to be aware of time?, clinic, etc.
f) How can we balance routine work, e.g., writing agendas?

Sessions:

a) Review suggested agenda drawn up by lead facilitator or use Tentative Agendas.
b) Who will do what?

Closing:

Each says what he or she has appreciated about each of the other team members during this planning session, or about the team as a whole.

Suggestions for Giving and Receiving Feedback Among Team Members

At the end of each session, or at least at the end of the day, take turns popcorn style:

1. **Have each person reflect on how they think they did**
   a) leading their exercise
   b) being supportive
   c) being creative

2. **Have others offer feedback for each person**
   a) starting with positives, then
   b) offering any ideas they may have for change

In offering feedback, it is important to:

1. Describe your reaction
2. Be specific
3. Speak to a behavior the person has the possibility of changing, e.g., sitting rather than standing when presenting an exercise.

In receiving feedback, remember:

1. We all have much to learn and can always improve — it's even possible we may be wrong.
2. We can even learn from misguided criticism.
3. Sometimes we are "stand-ins" for others in our critic's lives — we shouldn't always take things personally.
4. Each person is the final judge of what is valuable to him/herself.
5. We all have to accept much imperfection in ourselves and others — and try to live with it.

***At the end of the workshop*, start the team evaluation of the workshop by focusing on the following questions as a way to give team members time to interact and "unload":**

1. What did I do at this workshop that I am most proud of?
2. Affirm team members. What did my team members do that was **HOT—SIZZLING—CREATIVE?**
3. What constructive guidance can I offer to team members in regard to their facilitating during the workshop?
4. On what issues do I need reassurance from my team?
5. How have I seen myself grow as an AVP facilitator in this workshop?

Respect Everyone   Listen and Love   Trust the Process

PACKING FOR A WORKSHOP

Affirmation Poster Material

AVP Flyers

AVP Manuals

Ball of Yarn

Koosh Balls, Bean Bags
or tiny bean bag animals (5)

Blindfolds (12)

Broken Squares

Candles/Tapers/Matches

Cardboards for Writing

Certificates (25)

Dots

Feeling Cards

Feeling Plates

Lilypads (old newsprint)

Mandala

Markers (8 lg/several colors)

Match Up Slips

Masking Tape

Name That Tune Slips

Newspaper (40 sheets)

Newsprint (25 sheets)

Notebook or Scrap Paper

Pencils (30)

Pens (30)

"Perception" Pictures

"Picture Sharing" Pictures

"People Treasure Hunt" Sheets

Sand Pan

Shakers (2)

3 X 5 cards (or half sheets)

Tic Tacs (4 boxes)

TP Guides (sheets)

TP Guides (cards)

Timer

Video

Win/Win Scenarios

PREPARED POSTERS
(for example)

Ground-Rules/Agreements
for Workshop

Feeling Statements

Red-Yellow-Green

Win/Win

Workshop Agendas
Workshop Agendas
Workshop Agendas
Workshop Agendas
Workshop Agendas
Workshop Agendas
Workshop Agendas
Workshop Agendas
Workshop Agendas
Workshop Agendas
Workshop Agendas
Workshop Agendas
Workshop Agendas
Workshop Agendas
Workshop Agendas

SECTION D

WORKSHOP AGENDAS

Introduction to Workshop Agendas

Tentative Agendas for Youth Basic

Tentative Agendas for Youth Advanced

INTRODUCTION TO WORKSHOP AGENDAS

The tentative agendas given here are based on agendas that have proved successful in previous youth workshops. Naturally, in the course of the actual workshop things may come up which may require a deviation from the tentative agendas—then a change is made. Flexibility is a must in workshops with youth as it is in all AVP workshops.

These tentative agendas give a rough idea of what exercises might be done. They also establish a rough idea of the order in which the exercises might be used. In schools, working with a tentative agenda can be very helpful.

It has also been found helpful to use "expanded agendas" in schools where planning time is limited. Each session is expanded to a full page. This leaves space to note the themes of the session and the expected times for the various activities. It also provides room to write in any changes to agendas and to take notes.

Having a few "fillers" in mind is a wise plan. Sometimes an exercise one expects to take 30 minutes only takes 20. Advanced planning is always helpful when deviations arise. In Tentative Agendas for Youth Basic - C, for instance, the exercise Listening and Brainstorming Do's and Don'ts might be considered a "filler." It does provide action but if time is short, it can be cut. Reflective Listening can stand by itself. The same might be said of Power Trip and Ice Cream. If time is short, one or both could be cut.

Some exercises, which cover much of the same material, may have two or more versions, for example, Choices I and Choices II. Different facilitators have different styles, so make a choice! The same is true for People's Perceptions I, II, III, and IV.

Sometimes one exercise is expected to be followed by another. Goal Setting Part I is expected to be followed by Goal Setting Part II. Sometimes splitting an exercise into parts is suggested as an "option" in the *Notes* (see Buttons and Things I Hear(d) Over and Over).

Different "options" are suggested in other *"Notes."* For example Violence Brainstorm (w. Options) gives three options.

Sometimes certain exercises are chosen because some participants have been exposed to some AVP before they participate in a Basic Workshop. In the Walton School System, for example, students are involved in mini-programs as 10, 11 and 12 year-olds. Tentative Agendas for Youth Basic - A was devised to build on this previous experience.

It may seem unusual to have all six sessions for an Advanced Workshop tentatively planned. Frequently young people's goals are rather general. Goal Setting Parts I and II takes this into account. If a weighty focus topic does emerge, changes are made.

Many other exercises are useful for Advanced Workshops with youth, e.g., Addiction, Choices for Advanced, Fairy Tale Theatre, Fish Bowl Intervention, I Want I Want, and Labeling.

All of the agendas that follow are tentative. Pick and choose and develop your own favorites!

TENTATIVE AGENDAS FOR YOUTH BASIC - A

SESSION 1 (8:30 - 11:15)
Welcome, Team Intros and Agenda Preview
Opening Talk:
- Nature/Process
- 3 AVP "Ways
- Housekeeping
- Suggested Ground Rules/Agreements I

Adjective Name Game and 2 more "Ways" ("forgot sign" and "twinkling/thumbs up")
Two Chairs
Peoples' Perceptions I
L&L: Ethnic Food Cart/Sneakers (AKA Vegetable Cart)
Break
Violence Brainstorm (w. Option 3)
Choices I
Concentric Circles
Evaluation

SESSION 2 (2:00 - 2:30)
Agenda Preview
Gathering: My favorite positive word is....
Reflective Listening (include brainstorming)
Sharing Stories
Go-Around: Right now I'm feeling...
L&L: Elephant and Palm Tree
Break
Creative Construction
Evaluation

SESSION 3 (8:30 - 11:15)
Agenda Preview (and possibly Wha' Cha' Doin?)
Gathering: My idea of a good friend is ...
Power Trip
Ice Cream
Lots of Dots
L&L: Pattern Ball (AKA Ball Toss)
Break
Broken Squares
Transforming Power Combo
Tic Tac Challenge
Evaluation

SESSION 4 (12:00 - 2:30)
Agenda Preview
Gathering: Something most people don't know about me is...
Feeling Faces, Categories and Layers
Feeling Chair
L&L: Red Handed or Who's the Leader?
Break
Win/Win Process
Territory
Evaluation

SESSION 5 (8:30 - 11:15)
Agenda Preview
Gathering:
Role Plays - Intro and Brainstorm
Role Plays - Preparation
Role Play 1 (see R.P. - Pre-Running Notes and R.P.- Running and Debriefing)
L&L: Alligator (AKA Crocodile) and Frogs
Break
Role Play 2
Role Play 3
Invitation to Rainbow Lunch
Evaluation
Rainbow Lunch

SESSION 6 (12:00 - 2:30)
Agenda Preview
Gathering: Discuss Rainbow Lunch
AVP Posters
Trust Walk or another trust exercise
Silent Brainstorm: What is Nonviolence? (see Violence Brainstorm, Option 3)
Written Evaluation
Break
What's Next?
Certificates
Closing: Yarn Web

TENTATIVE AGENDAS FOR YOUTH BASIC - B

SESSION 1 (Fri 7-10 pm)
Welcome, Team Intros and Agenda Preview
Opening Talk
Adjective Name Game
L&L: Big Wind
Break
Gathering: Something I've always wanted to do
Violence (brainstorm/discussion)
L&L: Whass'up?
Concentric Circles (quickly elicit listening behaviors first)
Evaluation
Closing: High School Name Crunch (AKA Texas Hug)

SESSION 2 (Sat 8:00-10:00 am)
Agenda Review
Gathering: My favorite hiding place
Nonviolence (brainstorm/discussion)
L&L: A What? (2 leaders)
Secret Spot
Power Trip
Closing: Rainstorm

SESSION 3 (Sat 10:30-12:30 pm)
Agenda Preview
Gathering : Best present I've ever received (doesn't have to be tangible)
L&L: John Brown's Baby
Transforming Power (intro/guidelines)
Quick Decisions
L&L: Ball Toss
Evaluation II/III
Closing: Machine (in exercise section)

SESSION 4 (Sat 2:30-5:30 pm)
Agenda Preview
Gathering: A relationship in my life I'd like to transform
L&L: Name That Tune
Broken Squares
Return to Violence/Non Violence (mini / team talk / discussion)
L&L:Crocodile and Frogs
Break
L&L
Role Plays (AKA Possibilities)
Evaluation
Closing: Affirmation Pyramid

SESSION 5 (Sat 7-10 pm)
Agenda Preview
Gathering: My favorite animal and why
L&L: Bump Tag
2 or 3-question interview [3 times in pairs, 10 min each time]
L&L: Vegetable Cart

Introduce Affirmation Posters
Evaluation
Closing: Bonfire

SESSION 6 (Sun 8-11 am)
Complete affirmation posters
Agenda Preview
Gathering: What I'd like to tell my family about this workshop
Who Am I Becoming?
L&L: Ms. Mumbly
Unanswered Questions
What's Next?
Written Evaluation
Closing: Yarn Toss

TENTATIVE AGENDAS FOR YOUTH BASIC - C

SESSION 1 (8:30 - 11:45)
Welcome, Team Intros and Agenda Review
Opening Talk:
  Nature/Process
  3 AVP "Ways
  Housekeeping
  Suggested Ground Rules/Agreements II
Adjective Name Game 2 more "Ways" ("forgot sign" and "twinkling/thumbs up")
Two Chairs (volunteering and right-to-pass)
L&L: Ethnic Food Cart (AKA Veg. Cart)
Break
People's Perceptions II or IV
Violence Brainstorm (w. Option 1)
Concentric Circles (confidentiality)
Choices II (if time permits)
Evaluation

SESSION 2 (12:15 - 2:45)
Agenda Review
Gathering: A place I really like is ... because...
Choices II (if not done)
Sharing Stories
Go-Around: Right now I'm feeling...
L&L: Elephant and Palm Tree or ?
Break
Broken Squares
Listening and Brainstorming Do's and Don'ts and/or Reflective Listening
Evaluation
Closing: Intro partners or Affirmation Pyramid

SESSION 3 (8:30 - 11:45)
Agenda Review
Gathering: I feel good about myself when...
Power Trip
Transforming Power
L&L: Back to Back (Modified)
Break
Lots of Dots
Feeling Faces, Categories and Layers
Feeling Statement Cards
Role Plays - Intro and Brainstorm (and vote)
Evaluation

SESSION 4 (12:15 - 2:45)
Agenda Review
Gathering: Mind Bag
Red Yellow Green
Feeling Situations for Basic
L&L: Pattern Ball (AKA Ball Toss)
Break
Role Plays - Intro and Brainstorm (if not done)
Territory (if time permits)
Win/Win Process (if time permits)
Creative Construction
Evaluation
Closing: Texas Hug

SESSION 5 (8:30 - 11:45)
Agenda Review
Gathering: Wha' Cha' Doin?
Territory (if not done)
Win/Win Process (if not done)
L&L: Crocodile (AKA Alligator) and Frogs
Break
Tool Box (AKA Co-op Posters)
Role Plays - Preparation
Role Play 1 (see R.P. - Pre-Running Notes and R.P.- Running and Debriefing)
Trust Walk
Evaluation
Rainbow Lunch (optional)

SESSION 6 (12:15 - 2:45)
Agenda Review
Gathering: Something I like about this group of people is...
Role Play 2
L&L: Pretzel
Break
Unanswered Questions? (Fish Bowl Modified)
Who Am I Becoming? Modified
What's Next?
Written Evaluation
Certificates
Closing: Yarn Web

TENTATIVE AGENDA FOR YOUTH ADVANCED - A

SESSION 1 (8:15 - 11:45)
Welcome, Team Intros and Agenda Review
Opening Talk:
Process: general nature
Housekeeping: anything special?
Ground Rules: Generic
AVP "Ways" reviewed
What's In A Name (Adj.Name Game Mod.)
In Common
Point of View
L&L:Big Wind or Who're Your Neighbors?
BREAK
Biographies
Focusing On Violence/Nonviolence
L&L: Line Up 1
Goal Setting Part I
Evaluation

SESSION 2 (12:15 - 2:40)
Agenda Review
Gathering: Picture Sharing
Facts and Feelings
Triangles For Advanced
L&L: Touch Blue
BREAK
Goal Setting Part II
L&L: Line Up 2
Role Plays - Introduction and Brainstorm
Things I Hear(d) Over and Over Part I
Evaluation
Closing: World Ball

SESSION 3 (8:15 - 11:45)
Agenda Review (and Affirmation Posters)
Gathering: Something most people don't know about me is...
Crossover
Let's Go Swimming
L&L: Fire on the Mountain
BREAK
Things I Hear(d) Over and Over Part II
Buttons Part I
L&L: Back to Back; Hand to Knee
Buttons Part II
Evaluation

SESSION 4 (12:15 -2:40)
Agenda Review
Gathering: Mirror Circle: I'd like to see myself as...
TP Mandala (or TP Queries)
Feeling Circles
L&L: Pattern Ball (AKA Ball Toss) (w. challenges)
BREAK
Points of View
Hassle Helps
Evaluation
Closing Circle: A What?; Handshake/High Five

SESSION 5 (8:15 - 11:45)
Agenda Review
Personal Space and Gathering:
My space is important because....
Role Plays - Preparation
Role Play 1 (see R. P. - Pre-Running Notes and R.P. - Running and Debriefing)
L&L: Pruee
BREAK
Role Play II
Trust Falls in Pairs, Trios and Circle
Guided Reflection
L&L: Noah's Ark I
Evaluation

SESSION 6 (12:15 -2:40)
Agenda Review
Gathering: I think my goals.......
Risking Change
Unanswered Questions (Fish Bowl Mod.?)
L&L: Jail Break
BREAK
Who Me?
L&L: Earthquake
Talk in the Dark
Where Do We Go From Here?
Written Evaluation
Certificates and Affirmation Posters
Closing Circle: Rainstorm

TENTATIVE AGENDA FOR YOUTH ADVANCED - B

SESSION 1 (Fri. 7-10 PM)
Welcome, Team Intros Agenda Review
Opening Talk and Guidelines
Adjective Name (and why chosen)
Gathering: One word/phrase.... "How I am different from when I first experienced AVP"
L&L: Bonnie
TP Mandala
Queries (Define "queries")
"What questions/concerns do I have about alternatives to violence"? Discuss in small groups; each individual writes a query on 5"x24"strip of newsprint, return to full group, (don't debrief at this point).
BREAK
Convergence (AKA Consensus on theme)
Have volunteers post queries
Sort and group similar queries
Common threads?
Themes for weekend?
L&L: A What? (High 5 and hug)
Closing: Bonfire

SESSION 2 (Sat. 8:15-2:30)
Agenda Preview
Gathering: "A time I lost faith in myself as a nonviolent person, and how I regained it"
Applying AVP
(making "bumper stickers" in pairs)
Concentric Circles
Something about the gathering that touched me
Someone I was dying to respond to
Who did I want to comfort the most and why
What do I want from another person when I am angry
BREAK
Stereotyping (or similar exercise)
L&L: Crocs and Frogs
Evaluation
Closing: (Name of School) Crunch!
(AKA Texas Hug)

SESSION 3 (Sat 5- 7:45 PM)
Agenda Preview
Gathering: Weirdest food I ever ate!
Visualization (relating to the theme)
Wacky Wishes (AKA Goal /Wish)
L&L: Ball Toss
Another exercise relating to theme
Evaluation
Closing: Hug line

SESSION 4 (Sun 8:15-11:15)
Agenda Preview/ Inspirational reading
Gathering: What brings peace to me?
Don't stop thinking about tomorrow! (One question at a time/answer around circle)

1. What do you have to offer?
2. What have others said they value about you? (Whether you believe it or not)
3. What are you taking from your school?
4. What do you leave as a legacy for those who follow you at this school?

L&L:
What's Next?
Written Evaluation
Closing

Note: This agenda was used with young people about to graduate; their theme was uncertainty/change, especially how to keep faith in self and AVP.

Elementary and Middle School Program Development
Elementary and Middle School Program Development
Elementary and Middle School Program Development
Elementary and Middle School Program Development
Elementary and Middle School Program Development
Elementary and Middle School Program Development
Elementary and Middle School Program Development
Elementary and Middle School Program Development
Elementary and Middle School Program Development
Elementary and Middle School Program Development
Elementary and Middle School Program Development
Elementary and Middle School Program Development
Elementary and Middle School Program Development
Elementary and Middle School Program Development
Elementary and Middle School Program Development
Elementary and Middle School Program Development
Elementary and Middle School Program Development
Elementary and Middle School Program Development
Elementary and Middle School Program Development
Elementary and Middle School Program Development
Elementary and Middle School Program Development
Elementary and Middle School Program Development
Elementary and Middle School Program Development
Elementary and Middle School Program Development
Elementary and Middle School Program Development
Elementary and Middle School Program Development
Elementary and Middle School Program Development
Elementary and Middle School Program Development
Elementary and Middle School Program Development
Elementary and Middle School Program Development
Elementary and Middle School Program Development
Elementary and Middle School Program Development
Elementary and Middle School Program Development
Elementary and Middle School Program Development
Elementary and Middle School Program Development
Elementary and Middle School Program Development
Elementary and Middle School Program Development
Elementary and Middle School Program Development
Elementary and Middle School Program Development
Elementary and Middle School Program Development

SECTION E

ELEMENTARY AND MIDDLE SCHOOL PROGRAM DEVELOPMENT

Introduction to Elementary and Middle School Program Agendas

Elementary School Sample Lesson

5th Grade (10 year-olds) Mini
6th Grade (11 year-olds) Mini
7th Grade (12 year-olds) Mini

This is a separate section since Elementary and Middle School Programs do not generally include workshops (as they are defined in AVP) but rather are more general programs.

INTRODUCTION TO ELEMENTARY AND MIDDLE SCHOOL PROGRAM AGENDAS

ELEMENTARY SCHOOL PROGRAM AGENDAS

At the elementary level (6-8 year olds), the AViS program in Buffalo, NY focuses first on the teachers and does workshops with them, followed by classroom demonstrations, as in the sample school lesson below.

ELEMENTARY SCHOOL SAMPLE LESSON

A 45 minute lesson can be as simple as:

Gathering:	My favorite animal
Adjective Name Game:	(A Language Arts lesson on Adjectives!)
L/L:	Ball Toss
Closing:	One word that says how I feel right now (provides an opportunity to clarify what a feeling word is)

MIDDLE SCHOOL PROGRAM AGENDAS

The first three agendas listed below were devised for the Walton, New York, School district. They are still in use as of this printing.

As with the agendas in the section "Workshop Agendas," the agendas in this section are given simply as samples. They do give an idea of the possible flow of various exercises.

Many of the same concepts occur in all three agendas; however, different exercises were chosen to address the concepts at different age levels. The same concepts are found in the Basic and Advanced agendas, but again using different exercises.

Listening and cooperation skills are introduced in the 5th grade. They are developed further at both the 6th and 7th grade levels. Feeling statements are presented in the 6th grade and continued in the 7th. All three concepts are related to the Win/Win process, which is presented in both 6th and 7th grades.

The agendas that follow are:
5th Grade (10 year-olds) Mini - 1 Session (about 1 hour)
6th Grade (11 year-olds) Mini - 4 Sessions (about 6 hours) (done over 4 days)
7th Grade (12 year-olds) Mini - 3 Sessions (about 6 hours)

5th Grade (10 Year Olds) Mini - 1 Session (About 1 Hour)

Agenda:

Welcome, Team Intros and Agenda Review	05
Opening Talk: (Suggested Ground Rules, Clinic, Quiet Sign and Hurricane)	05
Adjective Name Game (Modified)	10
L&L: Vegetable Cart	10
Cooperative Drawing	15
Evaluation	05

6th Grade (11 Year Olds) Mini - 4 Sessions (About 6 Hours)
(Done Over 4 Days)

Session 1 (about 80 minutes)

Welcome, Team Intros and Agenda Review	05
Opening Talk: (Suggested Ground Rules, Clinic, Quiet Sign and Hurricane)	05
Adjective Name Game	15
In Common	10
L&L: Ethnic Food Cart	10
Break	05
Gathering: One of my favorite foods is...	05
Parallel Construction	15
Evaluation	05

Session 2 (about 80 minutes)

Agenda Review	01
Gathering: Something I do well is...	05
Paraphrasing	10
Feeling Faces and Cards	15
L&L: Elephant and Palm Tree	10
Break	05
Machines or Co-op Monsters	15
Evaluation	05

Session 3 (about 100 minutes)

Agenda Review	05
Gathering: If I could be an animal I'd be a ...because...	10
What Color is Conflict	15
L&L: Red Handed	10
Break	10
Heartbroken Chris/Pat	20
Paper Tiger (if there's time)	15
Evaluation	05

Session 4 (about 100 minutes)

Agenda Review	05
Gathering: A place I really like is...because...	10
Win/Win Intro	20
L&L: Who's the Leader	10
Break	10
Brainstorm or Rap Session: "Where Do 6th Graders Get Hassled"	15
Co-op Posters	20
Closing: One thing I'll remember about AVP is...	05

7th Grade (12 Year Olds) Mini - 3 Sessions (About 6 Hours)

Session 1 (about 120 minutes)	
Welcome, Team Intros and Agenda Review	05
Opening Talk:	
Suggested Ground Rules Version I, Clinic, Quiet Sign and Hurricane	05
Adjective Name Game Modified	15
Circle Game	10
Lots of Listening	25
L&L: Howdy, Howdy (AKA Whass'up, Whass'up)	10
Break	05
Feeling Scenarios	25
(Changes 1, 2, 3)*	15
Evaluation	05

Session 2 (about 95 minutes)	
Agenda Review	01
Gathering: Someone I respect is ... because...	15
Construction Gang	25
L&L: Ethnic Food Cart - or - Who's the Leader?	10
Break	05
Win/Win Friday Night or Win/Win Comics	20
(Head, Heart, Hand)*	15
Evaluation	05

Session 3 (about 80 minutes)	
Agenda Review	01
Gathering: One reason I like living here is ....because...	10
Garbage Bags	30
L&L: Noah's Ark	10
Break	05
(Make a Difference)*	10
Evaluation	05
Closing (Affirmation Pyramid? or a filler?)	10

"Treat Time"? (At dismissal; goodies might be shared and other L&L's played)

* These may be considered "fillers."

SECTION F

AGENDA FUNDAMENTALS WITH THEIR EXERCISES

AGENDA FUNDAMENTALS WITH THEIR EXERCISES
AGENDA FUNDAMENTALS WITH THEIR EXERCISES
AGENDA FUNDAMENTALS WITH THEIR EXERCISES
AGENDA FUNDAMENTALS WITH THEIR EXERCISES
AGENDA FUNDAMENTALS WITH THEIR EXERCISES
AGENDA FUNDAMENTALS WITH THEIR EXERCISES
AGENDA FUNDAMENTALS WITH THEIR EXERCISES
AGENDA FUNDAMENTALS WITH THEIR EXERCISES
AGENDA FUNDAMENTALS WITH THEIR EXERCISES
AGENDA FUNDAMENTALS WITH THEIR EXERCISES
AGENDA FUNDAMENTALS WITH THEIR EXERCISES
AGENDA FUNDAMENTALS WITH THEIR EXERCISES
AGENDA FUNDAMENTALS WITH THEIR EXERCISES
AGENDA FUNDAMENTALS WITH THEIR EXERCISES
AGENDA FUNDAMENTALS WITH THEIR EXERCISES
AGENDA FUNDAMENTALS WITH THEIR EXERCISES
AGENDA FUNDAMENTALS WITH THEIR EXERCISES
AGENDA FUNDAMENTALS WITH THEIR EXERCISES
AGENDA FUNDAMENTALS WITH THEIR EXERCISES
AGENDA FUNDAMENTALS WITH THEIR EXERCISES
AGENDA FUNDAMENTALS WITH THEIR EXERCISES
AGENDA FUNDAMENTALS WITH THEIR EXERCISES
AGENDA FUNDAMENTALS WITH THEIR EXERCISES
AGENDA FUNDAMENTALS WITH THEIR EXERCISES
AGENDA FUNDAMENTALS WITH THEIR EXERCISES
AGENDA FUNDAMENTALS WITH THEIR EXERCISES
AGENDA FUNDAMENTALS WITH THEIR EXERCISES
AGENDA FUNDAMENTALS WITH THEIR EXERCISES
AGENDA FUNDAMENTALS WITH THEIR EXERCISES
AGENDA FUNDAMENTALS WITH THEIR EXERCISES
AGENDA FUNDAMENTALS WITH THEIR EXERCISES
AGENDA FUNDAMENTALS WITH THEIR EXERCISES
AGENDA FUNDAMENTALS WITH THEIR EXERCISES
AGENDA FUNDAMENTALS WITH THEIR EXERCISES
AGENDA FUNDAMENTALS WITH THEIR EXERCISES
AGENDA FUNDAMENTALS WITH THEIR EXERCISES
AGENDA FUNDAMENTALS WITH THEIR EXERCISES
AGENDA FUNDAMENTALS WITH THEIR EXERCISES
AGENDA FUNDAMENTALS WITH THEIR EXERCISES
AGENDA FUNDAMENTALS WITH THEIR EXERCISES

Opening Talk and Suggested Ground Rules/Agreements

Transforming Power

Feeling Statements (AKA "I" Messages)

Win/Win

Role Plays

Trust Activities

These six concepts are so fundamental to AVP that we have given them their own section.

Following AVP process, each concept is preceded by introductory material and has accompanying exercises so each idea can be presented experientially rather than through lecture.

Of course, every workshop will not include all six elements. While every AVP workshop will include an Opening Talk and some presentation of Transforming Power, the facilitating team will decide the structure of the rest of the workshop depending on the needs of the group.

OPENING TALK AND SUGGESTED GROUND RULES/AGREEMENTS
Introductory Material

In Youth Workshops it's wise to keep the Opening Talk brief and upbeat. You don't want to lose the participants in the first few minutes.

Splitting the talk among team members follows the idea of not talking "too long or too often." It also provides variety. Moreover, it models teamwork and provides a way for the participants to begin to know all the members of the team.

A sample Opening Talk as an exercise follows. It is divided into six sections. The sections can be divided among team members in whatever way suits the team.

Two versions of presenting the Suggested Ground Rules/Agreements follow the Opening Talk exercise. These exercises about Ground Rules/Agreements are prefaced with the word "Suggested" to indicate that they are open to discussion, revision, and additions. They are also "rules" that participants will "agree" to follow, rather than have them imposed by facilitators, which is reflected in what they are called. It is hoped that participants will make them their own to make the workshop a safe and comfortable place to be.

Some programs, such as AViS, usually suggest only three basic guidelines:

CONFIDENTIALITY
NO PUT DOWNS
LISTEN RESPECTFULLY

Each term is described in a manner appropriate for the group (adults or students)
NO PUT DOWNS encourages affirming words and behavior
LISTEN RESPECTFULLY includes no side-talk, no interruptions, offering differing opinions without arguing, not hogging the floor when speaking.

Some facilitators prefer to simply discuss these three ideas in the first session with no written material. The points are then put on newsprint and posted for the second session.

In an Advanced workshop, the guidelines could be posted at the beginning OR the facilitator could ask participants if they recall the guidelines from their first workshop and carry on from there.

Note:: Any of these styles allows facilitators to ask if there are any ground rules/agreements the participants want to suggest or to add to as workshop behavior demands.
Regarding confidentiality: *You may wish to ask if anyone in the group is a "mandated reporter" whose position requires that s/he report certain situations such as abuse.*

Exercises

Opening Talk
Suggested Ground Rules/Agreements 1
Suggested Ground Rules/Agreements 2

OPENING TALK

Purpose: To set the stage for the workshop by telling participants a little bit about the history and nature of AVP and discussing some logistics of the workshop.

Time: About 10 minutes

Materials: A sheet entitled "Unanswered Questions," and a list of "Suggested Ground Rules/Agreements," (version depends on which exercise you choose.)

Procedure: Set Up:

1. Someone has probably already welcomed the group but tell them again how glad you are that they've come. (Let your enthusiasm show!) Explain that the Opening talk is just to let participants know a little bit about AVP before the main part of the workshop begins. Different facilitators will do different parts of the Talk so the group can get to know the team.

2. ***History:*** AVP started in 1975 in Greenhaven Correctional Facility in New York State. The prisoners found it very helpful and it began being offered in other facilities. It also started to be offered in communities and community people found it helpful. More recently it started in schools. In fact, it is partly because of prisoners saying they wished they had done AVP when they were younger that got it started in schools. Now AVP is done in over 40 states and it's even gone international.

3. ***Nature/Process:*** AVP holds that there is good in everyone and that in a group of people like us there is a great deal of wisdom. In AVP, everybody is both a learner and a teacher. The facilitators don't have the answers.

   The facilitators will introduce exercises or activities. Then the group will do the exercises and afterward people will talk about what happened and how it might relate to their life. We learn by sharing life experiences.

   If a serious problem arises in sharing our experiences, a facilitator can point out available resources. Facilitators are not counselors or therapists.

   During the exercises a question may arise. If there isn't enough time to answer it immediately, it can be put on the "Unanswered Questions" sheet (point it out.) Then it can be discussed at a later time.

4. ***AVP Ways***: AVP has certain "ways" that are used during the workshop. One is a silence signal. Some exercises involve people talking in small groups. If a facilitator wishes to get everyone's attention s/he will raise one arm. When others see the arm raised, they will raise their arm and finish the sentence they're saying. Then the facilitator will be able to give the next direction.

   Then there's a "clinic." Sometimes facilitators may wish to talk something over with other facilitators. One of the facilitators will call, "Clinic," and all will get together, probably in the middle of the circle. (Call one and do it)

Sometimes if we've been sitting and need to be energized, someone can call "Hurricane." If "Hurricane" is called, everyone has to get up and change seats. Anyone may call a "Hurricane," but we would ask that it not be called right in the middle of someone's statement and not more than once by each participant. (Call "Hurricane," and do it.)
Note: You may want to wait until you do "Big Wind" to explain this point.

5. ***Housekeeping:*** Here mention such things as the following: location of the bathrooms; regulations regarding the facility in which the workshop is being held; time frame for snacks and meals and sessions; smoking stipulations.

   Ask if anyone has any special needs. Someone may be allergic to certain scents; someone may have a back problem and may have to stand often; people of the Muslim faith may need time for prayers, some may have certain dietary restrictions, etc. It might be less awkward/embarrassing if this information is ascertained ahead of time, especially when the team has to make provision for these needs.

6. ***Suggested Ground Rules/Agreements:*** (Proceed with whichever method you choose.)

SUGGESTED GROUND RULES/AGREEMENTS 1

Purpose: To suggest ground rules that will make the workshop a good safe place to be. To ask participants if such ground rules "will work for them."

Time: 10 minutes

Materials: a sheet posted with the following ***Suggested Ground Rules/Agreements:***

- We are here as equals - everyone's ideas are important
- We look for the good in ourselves and others
- We avoid put-downs - even as jokes
- We have the right to pass
- We volunteer only ourselves
- We will risk speaking up, but not too often or too long
- We keep personal things confidential

Procedure: **Set Up:**

1. Refer to the Suggested Ground Rules/Agreements sheet and explain that they have developed over several years. They help make the workshop a safe place to be. Read them out loud, **briefly** explaining each one.

2. Ask if there are any questions regarding any of them.

3. Ask if the participants have any they would like to add.

4. Ask if everyone agrees to try to keep these ground rules.

5. Whoever feels a ground rule isn't being kept may say "ouch" as a reminder. "Ouch" could also be written on the Suggested Ground Rules/Agreements poster.

Note: The original AVP list of Ground Rules has been changed slightly.

Many of the Ground Rules are experienced in Session 1. This can be pointed out at the end of the session: Adjective Name Game uses "We look for the good..." and "No put-downs"; Concentric Circles involves "confidentiality," (etc.). Or, you might ask the participants which activities tie into which ground rules.

SUGGESTED GROUND RULES/AGREEMENTS 2

Purpose: To suggest some ground rules that will make the workshop a safe place to be. To ask participants if they would like to add others. To ask participants if such ground rules "will work for them."

Time: 10 minutes

Materials: A sheet posted with the following ***Suggested Ground Rules/Agreements:***

- We are all here as equals — everyone's ideas are respected.
- We'll look for and affirm the good in ourselves and others.
- We'll avoid put-downs of ourselves and others, even as jokes.
- We all have the right to speak without interruption, but not too often or too long.

Procedure: **Set Up:**

1. Refer to the Suggested Ground Rules/Agreements sheet and explain that they have developed over time. They help make the workshop a safe place to be.

2. Read the first ground rule and ask if there are any questions. You may want to clarify that "equal" means that we are here as people, not as students or teachers or nurses or custodians, etc., or as older/younger, just as people.

3. Ask someone to read the second and third ground rules and ask if there are any questions. Ask how we might "affirm" ourselves and others.

4. Ask someone to read the fourth ground rule. Ask what is meant by "interruption." <u>If</u> side conversations are not mentioned you might try the following: Ask a volunteer to describe what s/he has done since getting up that morning. When the volunteer starts talking, you start a mock side conversation with someone next to you. Do this just for 30 seconds and then call "cut." Then ask the volunteer who was speaking how s/he felt when you had this side conversation. The volunteer might not be bothered but others are likely to say that they don't like it when this happens to them.

Processing:

- Would anyone like to add any other ground rules?
- Will everyone try to keep the ground rules? Will this be hard?

Note: Whoever feels a ground rule isn't being kept may say "ouch" as a reminder. "Ouch" could also be written on the Suggested Ground Rules/Agreements poster.

Remaining ground rules are generated later. "Right to pass" and "Volunteering selves" are dealt with in Two Chairs. "Confidentiality," in Concentric Circles.

If someone has a reluctance about doing Adjective Name Game, you could ask at that point if the group might like to add something like, "We all have the right to pass" to the Suggested Ground Rule/Agreements list.

After doing "Two Chairs," you might ask if the group would agree to adding "We'll try to take risks" to the list.

TRANSFORMING POWER
Introduction

One thing to keep in mind in introducing this concept is that students tend to be turned off by lectures. Presentations that are active and colorful seem to prove more acceptable. Involving students in discussion and/or "taking a stand" is particularly effective.

Some programs for youth which are very similar to AVP don't even use the phrase Transforming Power. HIP (Help Increase the Peace), for instance, discusses the same concept but refers to it as "THINK HIP."

Facilitators who work with youth have varied opinions as to important points to make when presenting the concept of Transforming Power. Below are a sampling of such opinions.

OPINIONS
Larry Apsey, one of the founders of AVP, used to speak of the fact that we could be transformed by the renewal of our minds. Hence he spoke of a "transforming power for peace."

Cynthia MacBain and inside facilitators, (AVP-NY)

The following simple explanation can be written on newsprint and posted to be referred to during the workshop.

To "transform" is to "change the shape of"
Each one of us has the power to change the shape of a situation
- -in a negative direction toward a violent outcome
- -in a positive direction toward resolving conflict(s)

In AVP, we use the term "Transforming Power" to mean the power we have to change the shape of a conflict situation in a POSITIVE DIRECTION toward the PEACEFUL RESOLUTION of conflict.

The guides we have for discovering and using that power are

1) the desire to have a conflict resolved (rather than to hurt, "win," or "pay back" another person);
2) the belief that there is something of value in all of us, and we may have to reach inside and pull it out.

Fenna Mandolang

In the words of a teenager, "**Transforming Power** is the opposite of the power of violence. When someone is annoying or violent, it is easy to get mad at them. That's the power of violence. Transforming Power is the power to change a situation so that it becomes a manageable or, maybe, even a constructive situation. It is the power of truth, the power of caring, the power of respect. Transforming Power means you have to be open to all kinds of solutions: surprise, humor, patience, persistence, or being serious. Using Transforming Power is hard because it isn't letting people take advantage of you. It requires strength, courage, self-respect, and respect for others. It isn't safer than violence; it involves taking risks. It's just a choice between different kinds of risks."

Excerpted from "Bringing Nonviolence Workshops to Schools" by Fenna Mandolang, a student HIP facilitator. Friends Journal, August, 1997. Used with permission.

Florence Mc Neil (AVP, Walton, NY):

It's helpful to ask, "What does 'transform' mean, anyway?" as you begin this topic. This will involve participants immediately.

One way to describe TP is to refer to it as the ENERGY it takes to move away from the things we see on the "Violence" Brainstorm.

Nonviolence is not a wimpy life-style. It takes a lot more courage to work for a peaceful resolution than it does to get into a fight.

Even though people take an AVP workshop, it does not mean they won't experience conflict in their lives. The Guidelines to Transforming Power may help us consider some different responses to conflict.

Some of these guidelines are more difficult to use than others. People may doubt if some of the guidelines are even possible to use, at least for them. If people are willing to try even some of the guidelines, it's a positive step.

Some people expect that those who've participated in an AVP workshop will do everything 'right.' Students often hear, "You've done AVP and you're still acting like THIS?"

AVP does not provide a quick fix. It presents a direction we can choose to follow, rather than instant arrival at perfection.

Trying to live in an AVP fashion is trying to walk in the direction of a different way of dealing with life.

ADDITIONAL SUGGESTIONS FOR INTRODUCING TRANSFORMING POWER

Audrey Mang (AViS, Buffalo, NY):

We have found that introducing Transforming Power works best when there is as little lecture as possible. We will use the Transforming Power exercise (which follows) or simply present the Guides to Transforming Power and ask participants to talk about whichever of the guides speaks to them. It is important to do this "popcorn" style, rather than going around the circle, so that as the entire group considers the guides, people can speak when they feel moved.

Kate Ryan (AVP, Delhi, NY):

The guide "Expect the Best" may be unwise to use when working with young people. "Be Open to the Positive," might be a good replacement. This may seem overly cautious but the word "expect" really denotes, for some, the belief that something will definitely happen. It's certainly important to approach any situation hoping for a good outcome and not fearing a bad, but "expecting" anything may leave you terribly disappointed if what you expect doesn't happen.

Avoiding such disappointments is particularly important for youth who've experienced many disappointments already. Moreover young people who are already confronting a myriad of problems, such as poverty, drugs, crime, stereotyping, are quite likely to laugh at the idea of "expecting the best." They're more likely to at least consider the possibility of "being open to the positive."

EXERCISES

In the following pages are several exercises which suggest ways of presenting the concept of Transforming Power. They are formatted like exercises for consistency. New facilitators and facilitators who may not facilitate often seem to find this consistency of presentation helpful.

They are placed in this section for easier comparison with some opinions above. The exercises include:

TRANSFORMING POWER - might be used in a Basic Workshop where you expect many participants will go on to do an Advanced Workshop.

TRANSFORMING POWER AND SELF - this includes accompanying sheets, You Are Wonderful, and Forming the Ideal Self.

TRANSFORMING POWER MANDALA - for an Advanced

TRANSFORMING POWER COMBO - might be used in a Basic workshop where you think very few participants will go on to do an Advanced Workshop.

TRANSFORMING POWER QUERIES FOR ADVANCED (or possibly T4F) - this includes a sheet, Queries Concerning Transforming Power.

Following the exercises are four sheets which are referred to in several exercises, namely:

- Skits for Transforming Power
- Directions for Making a TP Mandala
- Guides to Transforming Power
- Wallet Cards with Guides.

TRANSFORMING POWER

Purpose: To introduce the concept of Transforming Power as used in AVP.

Time: About 30 minutes

Materials: TP Guides posted on newsprint and TP Guide cards for all

Procedure: **Set Up:**

1. You might begin by saying that Transforming Power is a phrase AVP uses to describe the energy involved in changing a potentially violent situation into a nonviolent situation or in moving from the Violence Brainstorm to the Non-Violence Brainstorm.

2. Explain that two facilitators will do a skit that shows Transforming Power in action. (see attached sheet)

3. Individual facilitators may wish to give their views or stories about TP.

4. After steps 2 and/or 3 hand out the TP Guide cards. Say that the guides may help a person be open to Transforming Power. Ask people to read the Guides and Help Along the Way, either from the cards or the poster.

5. Ask if any of the "Guides" or "Helps" were seen in the skit or heard in the stories. They may also have been used in some of the participants' stories told in the Sharing Exercise

Processing:

- Do you think you might be able to use any of these "Guides" or "Helps" in your life?
- Would some of the "Guides" or "Helps" be difficult to use?
- Does the idea of Transforming Power seem wimpy? impossible?

Note: This is an exercise that works well shared by two or all facilitators.

Many participants may think that Transforming Power is unrealistic or wouldn't be possible in their situation. That's all right. We have to "trust our inner sense of when to act."

TRANSFORMING POWER AND SELF

Purpose: To present the concept of transforming power through experiential and group process.

Time: 75 minutes (Step 1 — "You Are Wonderful," 20 minutes; Step 2 — "Forming the Ideal Self," 30 minutes; Step 3 - "Building Blocks to TP," 25 minutes)

Materials: "You Are Wonderful" sheet; slips with each task for "Forming the Ideal Self"; about 30 (4"x10") cards with the TP Guidelines (or Building Blocks to Transforming Power) printed, one to each card (make duplicates of the more popular ones); wallet size cards for all; markers; newsprint.

Procedure: **Set Up**

1. Familiarize yourself with the content of Step 1: "You Are Wonderful" (following). Read the text and/or ask questions about each part of the body, mind and spirit sections, such as: What is the prettiest sight you have ever seen? (eyes)
   - What kind of music do you like? (ears)
   - Do you like to sing? What is your favorite song? (voice)
   - What happened at your last birthday? (mind, past event)
   - Can you imagine swimming next summer? (mind, future)
   - Have you ever helped someone who was hurt? (spirit)
   - Keep the talk moving and directed. End with the point, "You are a wonderful miracle."

2. Follow the directions on Step 2: "Forming the Ideal Self" (following).

3. After groups have completed the tasks in Step 2 (Forming the Ideal Self), begin Step 3 by spreading out the 30 cards with the TP Guidelines (or Building Blocks to Transforming Power) on the floor. Say that these guides (Building Blocks) may help us to become closer to our ideal selves. As such we may help transform situations by allowing Transforming Power to work through us.

4. Ask each person to pick up a card and say why s/he thinks it may be useful.

5. Hand out wallet size cards as you collect the large cards and thank all for their input.

Step 1 - You Are Wonderful!

Thinking about all of you, we really want each and every one of you to know **HOW WONDERFUL YOU ARE!** Let's think about that for a while. Just look at how wonderful you are.

Put your hand over your heart.

Can you feel it pounding? It's sending streams of blood all through your body to energize it. Isn't that amazing?
Guess how many miles of tubing your heart fills with your blood?....About 60,000 miles of tubing!
Guess how many gallons of your blood your heart pumps in a year?....about 600,000 gallons each year!

Now, take a deep breath.

Doesn't that feel good? Your lungs are converting the oxygen from the air into fuel for your body. Doesn't that feel great!

Feel your tummy.

Your stomach is digesting food to give you new muscles, blood and energy. What a glorious machine you are!

Wiggle your fingers!

No other creature has the dexterity we humans have. Some of us can even play the piano, do artwork, fix machines. Our fingers are marvelous!

Feel your ears.

Floppy aren't they? But think what they can do. What are the things you can hear? Your mother's kindly voice? The cry of a baby? Someone singing sweetly? A rippling brook? How about a whole tremendous orchestra? What kind of music do you like? You can hear it! All kinds of sounds. What else can you hear? Amazing how your ears can do this!
Your ear has tiny fibers that pick up every sound. Guess how many fibers you have in an ear?....about 24,000 tiny fibers in each ear!

Touch your eyes.

Now there is a wonder! What can you see? A fluttering bird? A delicate flower? A misty sunrise? A spectacular sunset? All the colors of the rainbow? A million stars in a night sky? Everything beautiful and not so beautiful! What else can you see? How wonderful are your eyes!
Each eye has tiny receptors that pick up every little detail. Guess how many receptors you have?....about a hundred million tiny receptors in your eyes!

But then your mind is even more wonderful!

You can see in your mind's eye anywhere! Can you see in your mind: The front of your school? Your home? A place where you once took a vacation? Some sports stadium somewhere? Where else? You can see many places your mind can recall!
And your mind can also travel *back in time!* Can you see in your mind: When you were in a lower grade in school? When you had your last birthday?
And your mind can look *forward in time*! Can you imagine going home today after school? Graduating from high school some day?
So, with your amazing mind, you can travel both in *space and in time!*

More than that, your mind is your *power* with which you control your life. You can look at a situation and analyze it! You can judge what you think is best! You can decide which way to go! You can become captain of your ship! Yes, that way, you are in charge of yourself, you can **BE SOMEBODY!** That's what you want!

But the most stupendous and best part of you is not the body or mind. It is your INNER SPIRIT! Just think:

Can you comfort or care for someone who has fallen and scraped a knee?...Sure you can!

Can you be happy your friend is having a good birthday party?.....You bet you can!

Can you be kind to animals, maybe even a stray dog or cat?....Probably you have done it!

Can you sometimes "put yourselves in another's shoes" and understand how they feel?...Yes!

Can you forgive what a friend did to you and go on with the friendship?...Kids do that all the time!

There are "things of the Spirit" that you can do! What other "spiritual" things can you do?

Did you ever help someone with their homework?

Did you ever do something to stop an argument? You can do that!

Did you ever love someone, even if they were unkind to you?...You can do even that!

These Spirit-Abilities are the things that matter most, and make you the most beautiful!

So, you see, in *Body, Mind and Spirit* you are simply amazing. In fact, **YOU ARE A MIRACLE.**

And now, one other thing you might like to know. Do you know how far back your roots go? Lots of the stuff that you are made of like bits of iron, copper, carbon, etc., actually came from the stars of the universe! You are from stars! It took more than 12 billion years of creation to get all of you together! And here you are! What an opportunity you have!

In fact, you can make yourself more wonderful each day! By the things you decide to do, you are a part of this great creation process! By the things you decide to do, you are further building your body, your mind and your spirit everyday! Everyday, you can help to *transform* yourself into an ever more beautiful creature!

When you really know how wonderful you are, you become stronger, and able to handle even very difficult situations you may meet in life. You're better able to handle solutions to problems, too.

And you have the ***Power to Transform*** situations you run into - even help to transform the people around you. By the way you act, you can spread the way of being deep-down happy helping others, being more kind, avoiding violence and being peaceful.

Remind yourself, everyday, how very wonderful you are.
Be happy for who you really are!
And make the best of every day!

Step 2 - Forming the Ideal Self

The facilitator briefly defines the words *Transform* (to change) and *Power* (energy).
Each of us has the power to transform people and situations. Some things are more difficult to transform than others. If we try to transform other people, they may resent it. The best place to start with Transforming Power is to attempt to transform ourselves.

Divide the participants into six groups.
You do not need the same number in each group. Make copies of the tasks listed below and give each group a slip of paper with one of the tasks. Ask for a volunteer to be scribe and reporter of their project. S/he will record the suggestions, post the newsprint, announce the group task (reading aloud from the slip of paper), and then explain the group's conclusions. When you are finished, there will be six papers on the wall filled with good ideas about how to transform yourself.

IDEALS

Imagine yourself as the most wonderful and fulfilled person you can be.
Your task: On the top of your paper write — **I CAN BE:**
The task of this group is to list some words that describe that ideal person.

SPEECH

Recognize the power of your speech for evil, such as put downs, lying and abusive words; but also recognize the power of your speech for good.
Your task: On the top of your paper, write — **I CAN SAY:**
Then list words you can say that encourage others and help to develop good relationships.

BEHAVIOR

How can we act towards others to comfort them in their distress or calm them down when they are angry?
Your task: On the top of your paper, write — **I CAN ACT:**
Then list examples of good behavior you can use in your daily life, or whatever situation in which you find yourself.

USE OF TIME

Use your time and energy in activities that build you up rather than destroy.
Your task: On top of your paper, write — **I CAN USE MY TIME TO:**
Then list examples of good and constructive use of time.

EFFORT

There is energy inside you that can be used , with will power, in a steady pull to achieve a better direction.
Your task: On top of your paper, write — **I CAN ACHIEVE:**
Then list examples of goals you might work to achieve, how you might encourage help from others, and how you plan to overcome difficulties.

PEACE

Keep your mind tranquil and free from frantic desires, so as to tap inner strength.
Your task: On top of your paper write — **I CAN BE PEACEFUL:**
Then list ways to achieve inner peace.

Note: This is based on the concept of the eightfold path of Buddhism.

TRANSFORMING POWER MANDALA

Purpose: To help people consider the place of TP in their lives.

Time: About 20 minutes

Materials: 13-piece mandala made from neon poster board in various colors (see Directions for Making a TP Mandala).

Procedure: **Set Up:**

1. If TP guides have already been covered, give a brief reminder of TP:
   a) the **potential** to change situations to be less violent;
   b) we can **choose** to be open to the possibility of acting differently.
   If the Guides have not been used yet, this same brief introduction is appropriate.

2. Place the TP circle on the floor in the center of the group.

3. Lay out the remaining pieces around the circle, reading each one as you lay it down.

4. Ask participants to consider which technique is the one they are most likely to use or the one they are most comfortable with.

5. Ask them to stand up and go and stand by that guide. It's fine if several people choose the same guide. It is easier to see what people have chosen if they hold the guides up in the air.

6. Depending on the size of the group and time, go around and ask people to say their name and what they have chosen. You might ask if others in the group who know them think of them as exhibiting the behavior they have chosen. No one's opinion is wrong, but external and internal perceptions can differ. This can get complicated to do standing if the group is large.

7. Ask people to be seated and consider which one of the guides is hardest for them. Stay seated and have everyone share this choice.

Processing:

- Did you find this easy or difficult?
- Did you have anything in common with others?
- Would you tell us about any interesting differences or observations?

Note: Be clear that any of these behaviors ***taken to extreme can have negative effects.***

TRANSFORMING POWER COMBO

Purpose: To provide a colorful, active introduction to the concept of Transforming Power.

Time: 30 - 40 minutes.

Materials: The "Violence" brainstorm; a colorful poster of the TP Guidelines posted; TP cards printed on bright heavy paper; a copy of the guidelines on individual pieces of colorful circular pieces of poster board - (see Directions for making a TP Mandala.)

Procedure: Set Up

1. Do a brief TP Talk, (a couple of sentences from each team member works well, - not a lecture or you'll lose the group's attention). One way to describe TP is to refer to it as the ENERGY it takes to move away from the "stuff" on the "Violence" brainstorm.

2. It seems important to point out that nonviolence is not a wimpy lifestyle. It takes a lot more courage to work for a peaceful resolution than it does to get into a fight. We're not pretending that you take AVP and that's the end of conflict in your life. We're looking at some different responses to conflict.

3. Do the Marge Swan skit (see Skits for Transforming Power).

4. Hand out the TP cards. Read the Guidelines to TP out loud, popcorn style. Ask which guidelines were used by Marge Swan.

5. Put the TP circle on the floor in the middle of the circle of participants and scatter the Guideline pieces around it.

6. Ask the participants to stand near a guideline that "speaks" to them, maybe one they have tried or one that makes sense to them.

7. When everyone has "taken a stand," ask if someone would like to say why s/he chose that particular guideline. What does it mean to her/him?

8. When everyone who would like to speak has spoken, sit down.

Processing:

- Do some of the Guidelines seem hard to do?
- Which are the hardest?
- Might you be willing to try some?

Note: The action of "taking a stand" can make this exercise more effective than sitting, thinking and talking.

The processing questions provide a chance to talk about AVP as a direction we can choose to go in rather than instant arrival at perfection.

Students often hear, "You're in AVP and you're still acting like this?" They need to know how to respond. AVP is not a quick fix. It's a walk in the direction of a different way of life.

TRANSFORMING POWER QUERIES FOR ADVANCED

Purpose: To consider queries or questions concerning the concept of Transforming Power; to make these queries (and hence TP) more real by creating skits about some of them.

Time: 30 - 40 minutes.

Materials: Copies of "Queries Concerning Transforming Power" for everyone (attached).

Procedure: Set Up

1. Explain that people will work in four small groups. Each group will first discuss a group of 5 queries or questions that relate to Transforming Power. Then each group will make up a skit to illustrate one of its assigned queries.

2. Each group might refer to any brainstorm or goal concerning conflict that may have been discussed previously in the workshop to get ideas for their skit.

3. If there are no questions about the directions, divide into four small groups and begin.

Processing: (after each skit)

- Can any observer guess which of the 5 queries the group had, that the skit illustrates?
- How realistic was the approach taken?
- Might you be willing to try it?

Note: Having groups discuss 5 queries is less overwhelming than trying to deal with 20. Analyzing which query different skits illustrate makes everyone aware of all the queries.

QUERIES CONCERNING TRANSFORMING POWER

Group 1:

1. When threatened, do I think before I respond? Do I use my mind to direct my responses?
2. Do I respond nonviolently?
3. Do I talk myself into a nonviolent response in advance?
4. Do I stand my ground and let the other person know what's on my mind?
5. Do I look the other person in the eye and appeal to her/his reason?

Group 2:

1. Do I surprise the other person by doing or saying something unexpected which might make the other person respond more reasonably?
2. Do I forget about not liking the other person?
3. Do I hold onto my concept of my best self and apply it to the other person?
4. Do I put myself in the other person's shoes and speak to her/his best self?
5. Do I refuse to let words upset me and, at the same time, am I mindful of the words I use?

Group 3:

1. Do I avoid worrying about my own image?
2. Do I admit it if I am partly wrong to give the other person a chance to admit that s/he is partly wrong, too?
3. If I find the other person is right, do I say so and swiftly end the dispute?
4. Do I take a deep breath and use positive self talk such as "Easy does it."?
5. In a dangerous emergency, do I follow my gut reaction on whether to resist nonviolently or to withdraw?

Group 4:

1. While not welcoming hardship or suffering, are there some things I am willing to suffer for and thus win allies and maybe change the other person's perspective?
2. Do I realize I am never licked until I quit? When I have to wear down prejudice, do I try over and over again until I succeed?
3. Is my final goal to reach a win/win agreement with the other person?
4. Am I ready to practice these queries day after day until Transforming Power becomes my way of life?
5. Do I stay open to the positive?

SKITS FOR TRANSFORMING POWER

Marge Swan Skit

Narrator: This is a true story of a middle-aged woman who lived in New York City. She loved her area of the city. She had lived there all her life. Her neighborhood was becoming more crime-ridden however, and many of her friends thought she should move. She was determined to stay because she liked her community. This woman's name was Marge Swan. (Have skit start.) One night she was going home from the library. She was walking through Central Park carrying a heavy load of books. She became aware of heavy footsteps behind her. A man came up beside her and crowded her to one side.

Marge: (She turns and almost dumps the books in the man's hands and says with animation) I'm so glad you came along. My arms are aching from carrying these books. Would you help me carry them home? (They continue walking and she continues talking)

My apartment isn't very far. I can't tell you how much I appreciate your help.

This is my building. I can take the books now. Again, thank you. You helped me no end.

Man: Lady, that wasn't what I had in mind.

(The narration may be told by the person playing Marge Swan.)

Accidental Bump Skit

Narrator: This skit could take place anywhere — on a street, in a hallway, in a store. Our two actors are Mo and Jo.

Action: Mo and Jo might be walking along a street. Mo is distracted and accidentally bumps into Jo. S/he might step on Jo's sneaker.

Jo: Hey, stupid, why don't you look where you're going? You think you own the sidewalk?
You almost knocked me over. How clumsy can you be?

Mo: You know, you're right. I should have looked where I was going. Hey, I'm sorry. I got some heavy things on my mind. You all right?

Note: It's important to practice demonstration skits such as these at least a couple of times so everyone feels comfortable doing them.

DIRECTIONS FOR MAKING A TP MANDALA

1. Buy sheets of BRIGHT poster board of several different colors.

2. Make a circle about 6 - 8 inches across and print "Transforming Power" on it.

3. Make 12 arcs out of various colors. Print one or two key words on each piece.

   Inner circle applies more to self:
   - -- respect self
   - -- be patient
   - -- stay calm
   - -- be courageous
   - -- think before reacting

   Outer circle applies more to interactions with others:
   - -- affirm others
   - -- ask questions
   - -- use surprise
   - -- try humor
   - -- seek reconciliation
   - -- accept others as they are
   - -- take a risk

4. Below are small-scale samples of TP Mandalas.

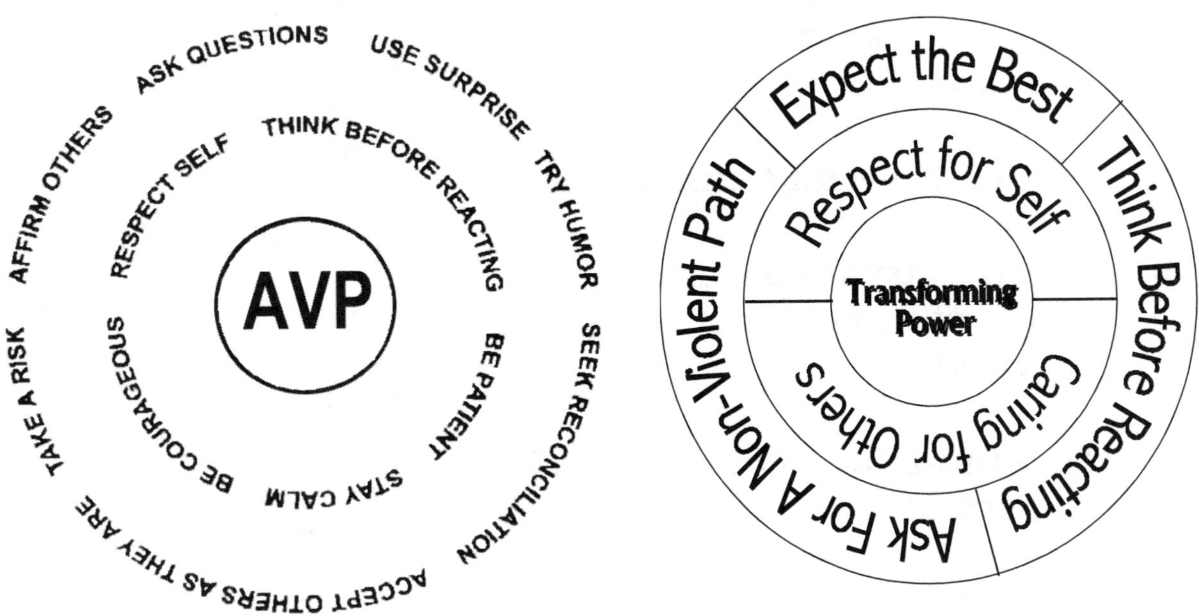

Note: Making a sample pattern out of paper that is easier to cut than poster board may prove helpful. It's not necessary to use the mandala shape. Bright moveable poster board pieces in shapes of your choice will do. Cover pieces with clear contact paper.

GUIDES TO TRANSFORMING POWER

1. **Find something you have in common.**
2. **Reach for the good in others.**
3. **Listen before you make judgments.**
4. **Base your position on truth.**
5. **Be ready to revise your position if it is wrong.**
6. **A position based on truth will give you courage to act.**
7. **If you can't avoid danger, face it creatively rather than violently.**
8. **Use surprise and humor.**
9. **Learn to trust your inner sense of when to act and when to withdraw.**
10. **Be willing to suffer for what is important.**
11. **Be patient and persistent.**
12. **Build community based on honesty, respect and caring.**

HELP ALONG THE WAY

- Build your own self-respect.
- Respect and care about others.
- Expect the best.
- Ask yourself for a nonviolent way. There may be one inside you.
- Pause—take time before you react.
- Don't threaten or put down.
- Don't rely on weapons, drugs or alcohol.
- When you have done wrong, admit it. Make amends if you can, so that you can forgive yourself, then let it go.
- Make friends who will support you. Support the best in them.
- Risk changing yourself.

WHAT IT FEELS LIKE

- The transforming power experience feels like: AHA !!!!!
- There is a spirit of caring.
- There is a letting go of something. (Patterns? Grudges?)
- There is a sharing of something.
- You feel right about it.
- You lose your fear if you had any.

1. Find something you have in common.
2. Reach for the good in others.
3. Listen before you make Judgments.
4. Base your position on truth.
5. Be ready to revise your position if it is wrong.
6. A position based on truth will give you courage to act.
7. If you can't avoid danger, face it creatively rather than violently.
8. Use surprise and humor.
9. Learn to trust your inner sense of when to act and when to withdraw.
10. Be willing to suffer for what is important.
11. Be patient and persistent.
12. Build community based on honesty, respect and caring.

1. Find something you have in common.
2. Reach for the good in others.
3. Listen before you make Judgments.
4. Base your position on truth.
5. Be ready to revise your position if it is wrong.
6. A position based on truth will give you courage to act.
7. If you can't avoid danger, face it creatively rather than violently.
8. Use surprise and humor.
9. Learn to trust your inner sense of when to act and when to withdraw.
10. Be willing to suffer for what is important.
11. Be patient and persistent.
12. Build community based on honesty, respect and caring.

1. Find something you have in common.
2. Reach for the good in others.
3. Listen before you make Judgments.
4. Base your position on truth.
5. Be ready to revise your position if it is wrong.
6. A position based on truth will give you courage to act.
7. If you can't avoid danger, face it creatively rather than violently.
8. Use surprise and humor.
9. Learn to trust your inner sense of when to act and when to withdraw.
10. Be willing to suffer for what is important.
11. Be patient and persistent.
12. Build community based on honesty, respect and caring.

1. Find something you have in common.
2. Reach for the good in others.
3. Listen before you make Judgments.
4. Base your position on truth.
5. Be ready to revise your position if it is wrong.
6. A position based on truth will give you courage to act.
7. If you can't avoid danger, face it creatively rather than violently.
8. Use surprise and humor.
9. Learn to trust your inner sense of when to act and when to withdraw.
10. Be willing to suffer for what is important.
11. Be patient and persistent.
12. Build community based on honesty, respect and caring.

1. Find something you have in common.
2. Reach for the good in others.
3. Listen before you make Judgments.
4. Base your position on truth.
5. Be ready to revise your position if it is wrong.
6. A position based on truth will give you courage to act.
7. If you can't avoid danger, face it creatively rather than violently.
8. Use surprise and humor.
9. Learn to trust your inner sense of when to act and when to withdraw.
10. Be willing to suffer for what is important.
11. Be patient and persistent.
12. Build community based on honesty, respect and caring.

1. Find something you have in common.
2. Reach for the good in others.
3. Listen before you make Judgments.
4. Base your position on truth.
5. Be ready to revise your position if it is wrong.
6. A position based on truth will give you courage to act.
7. If you can't avoid danger, face it creatively rather than violently.
8. Use surprise and humor.
9. Learn to trust your inner sense of when to act and when to withdraw.
10. Be willing to suffer for what is important.
11. Be patient and persistent.
12. Build community based on honesty, respect and caring.

1. Find something you have in common.
2. Reach for the good in others.
3. Listen before you make Judgments.
4. Base your position on truth.
5. Be ready to revise your position if it is wrong.
6. A position based on truth will give you courage to act.
7. If you can't avoid danger, face it creatively rather than violently.
8. Use surprise and humor.
9. Learn to trust your inner sense of when to act and when to withdraw.
10. Be willing to suffer for what is important.
11. Be patient and persistent.
12. Build community based on honesty, respect and caring. 1. Find something you have in common.

1. Find something you have in common.
2. Reach for the good in others.
3. Listen before you make Judgments.
4. Base your position on truth.
5. Be ready to revise your position if it is wrong.
6. A position based on truth will give you courage to act.
7. If you can't avoid danger, face it creatively rather than violently.
8. Use surprise and humor.
9. Learn to trust your inner sense of when to act and when to withdraw.
10. Be willing to suffer for what is important.
11. Be patient and persistent.
12. Build community based on honesty, respect and caring.

1. Find something you have in common.
2. Reach for the good in others.
3. Listen before you make Judgments.
4. Base your position on truth.
5. Be ready to revise your position if it is wrong.
6. A position based on truth will give you courage to act.
7. If you can't avoid danger, face it creatively rather than violently.
8. Use surprise and humor.
9. Learn to trust your inner sense of when to act and when to withdraw.
10. Be willing to suffer for what is important.
11. Be patient and persistent.
12. Build community based on honesty, respect and caring.

1. Find something you have in common.
2. Reach for the good in others.
3. Listen before you make Judgments.
4. Base your position on truth.
5. Be ready to revise your position if it is wrong.
6. A position based on truth will give you courage to act.
7. If you can't avoid danger, face it creatively rather than violently.
8. Use surprise and humor.
9. Learn to trust your inner sense of when to act and when to withdraw.
10. Be willing to suffer for what is important.
11. Be patient and persistent.
12. Build community based on honesty, respect and caring.

1. Find something you have in common.
2. Reach for the good in others.
3. Listen before you make Judgments.
4. Base your position on truth.
5. Be ready to revise your position if it is wrong.
6. A position based on truth will give you courage to act.
7. If you can't avoid danger, face it creatively rather than violently.
8. Use surprise and humor.
9. Learn to trust your inner sense of when to act and when to withdraw.
10. Be willing to suffer for what is important.
11. Be patient and persistent.
12. Build community based on honesty, respect and caring.

HELP ALONG THE WAY

- Build your own self-respect.
- Respect and care about others.
- Expect the best.
- Ask yourself for a non-violent way.
  There may be one inside you.
- Pause--take time before you react.
- Don't threaten or put down.
- Don't rely on weapons, drugs or alcohol.
- When you have done wrong, admit it, make amends if you can, so that you can forgive yourself, then let it go.
- Make friends who will support you. Support the best in them.
- Risk changing yourself.

HELP ALONG THE WAY

- Build your own self-respect.
- Respect and care about others.
- Expect the best.
- Ask yourself for a non-violent way.
  There may be one inside you.
- Pause--take time before you react.
- Don't threaten or put down.
- Don't rely on weapons, drugs or alcohol.
- When you have done wrong, admit it, make amends if you can, so that you can forgive yourself, then let it go.
- Make friends who will support you. Support the best in them.
- Risk changing yourself.

HELP ALONG THE WAY

- Build your own self-respect.
- Respect and care about others.
- Expect the best.
- Ask yourself for a non-violent way.
  There may be one inside you.
- Pause--take time before you react.
- Don't threaten or put down.
- Don't rely on weapons, drugs or alcohol.
- When you have done wrong, admit it, make amends if you can, so that you can forgive yourself, then let it go.
- Make friends who will support you. Support the best in them.
- Risk changing yourself.

HELP ALONG THE WAY

- Build your own self-respect.
- Respect and care about others.
- Expect the best.
- Ask yourself for a non-violent way.
  There may be one inside you.
- Pause--take time before you react.
- Don't threaten or put down.
- Don't rely on weapons, drugs or alcohol.
- When you have done wrong, admit it, make amends if you can, so that you can forgive yourself, then let it go.
- Make friends who will support you. Support the best in them.
- Risk changing yourself.

HELP ALONG THE WAY

- Build your own self-respect.
- Respect and care about others.
- Expect the best.
- Ask yourself for a non-violent way.
  There may be one inside you.
- Pause--take time before you react.
- Don't threaten or put down.
- Don't rely on weapons, drugs or alcohol.
- When you have done wrong, admit it, make amends if you can, so that you can forgive yourself, then let it go.
- Make friends who will support you. Support the best in them.
- Risk changing yourself.

HELP ALONG THE WAY

- Build your own self-respect.
- Respect and care about others.
- Expect the best.
- Ask yourself for a non-violent way.
  There may be one inside you.
- Pause--take time before you react.
- Don't threaten or put down.
- Don't rely on weapons, drugs or alcohol.
- When you have done wrong, admit it, make amends if you can, so that you can forgive yourself, then let it go.
- Make friends who will support you. Support the best in them.
- Risk changing yourself.

HELP ALONG THE WAY

- Build your own self-respect.
- Respect and care about others.
- Expect the best.
- Ask yourself for a non-violent way.
  There may be one inside you.
- Pause--take time before you react.
- Don't threaten or put down.
- Don't rely on weapons, drugs or alcohol.
- When you have done wrong, admit it, make amends if you can, so that you can forgive yourself, then let it go.
- Make friends who will support you. Support the best in them.
- Risk changing yourself.

HELP ALONG THE WAY

- Build your own self-respect.
- Respect and care about others.
- Expect the best.
- Ask yourself for a non-violent way.
  There may be one inside you.
- Pause--take time before you react.
- Don't threaten or put down.
- Don't rely on weapons, drugs or alcohol.
- When you have done wrong, admit it, make amends if you can, so that you can forgive yourself, then let it go.
- Make friends who will support you. Support the best in them.
- Risk changing yourself.

HELP ALONG THE WAY

- Build your own self-respect.
- Respect and care about others.
- Expect the best.
- Ask yourself for a non-violent way.
  There may be one inside you.
- Pause--take time before you react.
- Don't threaten or put down.
- Don't rely on weapons, drugs or alcohol.
- When you have done wrong, admit it, make amends if you can, so that you can forgive yourself, then let it go.
- Make friends who will support you. Support the best in them.
- Risk changing yourself.

HELP ALONG THE WAY

- Build your own self-respect.
- Respect and care about others.
- Expect the best.
- Ask yourself for a non-violent way.
  There may be one inside you.
- Pause--take time before you react.
- Don't threaten or put down.
- Don't rely on weapons, drugs or alcohol.
- When you have done wrong, admit it, make amends if you can, so that you can forgive yourself, then let it go.
- Make friends who will support you. Support the best in them.
- Risk changing yourself.

FEELING STATEMENTS
Introductory Material

The concept of Feeling Statements (AKA I-Messages) is an integral part of the AVP approach. The sample agendas include exercises for different levels. Having these exercises in one section may be helpful for planning new programs. Depending on the particular group in any given workshop, facilitators may pick and choose which exercises they'll use.

GENERAL THOUGHTS

The purpose for using Feeling Statements is to resolve a conflict without attacking a person. To do this, focus is placed on the situation and the consideration of what feelings arise in a person when a particular situation occurs. A Feeling Statement avoids blaming and/or judging. Blaming and judging escalate rather than resolve conflicts peacefully.

The FEELING STATEMENT FORMULA may include:

WHEN	describe the situation or behavior.
I GET/FEEL/AM	state the feeling, e.g., angry, hurt, discouraged.
BECAUSE	explain the result for yourself or the basis of your feelings without blaming others.
(*and possibly*)	
THEREFORE	explain what you'd like to see happen - working for an acceptable solution for each other.

The formula need not be used every time you speak to someone about what you consider to be a problem. It is very worthwhile to use the formula to clarify "where you're coming from" and subsequently to consider how you wish to try to solve your problem, remembering that what you consider to be a problem may not be a problem for another.

The first three steps of the formula needn't be considered in the order given. Any order is fine. Sometimes younger students are only able to identify the feeling(s) that swell up in them when a particular event happens. They may need time and maturity to determine why any particular feeling surfaces. Identifying feelings is important just in itself! Considering how to handle them is also a plus.

Introducing Feeling Statements as a way to clarify one's own state may be a wise approach with young people. Being able to say how they feel when a particular situation happens, just in front of the group, can be a positive experience. Knowing that others often feel the same way can be comforting. Having people share how they might handle their feelings is also important.

Many young people shy away from actually using a Feeling Statement directly to another person. This is definitely understandable. Feeling Statements make people vulnerable. The response to your stating your feelings may be, "I don't care how you feel."

Fearing such a response, people may clam up or fight or give up. Are these reactions positive? Considering such a question is worthwhile, as is considering whether we are responsible for how we handle our feelings.

The use of Feeling Statements might be more acceptable if seen as part of a bigger picture. Using Feeling Statements might be thought of as looking for common ground. To do this, preface the Feeling Statement with a phrase such as, "Look, could we talk about.....(*whatever*). I'd like to tell you what's going on with me and I'd like to hear how you're seeing things."

Though it may seem unnatural to avoid saying "you" in a Feeling Statement, people may understand why "you" is avoided by experiencing the simple "Hand Push" exercise. Just as a physical push is often followed by a retaliatory physical push, a verbal "push" like "You shouldn't" is often followed by a verbal "push" such as "Well, you shouldn't" or "You always." "You messages" like these which blame or deal with past history won't help defuse conflicts.

In the dictionary the word "feeling" refers to emotions, states of mind and comparisons. Examples of how we might express some of these are:

EMOTIONS	STATES OF MIND	COMPARISONS
I feel	*I feel*	*I feel*
mad (angry)	excluded	like an outcast
sad (hurt)	disrespected (dis'd)	like a turd
scared (fearful)	used	like a Ping-Pong ball
glad (joyful)	good	on top of the world

Feelings that are the least likely to be challenged or contradicted are those that fall under "Emotions." These come from the gut, not the head. People may say, "You shouldn't feel hurt." but you and only you know how you feel.

Some states of mind might imply a disguised "you message" and/or a judgment. It is important to point this out. Saying "I feel disrespected" to someone may imply "you disrespected me." If a participant expresses a "State of Mind," e.g., saying "I feel disrespected when someone cuts in front of me on the lunch line," a facilitator may paraphrase what was said. "I see. You think a person has disrespected you when they cut you on line. But how do you feel underneath? angry? hurt"? This usually helps people see the difference.

Though usually Feeling Statements try to avoid the use of "you," some people may feel this is too artificial. Suggest that they include the "you" with care. A great deal depends on the tone of voice one uses. If people truly are looking for common ground and preface their statement accordingly (see above), the "you" is more likely to be received with good will. Explaining the basis of your feelings in such a statement is also positive. For example:

I worry	when you drink/drug so much	because I love you and feel afraid that something will happen to you.
I feel inadequate	when you call me stupid	because I haven't done well in school and I don't have much confidence in my abilities.

Regardless of the care people take in expressing a Feeling Statement, those on the receiving end may not respond positively. Everyone's at different places at different times. It might be wise to warn young people of this reality. Of course, the person receiving the Feeling Statement may respond positively — at a later time. Regardless, sometimes just having an opportunity to say the Feeling Statement can be helpful for the speaker.

Understanding and incorporating Feeling Statements into one's life also takes time. It is unlikely that all of the above aspects of Feeling Statements can be conveyed in one or even two workshops. It may only be possible to plant a seed or two.

The use of the "feeling" faces or plates in many of the following exercises may seem redundant. However, holding a plate which shows a feeling seems to provide a bit of distance from the feeling itself and therefore makes it easier for people to talk about it.

EXERCISES

In the following pages are several exercises which suggest ways of presenting the concept of Feeling Statements. The exercises are referred to as such in the sample agendas. The exercises are listed in order from simplest to more complex (relatively speaking) rather than alphabetically.

The exercises include:

1) **FEELING FACES and CARDS FOR MIDDLE SCHOOL** - a short introduction for 11 year-olds
2) **FEELING SCENARIOS** - a continuation of 1) for 12 year-olds or a continuation of 4) and 5) for older students to practice forming feeling statements
3) **FEELING SITUATIONS FOR MIDDLE SCHOOLS** - an alternative or a backup for 2) for 12 year-olds
4) **FEELING FACES, CATEGORIES and LAYERS** - for a Basic (it can build on what's been presented in middle school, or stand on its own)
5) **FEELING STATEMENT CARDS** - for a Basic if "Cards" are not covered in a middle school program
6) **FEELING SITUATIONS FOR BASIC** - an alternative or a backup for 2) in a Basic
7) **FEELING STATEMENTS IN PAIRS** - another way to practice forming feeling statements
8) **FEELING CHAIR** - a way to practice forming/saying feeling statements to someone
9) **FEELING CIRCLES** - another way to practice forming/saying feeling statements to someone

Following these exercises are sheets used with several exercises and referred to in the exercises. They are entitled Feeling Faces Sheet, Feeling Statement Card Samples (this includes statements for both older and younger students) and Suggested Scenarios to Practice Feeling Statements.

Please note, the basic Feeling Statement Formula is given on page F-25. Unless noted, the exercises incorporate only the first three steps.

COMPLEMENTARY EXERCISES (found in the Exercise Section)

Hand Push might be used as an introductory exercise to Feeling Statements or to enliven more sedentary Feeling Statement exercises. ***Take the Blame Out*** offers another opportunity to practice forming feeling statements and to experience the downside of "you messages."

Choices I and II both consider different ways of handling feelings like anger and frustration. ***Facts and Feelings*** and ***Buttons*** allow for a deeper look at what may lie beneath some of our feelings.

FEELING FACES AND CARDS FOR MIDDLE SCHOOL

Purpose: To begin to examine feelings in general and to provide a brief introduction to Feeling Statements with cards.

Time: About 20 minutes

Materials: Paper plates with about 20 different faces and their corresponding feelings (see Feeling Faces Sheet) and a few blank plates; a poster with the basic Feeling Statement Formula: I feel...when...because...; four sets of fifteen cards (each set can be arranged in five Feeling Statements); each set has different statements [see Feeling Statement Card Samples])

Procedure: **Set Up**

1. Scatter the plates on the floor in the middle of the circle. Talk briefly about them. Does anyone see any feelings they have felt? Are any of these feelings hard to talk about? Are there feelings that need to be added? (If so, someone could write them on the empty plates.)

2. Point out the poster with the basic Feeling Statement Formula. Explain that it can help us figure out how we feel when certain things happen. It can also be used to tell someone else how we feel. Give an example: I feel angry when someone cuts in front of me on the lunch line, because it'll take me longer to get lunch.

3. Explain that in small groups, everyone will have a chance to make some Feeling Statements using flash cards. Each group will get fifteen cards. Five cards start with "I," five start with "when," and five start with "because." Putting one each of the three parts together will form a statement. Each group will work to form five Feeling Statements that people think make sense. People will also prepare to read them when they return to the big circle.

4. If there are no questions divide the participants into groups (if possible have groups of 5) and give one set of fifteen cards to each group. They may work on a table or the floor. If possible have a co-facilitator work with each group.

5. When all the groups are finished, ask them to return to the big circle and read their Feeling Statements.

Processing:

- Do any of these situations sound familiar?
- Might you be able to use such statements in real life?
- Might naming our feelings help us to deal with them better?

Note: It's not necessary to get too intense about the formula. Don't be surprised if some of the sentences formed are unusual. Keep it light. Feeling Statements will be used again in the Introduction to Win/Win.

FEELING SCENARIOS

Purpose: To have people form Feeling Statements for their own scenarios.

Time: About 20 minutes

Materials: Plates from Feeling Faces Sheet and a poster with the Feeling Statement Formula

Procedure: Set Up:

1. Scatter the plates (20-25) on the floor in the middle of the circle. Review the general Feeling Statements Formula. Remind people that previously they had formed Feeling Statements using "flash" cards. Now they'll try making their own Feeling Statements.

2. In a minute you'll ask everyone to walk around the plates. As people walk they'll think of a scenario or situation in which they feel a certain way. When they see a plate that corresponds to their feeling, they'll keep it in mind. When everyone has walked full circle, have them sit down.

3. Next, explain that people going "pop-corn" style can pick up a plate they've kept in mind. When they sit down again, they'll describe their scenario and use the plate to show how they feel in that situation. Then they'll explain why they feel that way, using the Feeling Statement Formula.

4. Model this yourself. Pick up "overwhelmed" and sit down. Say, "When someone bigger than I am yells at me, I feel overwhelmed because I don't know what to do." Then return your plate to the floor so someone else may use it.

5. If there are no questions, say that people may begin whenever they're ready.

Processing:

- Do you have feelings similar to others in similar situations?
- Would you be able to use a Feeling Statement to clarify how you feel? to explain to someone else how you feel?

Note: If not many students are forthcoming in explaining their own scenarios you might use the scenarios from FEELING SITUATIONS FOR BASIC or FEELING SITUATIONS FOR MIDDLE SCHOOLS as a backup.

It's very likely that the "because" part of the statement will involve a judgment rather than a result for self or the basis of the feeling. It's good to point this out and see if anyone can come up with a result for self or the basis of the feeling.

For younger students, do so lightly. Sometimes it might be better to simply say the feeling and leave out the "because" part of the statement at this age.

FEELING SITUATIONS FOR MIDDLE SCHOOL

Purpose: To practice forming Feeling Statements.

Time 15 - 20 minutes

Materials: Plates from Feeling Faces Sheet, a poster with the Feeling Statement Formula and a list of situations (see below or make your own)

Procedure: Set Up:

1. Scatter the plates (20-25) on the floor in the middle of the circle. Review the general Feeling Statements Formula (unless you've done this recently).

2. Explain that you will read a group of situations that may speak to some people. If someone feels a particular way about one of the situations, s/he may choose a plate (pop-corn style) that describes how s/he feels and explain why s/he feels that way giving a result for self or the basis of the feeling. (You may want to limit the number responding to 2 or 3)

3. Ask a fellow facilitator to model what you mean. Read: If someone cuts in front of me on the lunch line, I feel.....(bloop)....because....(blop). The facilitator might pick up "angry" and say: When someone cuts in front of me on the lunch line, I feel angry because it will slow me down in getting my lunch.

4. If there are no questions, continue by reading other situations such as :
   When I forget my homework, I feel.....because....
   When I get a commendation (sticker, prize) from a teacher, I feel .....because....
   When my friend gets a commendation and I don't, I feel.....because.....
   When I walk into a room where I don't know anyone, I feel.....because.....
   When my mom takes me to the grocery store with her, I feel.....because.....
   When I get a good grade on a test, I feel.....because.....
   When a teacher yells at me, I feel .....because.....
   When I hear adults yelling at each other, I feel.....because....
   When people tease me, I feel.....because.....

Processing:

- Do you have feelings similar to others in similar situations?
- Would you be able to use a Feeling Statement to clarify how you feel? to explain to someone else how you feel?

Note: It's very likely that the "because" part of the statement will involve a judgment rather than a result for self or the basis of the feeling. It's good to point this out and ask for suggestions. Try to do so lightly. Sometimes it might be better to simply say the feeling and leave out the "because" part of the statement at this age.

FEELING FACES, CATEGORIES AND LAYERS

Purpose: To examine feelings in general and to recall that often one feeling covers another.

Time: About 20 minutes

Materials: 20-25 plates from Feeling Faces Sheet, a couple of empty plates; 4 small signs (3x5 cards) with the words, "SAD," "MAD," "GLAD," and "SCARED," printed on them.

Procedure: **Set Up**

1. Scatter the plates on the floor in the middle of the circle. Ask a volunteer to pick up a plate that has a feeling on it that s/he has felt at one time or another. If a feeling they've felt is not there, they could write it on one of the empty plates. You pick up a plate, too.
2. When it seems that everyone who would like to has picked up a plate, hold your plate so all can see it. Give an example of a time when you feel this particular feeling. (e.g., "I feel angry when somebody cuts in front of me on the lunch line.")
3. Replace your plate and invite others to say when they feel what's on their plate. This can be done popcorn style or going around the circle. As they finish, ask them to return their plates to the floor since someone else may want to use them.
4. When all the plates are back on the floor, put the **SAD/MAD/GLAD/SCARED** cards on the floor, as if the circle were divided into four sections.
5. Ask everyone to pick up a plate and place it near the card they think best.
6. When movement stops, ask if anyone thinks any of the plates should be closer to a different card. For example, someone may have put "jealous" near "MAD." Someone else may think it should be closer to "SAD" or to "SCARED." Ask if there's a spot where it could be placed to show that "jealous" may involve being "MAD" "SAD" or "SCARED."
7. Would anyone like to move another plate or plates? Consider as in #6.
8. Ask if anyone has ever experienced feeling several feelings at once? For example, might "jealous" involve feeling "MAD," "SAD," <u>and</u> "SCARED," all at the same time? Might someone explain how this can be so?
9. Overlap the four plates to show how sometimes feelings may cover or mask each other. Others may wish to share their experiences with over-lapping feelings.
10. Ask if people ever show one face to cover up what they're really feeling, e.g., showing "good" or "happy" to cover up "hurt."

Processing:

- How do you feel about feelings?
- Is it easy to pinpoint exactly what we're feeling all of the time?
- Is it all right to have feelings like angry or mad?

Note: *If your participants have experienced Feeling Faces and Cards for Middle School and Feeling Scenarios and/or Feeling Situations for Middle School, steps 1 through 3 may not be necessary.*
If "angry" or "mad" were placed on the Brainstorm on Violence sheet you might also ask if feeling "angry" or "mad" is violent?
This exercise may generate wide differences of opinion since experiences of feelings are so personal. It may provide an opportunity for people to say why they feel and think the way they do.

FEELING STATEMENT CARDS

Purpose: To form Feeling Statements, to hear a good number of them and to consider the value of using them to deal with our feelings.

Time: 15 - 20 minutes

Materials: A poster with the Feeling Statement Formula, for 20 people have four sets of fifteen cards (each set can be arranged in five Feeling Statements; each set has different statements [see Feeling Statement Card Samples]).

Procedure: **Set Up**

1. Say that sometimes we have strong feelings about different situations. Sometimes it's hard to handle our feelings. We might try to express them using a Feeling Statement. Read or ask volunteers to read the Feeling Statement Formula that's posted.

2. Explain that in small groups, everyone will have a chance to make some Feeling Statements, using flash cards. Each group will get fifteen cards. Five cards start with "I," five start with "when," and five start with "because." Putting together one each of the three parts will form a statement. Each group will work to form five Feeling Statements that people think make sense. They will also prepare to read them when they return to the big circle.

3. If there are no questions, divide the participants into four groups and give one set of fifteen cards to each group. They may work on a table or the floor. If possible, have a co-facilitator work with each small group.

4. When all the groups are finished, ask them to return to the big circle with their group and read their Feeling Statements.

Processing:

- Do any of the situations described in the statements sound familiar?
- Might naming our feelings help us to deal with them better?
- Might you use such statements in real life?
- If you said such a statement to people you know, what do you think their response would be?

Note: Many people don't think they can use Feeling Statements in real life. Even if all a person does is to identify what s/he feels in a given situation, this can be helpful.

Don't be surprised if some groups form silly statements.

FEELING SITUATIONS FOR BASIC

Purpose: To practice forming Feeling Statements.

Time 15 - 20 minutes

Materials: Plates from Feeling Faces Sheet, a poster with the Feeling Statement Formula and a list of situations (see below or make your own)

Procedure: **Set Up:**

1. Scatter the plates (20-25) on the floor in the middle of the circle. Review the general Feeling Statements Formula (unless you've done this recently).

2. Explain that you will read a group of situations that may speak to some people. If someone feels a particular way about one of the situations, s/he may choose a plate (pop-corn style) that describes how s/he feels and explain why s/he feels that way giving a result for self or the basis of the feeling. (You may want to limit the number responding to 2 or 3)

3. Ask a fellow facilitator to model what you mean. Read: If someone cuts in front of me on a cafeteria line, I feel..(bloop)..because..(blop). The facilitator might pick up "angry" and say: When someone cuts in front of me on a cafeteria line I feel angry because it will slow me down in getting my lunch. You might remind people that the "because" part of the statement explains the result for self or the basis of the feeling. It avoids judging and blaming.

4. If there are no questions, continue by reading other situations such as:
   When I forget an important meeting, I feel.....because....
   When I get a compliment, I feel .....because.....
   When I walk into a room where I don't know anyone, I feel.....because.....
   When someone in authority yells at me, I feel .....because.....
   When I do well at something, I feel.....because.....
   When someone gives me the finger, I feel .....because.....
   When people in my family yell at each other, I feel.....because....
   When people put me down, I feel.....because.....

Processing:

- How can you pinpoint the reason that you feel the way you do?
- Do you have feelings similar to others in similar situations?
- What would happen if you said a Feeling Statement to someone you know?

Note: Naturally many people may have trouble pinpointing the result for self or the basis of the feeling. It's much more likely that we say, "because it's wrong" or "because s/he shouldn't," etc. Even realizing that these are judgments can be helpful. Other members of the group might be able to suggest reasons that truly are results for self or the basis of the feeling.

FEELING STATEMENTS IN PAIRS

Purpose: To practice forming Feeling Statements

Time: 20 minutes

Materials: The Feeling Statement Formula posted; copies of the Feeling Faces Sheet for everyone; scenarios (see Suggested Scenarios to Practice Feeling Statements) printed on slips of paper (one per pair) or a sheet for everyone; paper/pencils

Procedure: **Set Up**

1. Explain that communication consists of sending and receiving messages. Messages involving feelings may be sent with "I"/feeling statements, or "you"/judgments.

2. "You"/judgment statements:
   a) put people down;
   b) tell people what is wrong with them;
   c) stop the conversation.

   For example:
   You only think of yourself and your friends.
   You should be nicer to me.
   You're always bugging me.

3. Feeling statements usually start with "I" and give information about me, my feelings and my needs in a way that shows respect and concern for others. Point out the Feeling Statement Formula and explain it briefly.
   Give some examples:
   I feel frustrated when the phone is often in use because I can't receive calls.
   I am thankful when people call me to say they will be late because then I don't worry.
   I was angry when you didn't return my calls because I needed your help.

4. Divide the group into pairs, distribute copies of the Feeling Faces Sheet, paper and pencils and one scenario (or the whole sheet) to do one of the following:
   a) Give each pair one scenario and ask <u>the pair</u> to develop and write down a feeling statement (using a feeling from the sheet) that could be used in the situation described.
   b) Give each pair one scenario and ask <u>each person</u> to write a feeling statement and read it to her/his partner, who may give advice on whether the statement <u>decreases</u> the tension in the situation.
   c) Give each person in the pair the list of scenarios and have each choose one and proceed as in "b" just above.

5. When all are ready, go around asking each person or pair to read the scenario and feeling statement they would use in the given situation. Affirm each one.

FEELING CHAIR

Purpose: To practice saying a Feeling Statement to someone else.

Time: 15 - 20 minutes

Materials: 2 extra chairs placed in the middle of the circle; the Feeling Statement Formula posted

Procedure: Set Up

1. Explain that this activity will give people a chance to practice saying a Feeling Statement to someone in their lives.
2. If necessary, review the Feeling Statement Formula.
3. Model, or have a teammate model, what will be done. Take one of the two seats in the center of the circle. Explain that you'll imagine that your (mother, brother, daughter, friend) is seated in the other chair. Say a feeling statement to that person e.g., "I worry when you drink/drug because I love you and feel afraid that something will happen to you."
4. Ask for comments. Does the statement judge? How might it be received? Are there any disguised "you" statements?
5. If there are no questions, ask everyone to think for a minute and consider if there is anyone to whom they would like to try saying a Feeling Statement.
6. After a minute or so, ask anyone who would like to try, to simply come up and sit in one of the chairs and continue as was modeled in #3 above.
7. After each person goes, ask questions as in #4 above.
8. After everyone who wishes to has had a turn, remove the chairs and process.

Processing:

- Has anyone any general comments?
- Is it easy or difficult forming Feeling Statements?
- Does it help you determine why you feel the way you do?
- Will a Feeling Statement necessarily lead to change in another's behavior?

Note: Another option is to have someone sit in the second chair and "Role Play" the speaker's "other person," reflecting back what the speaker says. This could be done from the start or after a few people have spoken to an empty chair. If you choose to do this, it would be wise to model the "reflecting back" when you introduce it.

FEELING CIRCLES

Purpose: To practice saying a Feeling Statement to others and to hear the others reflect back what we've said — a review for an Advanced.

Time: 15 - 20 minutes

Materials: The Feeling Statement Formula posted, a list of scenarios to read (See Suggested Scenarios to Practice Feeling Statements or make your own.)

Procedure: **Set Up**

1. Explain that this activity will give everyone a chance to practice saying Feeling Statements to people and to experience hearing the statements reflected back.

2. If necessary, review the Feeling Statement Formula.

3. People will be seated as if they were going to do Concentric Circles.

4. First those in the outer circle will listen to a scenario that you will read. They will consider themselves to be the "you" in the scenario. They will make a Feeling Statement and say it to the person opposite them. That person will reflect back what s/he heard. Have two facilitators model this (see *Note).*

5. If there are no questions, arrange the group as for Concentric Circles, read the first scenario and have the group do what you explained in #4 above.

6. Now ask those in the inner circle to move one chair to their right. Explain that this time the inner circle will try making the Feeling Statement, considering themselves to be the "you" in the next scenario. Then their new partner will reflect back what they heard. If there are no questions, proceed with a second scenario.

7. Now have the people in the outer circle move one chair to their right; continue as in #4 above.

8. Have each circle try three or four feeling statements. Have one scenario for each circle involve a positive situation. Then return to the full circle.

Processing:

- Did people relate to the situations given?
- Was it easy or difficult forming Feeling Statements without judging?
- Will a person always understand exactly what you say?

Note: To model what everyone will be doing, you might do the "option" in the Feeling Chair exercise, unless this was done already. It's wise to practice the modeling.

How Do You FEEL ?

sad
mad
glad
scared
lonely
mellow
overwhelmed
happy
disgusted
depressed
confused
bored
helpless
angry
surprised
worried
guilty
envious
uneasy
hopeful
sorry
upset
weary
excited
frustrated
ashamed
embarrassed
jealous

FEELING STATEMENT CARD SAMPLES

Using 5x7 cards of 3 different colors, make 4 sets with 5 Feeling Statements in each, as follows: Put the "feeling" section on pink cards;
the "when" section on blue cards;
the "because" section on white cards.
The first 4 sets below might be suitable for older students; the last 4 for younger. Shuffle the colors in each set before using.

"Feeling" - Pink	"When" - Blue	"Because" - White
I get confused	when people say, "take that look off your face"	because I thought I was just listening
I feel overwhelmed	when things pile up	because I can't figure out where to start
I get angry	when my tape isn't playable	because it's one of my favorites
I get hysterical	when we use that detergent	because it makes me itch
I worry	when people drink/drug so much	because I don't want them to get hurt
I get annoyed	when people tell me what to do	because I like to do things my way
I get edgy	when we eat there	because it gives me gas
I feel overwhelmed	when people shout	because then I have trouble listening
I am pleased	when I get compliments about my work	because I take pride in what I do
I get angry	when people turn things into jokes	because some things are serious for me
I get hurt	when people don't show up for a date	because it <u>seems</u> like they don't care
I feel satisfied	when I do well in practice	because it shows hard work is worth it
I feel guilty	when I don't do the things I should	because I'm letting others and myself down
I get frustrated	when people interrupt	because I lose my train of thought
I feel anxious	just before test results are announced	because if I get D or F I'll be off the team
I get frustrated	when people won't try something I suggest	because I like my opinions valued
I'm relieved	when people call to say they'll be late	because otherwise I'd worry
I get annoyed	when people call me stupid	because I don't always make mistakes
I feel scared	when people take reckless chances	because it could end in disaster
I feel vulnerable	when people know so much about me	because I don't know how they'll judge me
(*for younger students*)		
I get angry	when I don't get my own way	because I was told I'm special
I feel at ease	when everything is under control	because then I can handle things
I get bored	when I hear the same song over and over	after a while I don't hear anything
I feel calm	when the day is over	because now it's time to take it easy
I feel eager	to get started first thing in the morning	because then things look good
I feel friendly	when people wave	because they recognize me
I feel proud	when I have a good idea	because I like to contribute
I'm fearful	when I get bad grades	because I don't know what will happen
I get worried	when people don't keep my secrets	because it could be embarrassing
I feel silly	when I stand on my head	because everything is upside down
I get tense	when I haven't prepared for a test	because I want to do well
I feel glad	when people tell me I've done a good job	because it's nice to be appreciated
I feel afraid	when I don't know what will happen next	because it could end badly
I get angry	when people take advantage of other people	because the same thing has happened to me
I feel absurd	when I have to wear some things	because they seem so out of style
I'm cheerful	when I'm with my friends	because I know I'm accepted
I feel helpless	when I see bullies picking on other people	because I don't know how to stop them
I feel cool	when I try something new and it works	because my friends will want to try it too
I 'm glad	when people offer to do the dishes	because I have so much work to do
I feel free	when there's no one to give orders	because I know what needs to be done

Suggested Scenarios to Practice Feeling Statements

1. A loved one (child, parent, spouse) is expected home at 9, doesn't call and shows up at 11. You say...

2. You're "going with" someone. The two of you have gone to watch a basketball game and your friend spends a lot of time with someone else. You say...

3. You loan your car or bike to someone who returns it clean and polished. You say...

4. You and your friend were going to meet for pizza. Your friend doesn't show up. Next time you meet, you say...

5. You're on the phone and someone won't leave you alone, and keeps telling you to cut it short so s/he can use the phone. You say...

6. You've had a really rough week and a friend sends you a "cheer-up" card. You call and say...

7. A friend borrows a tape. Soda gets spilled on it so that it's ruined. You say...

8. It's a stormy night. You planned to go to an out-of-town game with a friend. Then the friend calls to say that s/he can't use the family car. You say...

9. You have a ton of work to do and someone offers to do the dishes for you. You say...

10. In a disagreement with a family member, s/he begins to yell in your face and gets really threatening. You say...

11. Your friend always says s/he wants to do things together, but always seems to make excuses when you suggest something you particularly enjoy (a hike, a movie, whatever) You say...

12. An older relative still calls you by a "baby" nickname and you really don't like it. You say...

13. Your boss continually calls you stupid. You finally decide to say...

14. Your father/mother/older sibling seems to want to make your decisions for you. You say...

15. Now that you are older, you have told your family that your bedroom is your own private space, but family members continue to enter without asking or knocking. Finally you say. . .

16. You and your friends are concerned with the way certain kids tell dirty jokes and talk about sex in public simply to get attention. So when you meet one of them, you say...

17. Your parents never seem to want you to stay out at night with your friends, so you say...

WIN/WIN
Introductory Material

The concept of **Win/Win** seems particularly important in youth programs. Some facilitators like to introduce it as early as possible and return to it in subsequent programs and workshops. Therefore several exercises dealing with **Win/Win** have been included in this manual.

The sample agendas include exercises for different levels. It is hoped that, as with "Feeling Statements," having these exercises in one section might be helpful in planning new programs.

Some programs for youth substitute the term Fair/Fair for **Win/Win**. A total **Win/Win** is not always possible in life. Fair/Fair would be a compromise which is truly acceptable to both sides in a conflict and not just an agreement that one or both sides "put up with."

EXERCISES
In the following pages are several exercises which suggest ways of presenting the concept of **Win/Win**.

The exercises include:

WIN/WIN INTRO FOR MIDDLE SCHOOL-
a complete **Win/Win** - the orange story for eleven year-olds.

WIN/WIN COMICS -
a pictorial representation of the **Win/Win** approach for twelve year-olds.

WIN/WIN FRIDAY NIGHT -
an alternative for either of the above

WIN/WIN PROCESS -
a modeling of the **Win/Win** Process followed by participants' skits for a Basic Workshop.

Following these exercises are the sheets:
Poster and Possible Intro to the **Win/Win** Process and
Suggested Scenarios for **Win/Win**.

COMPLEMENTARY EXERCISES
The **Win/Win** process involves the following:
"reflective (or mirror) listening,"
"feeling statements,"
"points of view," and
"brainstorming."
Exercises dealing with these concepts are included in sections F and G.

Several other exercises in section G also pertain to the **Win/Win** idea. They are: *Candy Kisses, Territory, Tic Tac Challenge* and *Hassle Helps.*

The first three might be used either before or after whatever introduction to **Win/Win** is used. They provide physical experiences that introduce and/or emphasize the possibility of **Win/Win**. Hassle Helps provides an opportunity to practice skills already considered in Red Yellow Green and/or **Win/Win**. It would probably be most appropriate for an Advanced Workshop.

WIN/WIN INTRO FOR MIDDLE SCHOOL

Purpose: To present the idea that some conflicts can end in a Win/Win, a result in which no one loses and everyone feels good.

Time: 20 minutes

Materials: Markers, a poster with the Win/Win Guidelines, and newsprint as follows:

	A	Outcomes	B
(with a sample outcome)		B runs away with it	

Procedure: Set Up:

1. Explain that two facilitators, A and B (indicated by masking tape), will role-play a conflict. Then the participants will brainstorm possible outcomes.
2. A and B each want the <u>last</u> orange in the house. A walks in and mimes taking an orange out of a fridge and putting it on a table. (Having a real orange can be helpful.) A turns away from the orange and B comes in and picks up the orange. A turns back and says, "Don't take that orange, it's mine." B, "Not now it isn't; it's mine." A, "I just took it out of the fridge." B, "Finders, keepers; losers, weepers." A, "Not this time; I had it first." Call, "Cut."
3. Ask, "what might happen here?" Brainstorm a few more possible outcomes than that recorded on the newsprint above.
4. Consider whether the outcomes are 'wins' or 'losses' for A and B. Label with smiling or frowning mouths, or curvy mouths if the outcome is a bit of both.
5. Without knowing why A and B want the orange, it's hard to know what will make A and B feel good about the outcome. Perhaps the Win/Win Process can help. Point out the chart. Ask if the group can think of some ways for A and B to cool off. Mention deep breathing if it isn't suggested. Have everyone try a couple of deep breaths, imagining that as they inhale they breathe in the positive, and as they exhale they let out the negative.
6. Repeat the role-play and then have A start the process by taking a deep breath and saying, "Hey, can we talk about this? I have to make cookies for Home Ec. Class and the recipe calls for orange rind." B says, "Well I had a lousy day at school and the orange looked like it would be nice and refreshing." A reflects, "You had a rough day and then I jumped on you because I was worried about making the cookies." B, "Yeah, I got mad and yelled back because I had a rough day at school. So you need this orange to make cookies." A, "Can we work this out some way?"
7. Ask the class to brainstorm solutions now that they've heard what A and B said. Ask A and B which solution would be a Win/Win for them. (see note below)

Processing:

- Did you hear A's and B's points of view and feelings?
- Did A and B use reflective listening?
- Do you think using the Win/Win Process would help in real life?

Note: It's important for facilitators to practice both the initial skit and the repeat. You may wish to ask the first two questions before step #7.
The group might suggest splitting the orange. Though not a total Win/Win, it's definitely positive and would be a Fair/Fair if both A and B feel good about it.

WIN/WIN COMICS

Purpose: To make stick figure comics in small groups that show the Win/Win Process.

Time: About 30 minutes

Materials: Poster paper or oaktag and pencils, erasers and markers for each small group; the Win/Win Process posted and a sample Win/Win Comic, (see attached), enlarged and with only the first frame showing (see following page.)

Procedure: **Set Up:**

1. Explain that in this exercise people will be working in small groups to make comics that show the Win/Win Process.

2. Show the sample comic with all but the first frame covered. Read the background and ask for volunteers to read what A and B are saying. After the first frame is read, ask what is likely to happen at this point. Probably the answer will be, "A fight." Uncover the next 3 frames and have volunteers read A's and B's lines. Then have the volunteers sit down.

3. Refer to the Win/Win Process and ask who in the sample comic started the Win/Win process. What in the Win/Win process was used?

4. Mention that in the sample comic, B could have started the process. Then A and B would have said different things. Explain that small groups will make a new comic in which B starts the process. Let B start it in the first frame right after A says, "Don't you shove me." Perhaps B could use "reflective listening."

5. If there are no questions, break into groups of 3 or 4. Assign working space, distribute materials and have them begin. Give them about 20 minutes.

6. When everyone comes back to the circle have the groups "show and tell."

Processing:

- Did you find this easy or difficult? What was easy? What was difficult?
- Do you think you could try the Win/Win Process in real life?
- Would the process work with strangers or only with people you know somewhat?

Note: Some groups may not show the process exactly. Encourage whatever is positive.

Sample WIN/Win Comic

Background: A is waiting to get on the bus. B and C are fooling around. B loses balance and falls backwards, bumping into A

WIN/WIN FRIDAY NIGHT

Purpose: To present the idea that some conflicts can end in a Win/Win, a result in which no one loses and everyone feels good.

Materials: Win/Win Guidelines posted; "points of view" for the X's and Y's (see below)

Time: 20 - 30 minutes

Procedure: Set Up:

1. In planning time, ask two teammates to be X and Y, who will explain to the participant X's and Y's their points of view and do a skit.
2. Have the group form pairs. Have the two people in each pair stand on opposite sides of an imaginary line that you indicate.
3. Call those on one side of the line the X's; call those on the other side of the line Y's.
4. Have teammate X gather the participant X's and explain X's point of view. Have teammate Y gather the participant Y's and explain Y's point of view.

   X's point of view: X's love to go to the movies. They don't like bowling. Actually they've tried bowling in the past and they're afraid of looking silly. They don't usually tell anyone WHY they don't want to go bowling.

   Y's point of view: Y's like the movies but also like bowling. They aren't great at bowling, but they think it's fun and funny. They enjoy active things and they'd like the X's to try bowling for a change.
5. After the X's and Y's hear their respective points of view, have them go back to their lines opposite their partners. Arrange the lines in a "V" formation so everyone can see facilitators X and Y who will stand at the wide end of the "V." Have the facilitators start a skit arguing over what they'd like to do on Friday Night.
6. Cut after just a minute or so. (They do <u>not</u> come to a Win/Win this time.) Then have the lines come together and ask the participants to act out the same Friday night argument with their partners. Cut after about 30 seconds or so.
7. Now read over the Win/Win Guidelines poster. Then ask facilitators X and Y to try the guidelines. First have them take a deep breath. Ask X to tell Y her/his point of view and how s/he feels about the problem. Ask Y to reflect back what X said.
8. Next ask the participants to take a deep breath and try what the facilitators just modeled. The X's speak and the Y's reflect what was said. (It's quite all right if they repeat pretty much what the facilitators said.) (Give about 30 seconds)
9. Now have facilitator Y tell facilitator X her/his point of view and how s/he feels and have X reflect back what Y said. Again, have the lines follow suit.
10. Lastly, have the pairs see if they can come up with ("brainstorm") some ideas to solve the problem so both people feel good about what they decide to do. Then have the pairs return to the circle.

Processing:

- Would some pairs like to tell what they decided to do?
- Do you think the Win/Win Process would work in real life?
- Would you be willing to try it?

Note: *It's important for facilitators X and Y to practice the skits used in Steps 5, 7, and 9 so that they model the process clearly, without being too wordy. After one pair says what was decided, you might ask if other pairs decided on the same thing. Then ask if any pair decided on something else, etc.*

WIN/WIN PROCESS

Purpose: To offer a specific process for working through a disagreement. The Win/Win Process seems especially appropriate for these days when competition is the word of the day and the idea that both "sides" can feel OK is unfamiliar.

Time: About 40 minutes, but be flexible because this exercise can generate good discussion in the small groups.

Materials: The "Win/Win Process" poster on newsprint and a sheet for each small group with "Possible Intro to the Win/Win Process"; a scenario for each of four groups (see Step # 6 and "Suggested Scenarios for Win/Win"), or write your own based on the group's Role Play brainstorm.

Procedure: **Set Up:**

1. Explain that the Win/Win Process is a way to work through a disagreement so that the two "sides" in the disagreement feel OK about the outcome. You may wish to refer back to "Territory" if the group has done that exercise.
2. The process has several steps. Point out the poster. The first step is "Cool Off," and one suggestion is given. Do a quick two-minute brainstorm for other ways to cool off when angry or frustrated or hurt, etc.
3. Ask volunteers to read the rest of the steps in the process.
4. Explain that two co-facilitators will do a skit using the Win/Win Process. Introduce the characters (have masking tape names on them), read the practiced scenario, and let the skit begin.
5. After the skit, ask the group to identify steps in the process that were used.
6. Break into small groups. With a group of 20, you might form four groups and have 2 groups do one scenario and 2 groups do another (see materials). Have a facilitator work with each group to prepare a skit using the Win/Win Process. Encourage the groups to practice their skit.
7. When everyone comes back to the circle, have two groups with the same scenario do their skits one after the other. Then ask for comments from the observers. Then have the other two groups do their skits and ask for comments from the observers.

Processing:

- Did you find this easy or difficult?
- In what situations in real life might this process be used?
- Would the process work with strangers or only with people you know ?

Note: Win/Win works best toward the end of a Basic Workshop since it uses "Feeling Statements" and "Reflective Listening" skills.

It is important for the facilitators illustrating the process to practice their skit in order to show all the steps.

In this exercise, skits are practiced to try to use all the steps; this is different from Role Plays, which are done in an impromptu or unrehearsed fashion.

Some groups may not use the process exactly. Encourage whatever is positive.

Suggest that they try to use the process in Role Plays

POSTER AND POSSIBLE INTRO TO THE WIN/WIN PROCESS

WIN/WIN PROCESS	
COOL OFF	BREATHE DEEPLY, etc.
EACH TELL THE OTHER HOW S/HE SEES THE PROBLEM	POINT OF VIEW
EACH SAY HOW S/HE FEELS ABOUT IT	FEELING STATEMENTS
EACH SAY WHAT S/HE HEARD	REFLECTIVE LISTENING
DISCUSS POSSIBLE SOLUTIONS	BRAINSTORM
BOTH CHOOSE A WIN/WIN	AGREE TO TRY IT

POSSIBLE INTRO TO THE WIN/WIN PROCESS (AFTER COOLING OFF)

Look, we don't seem to be getting anywhere.

Could we try something to see if we understand each other exactly?

Without name-calling or blaming, one of us would say how s/he sees and feels about the problem. Then the other would say what s/he heard.

Then we'll reverse this procedure.

Do you think we could try this?

(if the person agrees, ask..) "Would you like to go first or second?"

Suggested Scenarios for Win/Win

1. Jo finished working on an art/science project that s/he needs to show to a boss or teacher the next day. Jo put it in a box on the floor near the door. Suddenly a family member throws open the door which pushes the box into Jo's desk and squashes the project. Can there be a Win/Win?

2. Jo has been working in a new job for about a week. Jo's trying really hard but since everything is new Jo works slower than the boss wants. The boss therefore yells at Jo a great deal. Jo is discouraged, but can there be a Win/Win?

3. Mo differs with her/his sixteen year-old Jo as to a reasonable curfew time. Mo thinks eleven o'clock is good. Jo wants at least midnight. Can there be a Win/Win?

4. Jo goes into a pizza place, orders a plain pizza and stands waiting for it near the main counter. Mo comes in and also orders a plain pizza. A little time goes by and the owner brings out a pizza. Mo starts paying for it. Jo comes over and says, "Hey, that's my pizza." Do things escalate or can someone use the Win/Win Process?

5. Six weeks ago Jo, who is sixteen, went to a concert and came home two hours late at 2:00 AM. Since then Jo has been getting home on time. Now Jo wants to go to another concert. Mo, Jo's parent, says, "No way!" Is there any chance for a Win/Win?

6. One Saturday night, Jo and Mo go out with two other friends. The next Monday morning Jo storms up to Mo and says, "Where do you get off telling everybody what happened Saturday? " In fact, Mo didn't tell anyone anything. Is there any chance for a Win/Win?

7. Jo has been going out with Mo for two months. One night at a basketball game Jo goes out for a smoke. When Jo comes back, Mo is in a deep conversation with Chris. Jo gets angry. Does it escalate or can there be a Win/Win?

ROLE PLAYS
Introductory Material

In an AVP workshop, Role Plays are as near as we can get to real-life conflict situations. In Role Plays we create our own scenarios of "virtual" conflicts. Then we try to put what we've learned in the workshop into practice. Role Plays give us a chance to examine options and analyze results.

Skits are also used in some AVP workshops. Role Plays are different from skits. Skits are planned and rehearsed. When we plan a skit, we know what the outcome will be. The people in the skits have at least a rough idea of what they will say. This is so because skits are usually done to show a process such as Win/Win.

Role Plays do not have planned outcomes. Players do not practice any lines. In planning a Role Play, a group simply determines what the conflict is, where and when it is taking place, and who the characters are that are involved in the conflict. It is performed "impromptu," that is, without rehearsal.

Volunteers play the "characters" in the Role Play. People don't play themselves. In that sense, a Role Play is like a real play. But it's a play without lines and without a known ending.

The reason Role Plays are "impromptu" is to make the conflicts as "virtual" as possible. People don't rehearse in real life. They have to be creative on the spot. Role Plays give people a chance to try being "put on the spot" in a safe place to see how they'll do.

Regardless of the outcome of the Role Play, we can learn from it. We can see what might work and what might not work. We can ask, "Are there other ways?"

EXERCISES:
The information regarding Role Plays has been put in exercise format, first of all, to be consistent. Secondly, this allows the material to be considered in four parts. This provides participants and new facilitators with information a little at a time so it's not overwhelming.

The exercises include:

ROLE PLAYS - INTRODUCTION AND BRAINSTORM
ROLE PLAYS - PREPARATION
ROLE PLAYS - PRE-RUNNING NOTES
ROLE PLAYS - RUNNING AND DEBRIEFING

ROLE PLAYS - INTRODUCTION AND BRAINSTORM

Purpose: To find out which conflict situations the group would like to work on in Role Plays (some suggestions might also be used in skits - see notes)

Time: About 10 minutes

Materials: Newsprint and markers

Procedure: **Set Up:**

1. Explain that Role Plays will be used to give us a chance to try out new ways of dealing with conflict situations. A brainstorm will be used to create a list of perhaps 12 - 15 possible conflict situations, situations that are familiar to the group in real life.
2. The situations suggested needn't involve particulars. An example might be a conflict between a parent and child. A scribe would record only the words, "parent/child." The details will be decided on later.
3. As with all brainstorms, anything may be suggested without discussion until the brainstorm is finished. If there are no questions, begin the brainstorm.
4. At the end of the brainstorm, explain that 2 or 3 Role Plays may be done. Some situations might be used in skits, which are different from Role Plays. To get an idea of which situations interest the most people, take a rough vote.
5. Everyone may vote four or five times. Have someone read through all the situations. Then read one situation at a time and have the group vote on each one. Record the number of votes on the brainstorm. Explain that you'll discuss the results a bit later in the workshop.

Note: No processing is necessary.
Having several facilitators counting the votes is helpful.

If this brainstorm and vote can be done in an earlier session, some of the situations which receive a medium number of votes might be used as skits in the Win/Win exercise. Those with higher numbers of votes may be saved for the Role Plays.

Instead of voting by hand, you might give participants markers to check 4 or 5 topics they see as a priority. Or, you might give participants 4 or 5 stickers each and have them place stickers by their favorite topics. Several people can "mark" the brainstorm at the same time.

Sometimes, scenarios may be linked together. For example, a conflict scenario between "friend/friend" and another called "drugs" could be renamed, "friends and drugs." Such "linking" might take place as part of "Role Plays - Preparation."

In some situations, you may want to have a group choose from possible topics, rather than brainstorm. Some possible ones are:
Your pen is missing and you see someone else using a similar pen;
Your mother refuses to let you go to a party;
A friend is running away and wants you to go with her/him;
Another student attacks you. When you defend yourself the teacher sees you retaliating and blames you for the whole incident;
A friend brags to you about a gun he has purchased;
You and your brothers and sisters have an argument about what TV show to watch.

ROLE PLAYS - PREPARATION

Purpose: To explain the nature of Role Plays as used in AVP and to prepare for them in groups.

Time: 20 - 30 minutes

Materials: Newsprint and markers and a poster as follows:

In Planning for Roles Plays

- Try to limit the "play" to one scene.
- Make up names for the characters and put them on newsprint.
- Describe each character a bit, e.g., age, personality, interests.
- Don't plan the outcome.
- Have the situation be open to T.P.
- Don't play a role that's too close to your own life.
- Have volunteers play roles; make masking tape name-tags.
- Ask a volunteer to introduce the role play

Procedure: Set Up:

1. Decide beforehand as a team how many Role Plays it will be possible to do. Consider which conflict situations received the most votes. If necessary, consider whether any situations might be combined.

2. Explain the team's thinking to the group. If it is only possible to do two Role Plays and three situations received many votes, ask the group for input. Might two of the three be combined? Would the group like to re-vote on the three?

3. When it has been decided which Role Plays will be done, explain that everyone may choose which Role Play they would like to plan.

4. Everyone can have input in the planning even if they don't want to volunteer to play a role —to act.

5. Explain that roles plays are different from skits. We don't plan the outcome in Role Plays. We don't practice lines. We try to set up real conflict situations and give people a chance to try to solve the conflict on the spot.

6. Point out the poster and ask for volunteers to read it pop-corn style.

7. Have the groups working on the different Role Plays gather in different parts of the room. Have a couple of facilitators join each group as advisors, and begin.

Note: You can decide as a team when the Role Plays will be run. It might be wise to do them as close to preparation time as possible, so they remain impromptu. One can be run even if it's the only one ready. More preparation time can be given to other(s) at a later time.

ROLE PLAYS - PRE-RUNNING NOTES

Purpose: To explain briefly how Role Plays are run just before the running of the first Role Play.

Time: 5 minutes

Materials: None

Procedure: **Set Up:**

1. Before the first Role Play starts, say that since we don't know the outcome of the Role Play there may be some surprises. Some things may be funny. The observers/audience may laugh. This is understandable.

2. Ask the observers to be mindful and to try not to laugh so much it will distract the actors. Ask the actors to not take the laughter personally. It's the situation that people find funny, not the people who are acting.

3. Explain that a facilitator may call "Cut" at some point. The facilitator will ask the characters how they're feeling. The observers will also have a chance to question the characters.

4. The observers might also make suggestions to the characters. They might check the Guides to Transforming Power to see if any of the guides might be used. The actors may or may not wish to try such suggestions in a second take.

5. If there are no questions and if the Role Play group is ready, they may start.

Note: Any facilitator may give this information. It needn't be given by the facilitator(s) who worked with the Role Play group that's about to do its Role Play.

ROLE PLAYS - RUNNING AND DEBRIEFING

Purpose: To question the characters in a Role Play and, at the end of the Role Play, to help them come out of character.

Time: About 30 - 45 minutes including the actual Role Play.

Materials: A pad and pencil for the facilitator to make some notes

Procedure: **Set Up:**

1. Before the first Role Play starts, have some facilitator present material in "Role Plays - Pre-Running Notes."

2. Ask a narrator to introduce the characters and the setting of the Role Play, and have the Role Play begin.

3. If the action gets bogged down or the emotions of one or more characters seem too intense, call "Cut."

4. Ask the characters, one at a time, "How are you feeling right now?" Have them answer as the characters, right now. Don't let them fall into the past yet.

5. Ask the observers/audience if they have any questions for the characters. Also ask them if they have any suggestions for the characters. They might check to see if any of the Guides to Transforming Power could be used.

6. If there is time, ask the actors if they wish to try any suggestions in a second take. If the actors wish to, do "take two."

7. After the final "cut" or at the end, again ask the characters how they're feeling. Do the observers have any further questions for the characters? Try not to have this go on too long.

8. Taking the characters in turn, help them come out of their roles. Try to get people out of their roles fairly quickly. If someone is very emotionally involved, you might start with her/him. Otherwise, you may wish to de-role minor characters first so they can rejoin the circle. Ask each if s/he is ready to come out of her/his role. Then ask each to stand and take off the masking tape name-tag. Have them turn around. Say, "You are no longer 'Cool Character'; you are really, 'Jolly Joe'." Ask each to say her/his adjective name. You may wish to applaud each actor.

9. Offer each one a seat in the circle or have a co-facilitator do so. Put the masking tape name on the back of the character's chair and ask the real person e.g., "Jolly Joe" if s/he has any advice to give "Cool Character."

10. After everyone has been de-roled, ask everyone to give the actors a hand.

Processing:

- Was the Role Play realistic?
- Did anyone see Transforming Power ?
- Did any "actors" learn anything about themselves in playing the role they played?
- Was the Role Play helpful?

Note: It may help people come out of their roles if you touch them and help them turn around. The noise of the applause also helps actors come back to the real world. If some characters are very emotionally involved, applauding when they say their Adjective Name can be helpful. If the Role Play isn't too intense, you may wish to wait and applaud all the actors after all are de-roled.

If the Role Play has many characters, some of whom may be "by-standers," you may choose to de-role two or three at a time, and then ask if they wish to say anything to the characters they played.

Be prepared to remind everyone that, once people are out of their roles, they should no longer be referred to by the names of the characters they played.

TRUST
Introductory Material

Trust exercises help us to learn to trust and depend on our friends and to be trustworthy ourselves. It's wise that trust exercises be led by someone with experience. It's important for the entire team to discuss the trust exercise before it's done. The entire team is responsible for safety precautions and for judging whether a group has reached a level of trust in one another that makes these exercises emotionally safe for them. *It is not wise for a group that is untrusting to take part in these exercises.*

It's important to strike a note of seriousness when introducing trust exercises. Some people regardless of age may not immediately see that great care must be taken in trust exercises so nobody gets hurt either physically or emotionally. Some who are fearless themselves may have trouble understanding how others might not like to be blindfolded or might be less than enthusiastic about falling backward onto another's hands.

It is most understandable that some may be very hesitant about taking part in trust activities. Stressing people's right-to-pass is important. Since trust exercises don't usually occur before the fifth or sixth session of a workshop, people have probably shown other types of trust already. Speaking in front of a group, participating in "silly" L&L's and sharing stories and feelings all involve a sense of trust in the group. It is good to acknowledge this.

Having facilitators model trust exercises carefully is key. This can encourage participants to try them. Sometimes when a few people try an activity, others will try it too. Choosing one's own partner may also encourage a willingness to attempt an activity. However, if people are asked to choose their own partners, some participants may not be chosen. Then facilitators might offer to be partners with such participants. If some people choose not to take part, ask them to maintain a respectful silence during the course of the exercise.

EXERCISES: (listed in alphabetical order)

- TRUST BALANCES IN PAIRS AND CIRCLES
- TRUST FALLS IN PAIRS, TRIOS AND CIRCLES
- TRUST WALK

TRUST BALANCES IN PAIRS AND CIRCLE

Purpose: To provide an opportunity of being supported while being supportive.

Time: About 20 minutes

Materials: None

Procedure: Set Up:

1. Explain that both Trust Balances involve trusting that people in this group won't let anyone else in the group fall. It's important that people take this seriously so that no one gets hurt.
2. Say that two teammates will demonstrate the trust balance. As they do it, comment on the important aspects of it. First, the two face each other, put their toes together and hold each other at the wrists.
3. They establish eye contact and slowly lean back supporting each other. When both feel sure they're being supported, they slowly lower their bodies to sit on the ground. Then they rise up together slowly. They always maintain eye contact.
4. If there are no questions, have people choose partners, find some space in the circle and try it. Circulate with your teammates, coaching the different pairs.
5. After everyone who would like to has tried the balance in pairs, ask everyone to stand to try the circle balance. The circle balance requires an even number of people. Have teammates even things off.
6. Have people count off by 2's. Explain that this balance also involves holding wrists and supporting each other. First, the 2's will lean in, as the 1's lean out. Then both the 2's and the 1's will stand up straight. Then the 1's will lean in as the 2's lean out, and then, both will stand up straight - and so on.
7. Explain that you'll say when people are to lean and when they are to stand straight. Ask the two people on either side of you to support you so you can model this. Starting in the straight position, you'll model while saying slowly, "Lean, lean, lean and then stand straight; and lean, lean, lean and then stand straight," etc. If you are a 2, you would lean in first; if you are a 1, you would lean out first."
8. If there are no questions, begin. You may have to try it several times for everyone to feel comfortable. Be encouraging. It's not easy.

Processing:

- How did people feel being supported at the same time as being supportive?
- How does this relate to real life?

Note: It is important to go over this exercise with teammates in planning time.

Before having the whole group try the circle balance, you might want to model it with three other teammates in a circle of four before step # 6.

It is possible to do just one or the other of these by itself. The circle balance is a good closing for a session in an Advanced Workshop.

TRUST FALLS IN PAIRS, TRIOS AND CIRCLES

Purpose: To provide an opportunity to help us learn to trust and to be trustworthy.

Time: About 20 minutes

Materials: None

Procedure: **Set Up:**

1. Explain that the Trust Falls are serious. They give us a time to learn to trust and depend on others and a time to be trustworthy ourselves. Seriousness is necessary so no one is hurt. Some people may choose to pass. That's fine. We would ask, however, that everyone stay in the circle and be mindful observers.
2. Explain that this exercise starts in pairs. Have two facilitators model a trust fall as a pair.
3. Have one person stand behind the other. The one in front will be the "faller" and the one in back will be the "catcher."
4. The "catchers" put their feet, comfortably, one behind the other and have their knees slightly bent. They put the palms of their hands only about two inches away from the back of their "faller."
5. The "fallers" fold their arms across their chest, keep their feet together and their body stiff.
6. The "faller" says, "Ready to fall." The "catcher" replies, "Ready to catch." The "faller" then says, "Falling," and the "catcher" says, "Catching," and the "faller" falls. The "catcher" then gently pushes the "faller" upright. Try it.
7. The "catcher" then asks the "faller" if s/he would like to fall further back. If so, the "catcher" moves her/his palms perhaps four inches from the back of the "faller." Both must feel comfortable about increases. The same series of statements is repeated before each fall. Try this, with perhaps three increases.
8. Then both people turn around and reverse roles. It is good for facilitators to model this reverse. If there are no questions, invite people to pair with whomever they'd like and try it. Have co-facilitators circulate about the room as coaches.
9. After everyone who would like to has tried the fall in pairs, ask the group to return to the circle. Then have three facilitators model a fall in a trio.
10. The "faller" stands the same way. "Catchers" stand both behind and in front of the "faller," with the same body position as before. The "catcher" in front prepares to catch the "faller" on the upper arms.
11. The same series of statements is used. This time both "catchers" reply. The "faller" will fall backward first and then be gently pushed forward without stopping in the middle - to be caught by the front "catcher" and then gently pushed backward. The "faller" is rocked backward and forward by the "catchers," rather like the pendulum of a clock. Have the trio model it.

12. Invite others to try it. Mention that people in the trio can change roles. The "fallers" might like to try closing their eyes. After everyone who would like to has tried the fall in trios, return to the circle.

13. Explain that the Trust Fall in a Circle is similar to the Trust Fall in Trios except that there are more "catchers." The "faller" stands in the middle of a circle of about six "catchers." The "faller" stands as in the other two falls with arms folded, body stiff and feet together and firmly planted. Suggest closing eyes. A co-facilitator might model this. Say that when the "faller" falls, the "catchers" will gently move the "faller" around the circle, moving all the way around from one "catcher" to the next.

14. Invite volunteers to be "catchers." It would be good if some facilitators were catchers. Have the "catchers" form a tight circle. If there are no questions, have the "faller" start the series of statements. Be sure all the "catchers" respond, "Ready to catch."

15. Invite others to be either "fallers" or "catchers."

Processing:

- How did people feel as "fallers?"
- How did people feel as "catchers?"
- Does this relate to real life?

Note: It is important to go over this exercise with co-facilitators in planning time.

Co-facilitators should circulate around the room throughout the entire exercise.

Co-facilitators might give the directions for different parts of this exercise.

TRUST WALK

Purpose: To provide an opportunity to help us learn to trust and to be trustworthy.

Time: About 20 minutes

Materials: Blindfolds for half the number in the group; an obstacle course of chairs

Procedure: **Set Up:**

1. Explain that the Trust Walk is a serious activity. It gives us a chance to learn to trust and depend on others and a time to be trustworthy ourselves. It is important to be serious so no one is hurt.

2. This exercise is done in pairs. First one member of the pair will be blindfolded. That person's partner will guide her or him through an obstacle course, being very careful that the person who can't see does not get hurt.

3. Then, at the end of the course, people will switch roles. The person that was blindfolded becomes the guide. The guide will be blindfolded and guided back, through a new obstacle course.

4. With a teammate, model a couple of ways of guiding:
   a) Stand beside the blindfolded person and gently hold the person's bent arm under the elbow and wrist.
   b) When going through a very narrow space, step in front of the person, and have that person hold both of your forearms, as you walk backwards.

5. If there are no questions ask, people to choose partners and form a line of pairs, one pair behind the other. Ask teammates to be mindful of anyone who seems to be hesitant or who is not finding a partner. People may pass, but perhaps teammates could invite such persons to be their partners. Give a blindfold to each pair and have them decide who will be blindfolded first.

6. While pairs are doing this, have a teammate(s) help make an obstacle course. It needn't be too complicated or too long.

7. When all pairs are ready and in line, signal for silence.

8. Encourage people to talk to their partners, explaining what's around them, telling them if they have to step over something, etc. They might also have the blindfolded person touch something and try to guess what it is.

9. Have your teammate and partner go through the obstacle course first, with the teammate guiding. Plan the general route beforehand.

10. Stand at the front of the line and let the first pair go at least 6-8 feet before having the second pair start. Space the remaining pairs similarly.

11. When the first pair has finished the course, a co-facilitator can explain to others, as they finish, that they may now switch the blindfold.

12. When everyone is through the first course and while blindfolds are being switched, change the course slightly. When all are ready, have one pair start. This time you may have to show the first guide the path to take. Ask the following pairs to leave space between themselves and the pair before them.

13. As people finish the second course, have them rejoin the circle.

Processing:

- How did people feel being blindfolded?
- How did people feel being a guide?
- Does this relate to real life?

Note: It is important to go over this exercise with teammates in planning time.

If you plan to have pairs do something like go under a table, it is important to have a teammate at the table to be sure that guides warn their partners to keep their heads down, etc. Don't do this unless you are sure everyone is physically able.

If it's possible, you might try this outdoors.

SECTION G

EXERCISES

Introduction To Exercises

List of Exercises

Individual Descriptions
(in alphabetical order)

INTRODUCTION TO EXERCISES

Most of the exercises contained in this section can be found in other AVP manuals. They have been adapted somewhat to better meet the needs of younger participants. A few are new.

The exercises are arranged alphabetically. Some pertain to the same concept or concepts. The suggested agendas indicate the order in which they might be presented. In setting up your own agendas it's good to consider that some exercises work better before others, even if they pertain to the same concept. For example, it's better to present Secret Spot before Broken Squares.

The exercises are designed to fit the experiential learning process. This is based on the idea that:

EXPERIENCE SHOULD COME FIRST, CONCEPTS SECOND

It is great to keep this in mind when presenting exercises. It is for this reason that often the purpose of an exercise is NOT mentioned. After the exercise is experienced, participants can usually figure out the purpose of the exercise themselves.

It is important to present the instructions for the exercise as clearly and concisely as possible. Usually people are more apt to listen to the instructions without distractions when they are in the big circle. But, it's also a good idea to repeat the instructions after people have divided into small groups.

Involving participants as soon as possible is always helpful. For instance, if there is a poster to be read, you might ask for volunteers to read it line by line, pop-corn style, where one person starts and the next just pops in and continues.

When dividing into groups by counting off, you count by the NUMBER of groups you wish to form. For variety you might ask participants to choose their favorite season, or one of say five colors, to form four or five groups respectively. (This may not result in groups of equal number. If you want groups of equal numbers, you may have to ask for volunteers to re-place themselves.) To form pairs you may wish to count off by half the number of the whole group and have people find their corresponding number. (Also see *Dividing Into Groups* - Section I)

After presenting the exercise it's good to add, "Does the team have anything to add?" It's also wise to ask the participants, "Does anyone have any questions about the instructions?"

Generally it's good for facilitators to take part in exercises. Having a facilitator in each small group can help an exercise run more smoothly. However, there are some exercises, such as Broken Squares and Lots of Dots where facilitators might bias the results. (Of course a facilitator might fill-in in Broken Squares to complete a group of five, and play a very passive role.) It's a good idea to discuss this matter with your team beforehand.

Probably the trickiest part of facilitating is becoming skilled at the fine art of processing exercises. The key is to ask wise questions rather than making one's own comments about the exercise.

Four areas to cover with some corresponding questions are:

EXPERIENCES:

What HAPPENED? How were decisions MADE? Did anyone TAKE risks?

FEELINGS:

How did you FEEL doing the exercise? Relaxed? Anxious?

PERCEPTIONS:

Did it SEEM like everyone had a say? You too?

RELATING TO LIFE:

How is this LIKE real life?

More informal questions, and follow-up questions that address the same areas are:

EXPERIENCES:

How did that go for you? Can you tell us a little more about that?
Does (has) that ever happened to you or people you know?

FEELINGS:

I'd like to hear how you felt doing that exercise;

PERCEPTIONS:

Sometimes when.........happens people feel.......; What do you think about that?

RELATING TO LIFE:

Can you think of a time (times) in your life when you might try: (listening), (talking about feelings), (looking for a Win/Win) etc. ?

These questions needn't be asked in this order. Participants' responses to one question might lead to the most appropriate next question. Particular questions are suggested at the end of each exercise. When you're finished asking questions it's good to add, "Would any team members like to ask any other questions?"

Some responses lead to very productive discussions; others don't. In any case, to end discussion you might say, "Because our time is short we'll have to limit discussion to two or three more comments." Or, if a particularly "hot" topic comes up, put it on an "Unanswered Questions" sheet and explain that you'll get back to it later in the workshop.

Putting key words for the instructions for an exercise on one side of a 3x5 index card, and some key questions on the other side can be a great help. Facilitators don't have to have ace memories! And remember, you can always call, **"CLINIC."**

Consider "teaming" when presenting exercises. One facilitator might set up an exercise, another might process it. Use co-facilitators as scribes, or to model what's to be done.

Perhaps most important, **TRUST THE PROCESS!** Even if directions are very muddled, or if participants interpret them in a completely new way, in the end things usually work out (meaning that participants learn something).

Facilitators are only human, even old timers! "We do what we can." "What happens, happens." We learn experientially, too. Hopefully, a difficulty in one workshop will help us do better the next time.

LIST OF EXERCISES

Active Listening
Active Listening Techniques
in Triads
Addiction
Adjective Name Game
Adjective Name Game
Modified (AKA Jack in The
Box, What's in a Name)
Affirmation Pictures
APA Walk
AVP Posters

Biographies
Bonfire
Broken Squares
Buttons

Candy Kisses
Changes 1,2,3
Checkerboard Design
Choices I
Choices II
Choices And Consequences
Choices For Advanced
Circle Game
Clique Clash
Concentric Circles
(AKA Talking Circles)
Construction Crew
Cooperative Drawing
Co-op Monsters
Co-op Posters
(AKA Tool Box)
Creative Construction
Crossover

Escalator

Facts And Feelings
Fairy Tale Theater
Fishbowl Intervention
Strategy
Fish Bowl Modified
Focusing on
Violence/nonviolence

Garbage Bags
Goal Setting Part I
Goal Setting Part II
Guided Reflection

Hand Push
Hassle Helps
Heartbroken Chris
(Or Pat)

Ice Cream
In Common
It's How You Say it
I Want/ I Want

Labels
Let's Go Swimming
Life Beliefs
Listening And
Brainstorming Do's And
Don'ts
Lots of Dots
Lots of Listening

Machines
Marshmallows
Match up
Mind Bag (AKA Baggage)
Mind Set Chair
Mirror Circle
My Potential

Paper Bags
Paper Tiger
Parallel Construction
Paraphrasing
People's Perception I
People's Perception II
People's Perception III
People's Perception IV
People Treasure Hunt
Personal Space
Picture Sharing
Point of View
Points of View
Power Trip

Quick Decisions

Rainbow Lunch
Red Yellow Green
Reflective
Listening
Risking Change

Secret Spot
Sharing: "A Conflict
I Resolved
Nonviolently"
Sharing Stories
Six Point Problem
Solving
Stereotyping

Take The Blame Out
Talk in The Dark
Territory
Things I Hear(d)
Over And Over
Tic Tac Challenge
Triangles For
Advanced
Two Chairs
Two or Three
Question Interview

Violence Brainstorm
(With Options)
Voices Within

Wacky Wishes (AKA
Goal Wish Problem
Solving)
What Color Is
Conflict

Who Am I Becoming?
(Modified)
Who, Me?
Who Says I Am?

ACTIVE LISTENING

Purpose: To give participants practice in helping others to solve their own problems, by listening and reflecting back what was said and felt.

Time: 30 to 40 minutes

Materials: None

Procedure: **Set Up:**

1. Explain that active listening is an alternative to responses such as debating, analyzing, advising, judging, placating, distracting, ignoring or telling your own story - which can all be defensive reactions in the listener to strong feelings of helplessness, rage, fear or despair in oneself and others. The main essence of active listening is being available to others as an effective sounding board to help them work through an immediate crisis or decision.

   Active listening means really hearing and then restating in different words the content of what is said, reflecting the feelings that are being expressed, becoming clear about the concern the person has, and describing the behavior that is actually happening. It takes practice to do this.

2. Examples of non-listening (see above) can be modeled by team members. This may be done in a light-hearted way.

3. Suggest to participants that in listening they use not only their ears but also their eyes and their bodies. Since body language tells a lot about how a person is feeling, the listeners' body language will convey to the speaker how interested they are. As speakers, their bodies say how important things are to them, and whether their feelings fit with what they are saying.

4. Divide the group into pairs. Allow a moment for everyone to think of a problem to speak about, so that the partner can practice being an active listener. Then ask one person in each pair to sound off about a problem while the other person does active listening and gives feedback. Do not structure the time for feedback (as in the Basic Manual Listening Exercise), but let things flow naturally. After about 3 minutes switch roles.

Processing:

- Were you really listened to? How did that feel?
- Was it hard or easy to be the listener?
- As a listener were you able to suspend your own judgment about the speaker's problem?

ACTIVE LISTENING TECHNIQUES IN TRIADS

Purpose: To practice using the six Active Listening Techniques

Time: 50 minutes

Materials: A copy of the sheet "Techniques and Tasks for Active Listening in Triads" for each participant (see next page.)

Procedure: Set Up:

1. Review "Active Listening Techniques" as on the sheet mentioned above.
2. Divide the group into triads: one speaker, one listener and one observer. Review the "Observer Tasks" as on the sheet mentioned above.
3. Ask the speakers to talk for 4 minutes about something important to them while listeners practice active listening techniques and observers watch the interaction following Observer Task #1. You might suggest topics such as:
   Something you would like to change about yourself
   Something you would like to learn or improve
   The most difficult, frightening or embarrassing experience you've had
4. Call time at 4 minutes and process in triads according to Observer Tasks #2 and #3.
5. Have participants rotate roles and repeat steps 3 and 4 until each person has had an opportunity to be in each role.

Processing: (in full group)

- What are the benefits of "Active Listening Techniques" for the speaker? for the listener?

Techniques And Tasks for Active Listening in Triads

Active Listening Techniques

Encouraging	don't agree or disagree/use neutral words/vary voice tone
Clarifying	ask questions/restate wrong interpretation
Restating	restate basic ideas and facts
Reflecting	reflect speaker's basic feelings
Summarizing	restate major ideas and feelings
Validating	acknowledge value of issues/feelings show appreciation for speaker's efforts/action

Observer Tasks

1. **During the discussion between the speaker and the listener note:**
   What active listening techniques did the listener use?
   What did the listener do that was effective?
   What could the listener have done differently?

2. **When time is called ask the speaker:**
   What did the listener do that encouraged you to talk more?
   Was there anything especially helpful?
   Did the listener do anything that discouraged you from talking?
   How did you feel at the end of this discussion?

3. **Ask the listener:**
   What made it easy or difficult for you to listen?
   Which techniques were easiest/most difficult for you to use?
   Which active listening techniques would you like to practice more?

Techniques And Tasks for Active Listening in Triads

Active Listening Techniques

Encouraging	don't agree or disagree/use neutral words/vary voice tone
Clarifying	ask questions/restate wrong interpretation
Restating	restate basic ideas and facts
Reflecting	reflect speaker's basic feelings
Summarizing	restate major ideas and feelings
Validating	acknowledge value of issues/feelings show appreciation for speaker's efforts/action

Observer Tasks

1. **During the discussion between the speaker and the listener note:**
   What active listening techniques did the listener use?
   What did the listener do that was effective?
   What could the listener have done differently?

2. **When time is called ask the speaker:**
   What did the listener do that encouraged you to talk more?
   Was there anything especially helpful?
   Did the listener do anything that discouraged you from talking?
   How did you feel at the end of this discussion?

3. **Ask the listener:**
   What made it easy or difficult for you to listen?
   Which techniques were easiest/most difficult for you to use?
   Which active listening techniques would you like to practice more?

ADDICTION

Purpose: To recognize the process and path that addiction follows; to explore ways we can take control of our lives, whether dealing with our own addiction or that of others

Time: 30 - 40 minutes

Materials: Newsprint and markers enough for 4 or 5 groups; 2 pieces of newsprint as follows:

ADDICTION Causes	ADDICTION Effects perceived positive negative

Procedure: Set Up:

1. Ask, "Why do people get into using drugs, including alcohol? What draws us into those first steps in the direction of addiction"? e.g., use by family members, peer pressure. Record the responses in a brainstorm fashion under "Causes."

2. Next brainstorm effects, first considering "perceived positives" (e.g., if shyness led to trying drugs, the expected benefit might be "self confidence.").

3. What are some obvious "negative" effects? Might some negative effects occur later in life? (e.g., loss of job, loss of family, suicide, violence)

4. Might some of the "perceived positives" turn negative? Might self confidence turn to aggression and violence?

5. Ask for comments on the three brainstorms. Is drug/alcohol use a problem in our school? - homes? - community?

6. Explain that now small groups will brainstorm and try to find possible positive things that individuals, families and communities might do to change addictive behavior. Form groups, assign work places, distribute materials and have them begin. Let them know that they'll have about 10 minutes.

7. When the groups are ready have people return to the circle staying with their groups. Post the lists, have volunteers read them and ask for comments.

Processing:

- Are any of the positive suggestions happening now?
- Can we each get involved in some way?

Note: If possible, the group lists can be copied and given to anyone who wants a copy.

ADJECTIVE NAME GAME

Purpose: To learn each other's names and start affirming ourselves and others.

Time: About 15 minutes

Materials: None

Procedure: Set Up:

1. Explain that we're all going to use our first names in this workshop. Give participants a minute to think of an adjective (a word that describes) that starts with the same letter or sound as their first name. The adjective must be positive. Be extravagant! Give your own adjective and name as an example (Beautiful Brenda). If a person can't think of an adjective, ask the group to make suggestions and let the person make a choice.

2. Say that we'll go around the circle and each person will repeat the names of all those who went before and then give her/his own adjective name.

3. If there are no questions, begin.

Processing: (if you choose)

- How did you find that? How did it feel to be called something positive?
- If this was "strange," why might this be the case?

Note: Some people may really resist using an adjective name. If so, refer to the "right to pass" ground rule/agreement, or if you are generating ground rules/ agreements suggest that the "right to pass" be added to the list now.

If people choose a rhyming word as their adjective, or prefer to use their last name (e.g., Even Steven, Jolly Jones), go with the flow.

You should question adjectives that imply negative meaning (e.g., Crazy or Silly). If the word is positive to the individual, it should be accepted

With young children, it is helpful to clarify that an "adjective name" is like a "positive nickname."

Ask people to say their adjective name each time they speak. Then introduce <u>two more AVP ways</u>, the "forgot sign" and "twinkling" or "thumbs up."

ADJECTIVE NAME GAME MODIFIED
(AKA JACK-IN-THE-BOX, AKA WHAT'S IN A NAME?)

Purpose: To provide a shorter version of the Adjective Name Game.

Time: About 10 minutes

Materials: None

Procedure: **Set Up:**

1. Before starting, ask a co-facilitator to sit three seats to your right. S/he will be the first to start naming the three people who went before her/him.

2. Explain what an Adjective Name is as in # 1 of the regular exercise. If there are no questions, you may start, passing to your right. (Some may want suggestions for their adjective right away; others may wait until it's their turn. Go with the flow.)

3. When it comes to your co-facilitators turn, suggest making the game a little more challenging. Each person, starting with your co-facilitator, will have to name three people to her/his left. When those people are named, they will pop up and down like a Jack-in-the-Box. Ask your co-facilitator to start and when your name is called, pop up and down.

Processing: Questions that might be asked are:

- How did you find that?
- How does it feel being called something positive?

Note: This is often used in a mini program with sixth graders. It might also be used in an Advanced or a T4F for variety.

In an Advanced it can be called, "What's in a Name?" People would explain the origin of their names and say whether they liked or disliked their names. They would also tell why they chose their adjective names. Tell everyone that they might like to choose an adjective other than the one they used in the Basic. The rest of the exercise would be as above. (The "popping up" is optional.)

AFFIRMATION PICTURES

Purpose: To affirm ourselves, to help remember each others' names and to allow participants to become aware of individual preferences. This may be done just after the Adjective Name Exercise, especially with younger students.

Time: 30 minutes

Materials: One sheet 8 ½ x 11 plain paper for each participant, colored markers

Procedure: **Set Up:**

1. Hand out one sheet of 8 ½ x 11 paper to each participant.
2. Allow them to select their own colored markers.
3. Instruct them to put their own adjective name on the paper and to draw something on the paper that is important to them or says something about who they are.
4. After everyone has finished, ask them to rejoin the circle.
5. Each person then shows the other participants their picture, reading their adjective name and explaining what they drew on the paper and why.
6. After everyone has shared, participants will usually want to tape the pictures to the wall for everyone to see.

APA WALK

(A variation of "Assertiveness" from Level II manual)

Purpose: To actively investigate the concepts and influence of aggressive/passive/assertive behavior.

Time: 20 to 30 minutes.

Materials: None

Procedure: **Set Up:**

1. Divide into two groups on opposite sides of room. Have them line up along their side facing the center so there is a little bit of space around each person.

2. Ask them to assume an AGGRESSIVE mood. Suggest ideas to do this: think about getting even with someone; "get out of my way"; "don't tell ME what to do." Don't give a definition; have them respond as they understand the word.

3. Now, stand aggressively. How would your face look? How would you position your body?

4. Without touching anyone, walk across the room aggressively to the opposite side. (Some will feel awkward. Facilitators should all start walking to model).

5. Ask what that felt like PHYSICALLY (tense places, stomach, what were your hands doing?) What reaction did you have to those coming at you? Did you notice anything?

6. Shift mood to PASSIVE. (Again, suggest ideas without giving a definition.) Stand passively. What would you look like if you were feeling totally passive? Now, walk across the room passively without touching anyone. What did that feel like?

7. One more mood shift to ASSERTIVE. (Give time to get in the mood.) Stand in an assertive position. Walk across the room. Was that different from the other two? (Many will not know or be clear about this word. Don't define it; act it out! All facilitators should model).

Processing:

- Refer to previous activities (e.g., Secret Spot) and ask if anyone saw A/P/A behavior that took place; how about a real-life situation?
- Work out definitions for each.
  (Example: assertive = feel good about yourself without threatening/hurting others, or without being pushed around).
- Could do a "whip" on "Which am I?" and/or "Which I would like to be and why?"

AVP POSTERS

Purpose: To integrate themes such as affirmation, cooperation, and communication in the course of the last session of a Basic workshop as small groups illustrate what they think is important about an AVP workshop.

Time: About 1 hour

Materials: Oaktag or poster paper (2'x3' is big enough, but smaller works fine), scissors, glue, tape, markers, and a table full of "collage" materials e.g., colorful construction paper, ribbon, photos from magazines, (not whole magazines which may be distracting), colored toothpicks, popsicle sticks, cotton balls, rick-rack, etc. Heavy items like macaroni tend to fall off.

Procedure: **Set Up:**

1. Explain that this exercise involves making posters that illustrate what an AVP Workshop is all about. The posters will be hung up in some appropriate place (e.g., the school hall or a local library).

2. In small groups people will discuss what about the AVP workshop has been important for them. They might use a go-around to start their discussion.

3. When each group has finished its discussion the group can collect materials to illustrate its ideas on a poster. Explain that everyone may have to share materials.

4. If there are no questions, tell them they'll have about 40 minutes for the entire project - both discussion and creation of the posters. Then divide participants into four groups and have them begin.

5. When the posters are finished, have people return to the circle in their groups to show and explain their work. (This last step usually suffices for processing.)

BIOGRAPHIES

Purpose: To help people begin the process of looking within, to build community.

Time: About 20 minutes

Materials: None

Procedure: **Set Up:**

1. Explain that in this exercise we'll be working in groups of three. Each of the three will be given about five minutes to tell the story of her/his life. When the first person has spoken for the allotted time, you'll signal by raising your hand. The two listeners may then ask clarifying questions for about two minutes. Again you'll signal when time's up and the second person may start.

2. Stress that people may omit whatever they want from their life stories, and may decline to answer any questions. The biographies will not be shared in the big circle.

3. Ask people to form their own trios, preferably with others they don't know too well. If there are no questions about the instructions ask them to begin.

Processing:

- Did you find this easy or difficult?
- Did you have anything in common with your partners? (No one has to mention what the commonality is.)
- Were the differences interesting?
- How important are people's biographies in forming their "Point of View?"*

Note: It is handy to place this exercise after the exercise "Point of View."

Some young people think they haven't a very long biography. Urge them to try. If they get stuck suggest that they tell about the scariest time in their lives.

This exercise is adapted from the AVP Level II Manual.

BONFIRE

Purpose: To bring closing to an Advanced Workshop

Time: 30 minutes

Materials: A large pan or dish with enough clean sand to support candles, four sturdy candles (Sabbat or kitchen utility) and "twinkle candles" (long and thin, like a wick dipped in wax) so that each person will have one candle.

Procedure: **Set Up**

1. Place the pan of sand in the middle of the circle. Ask the group to sit on the floor. Put the lights out.

2. Speak about the energy of the workshop - the light and warmth generated by sharing our thoughts and feelings. This closing circle can help us remember this energy.

3. Pass the "twinkle candles" around the circle. Explain that you asked four people to help with the lighting of the candles, so they could practice.

4. Light the four sturdy candles. Have them light the other candles being sure to hold the sturdy candles upright.

5. As everyone sits holding a candle, mention that we are all individuals but we can create more of a glow if we work together.

6. Invite them to place their candles in the sand, going from the middle of the pan to the edges. Suggest going pop-corn style, with those holding sturdy candles going first. Everyone needs to be aware of leaving space for others so no one gets burned. If they would like to say something, they're welcome to do so.

7. Sit quietly until the thin candles burn down (about 5-7 minutes). Then mention that even though the candles go out, we can still keep the light going in our hearts.

8. Explain that people may leave as they wish going as quietly as possible.

Note: For people to leave as they wish, certificates and any business must be completed before the Bonfire.

BROKEN SQUARES

Purpose: To give people a chance to cooperate in completing a challenging task.

Time: About 40 minutes

Materials: Sample squares and sets of broken squares for each group of five (or four) participants - see attached sheet for samples (they vary for five or four). Instructions for observers - see below.
Fairly good size tables for each group arranged so participants can sit on the outside of them for processing (use the floor if tables are not available).
A poster:

YOU MAY	YOU MAY NOT
offer a piece or even a whole square to someone else	talk
or	gesture
accept a piece or a whole square offered to you.	take from others
	throw pieces into the center or
	show another where to put a piece.

Procedure: Set Up:

1. Explain that this exercise is a challenge! People will work in small groups. Each person in the group will be given an envelope containing pieces of cardboard that may be used to make squares. Show the pieces from one envelope and show a sample square.

2. The task for each group is to work cooperatively, so that each person will end up with a square in front of her/him. Stress that it is important that the group end up with five squares.

3. The challenging part is that the task must be done according to certain rules. Point out the poster and read or ask for volunteers to read the rules.

4. If there are no questions, form groups and assign each group a workspace.

5. Explain that co-facilitators or extra participants will act as observers in each group. (Give them a sheet with instructions.)

6. Mention that many different squares may be formed with the pieces given but only five (or four) particular squares will allow everyone at the table to have a square.

7. After everyone is arranged, with the help of co-facilitators hand out envelopes and sample squares to each group and have everyone begin.

8. Circulate around the room. If frustration level is increasing greatly, and if someone has a square other than one of those needed, you might repeat # 6. You might bring a group's attention to the sample square if someone seems to be trying to form a square that's too big.

9. If one group finishes before others, ask that group to be quiet.

10. When everyone is finished, have everyone stay with their group and face into the circle. Ask for reports from the observers before general group discussion.

Processing:

- How did you feel about this challenge?
- Was it difficult to follow the rules?
- How do people feel about being helped?
- Does this exercise remind you of real life situations?
- Does this exercise give you any thoughts about solving other group problems?

Note: It's important for all the groups to finish if possible. Sometimes just a little hint such as those mentioned in #8 might be helpful.

This exercise might be co-facilitated. One person might explain the task, point out the rules and do the processing; the other could manage the grouping and the distribution of materials. Both could circulate.

If a group thinks they are missing pieces, check the envelopes. (Note: For groups of five there are fifteen pieces in all and each square is made with three pieces. This fact should NOT be mentioned to the group.)

If a person has done the exercise before, s/he might be an observer. In a pinch, to form a group, someone who has done the exercise before might do it again - most people don't remember the five squares needed. Even a facilitator could sit in and play a passive role.

Instructions for Observers

Encourage people to keep the rules.
Watch to see if people are:
- actively involved in the task,
- willing or reluctant to share pieces,
- concerned about others
- using the sample square,
- frustrated.

Might someone have finished a square and then just watched?
Was there a turning point, e.g., someone giving away an entire square, which led to completion?

Try to be as positive as possible when giving your report.

Making the Squares for Broken Squares

A complete set of squares consists of five envelopes containing pieces of cardboard which has been cut into different patterns and which, when properly assembled, form 5 squares of equal size. One set is provided for each group.

To make a set, cut out five cardboard squares of ***equal*** size (about six by six inches). Mark the squares as shown below:

The lines should be drawn so that all pieces with the same shape will be ***exactly*** the same size. After drawing the lines, cut each square into the smaller pieces that will make up the puzzle. Mark five envelopes with the letters A, B, C, D, and E. Distribute the puzzle pieces in the envelopes.

Each Square is 6" x 6"

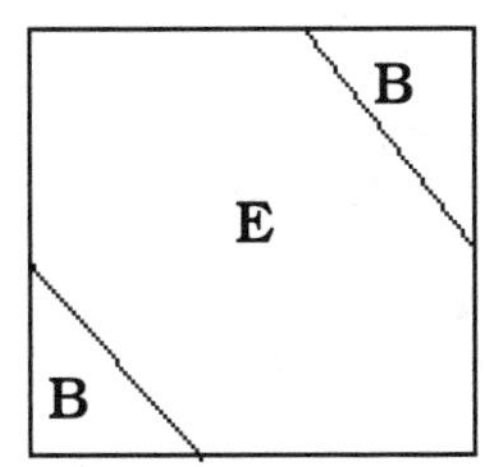

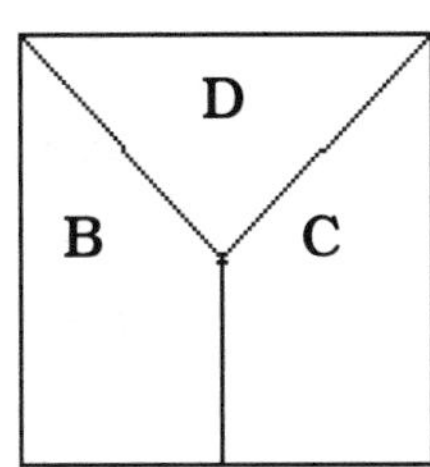

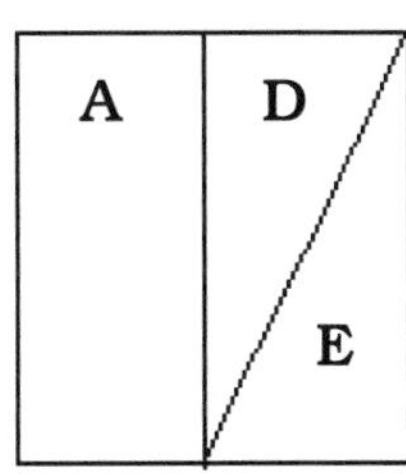

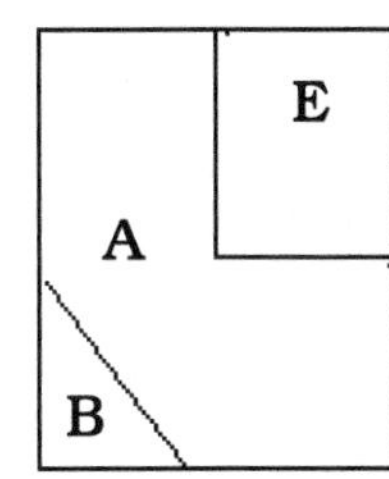

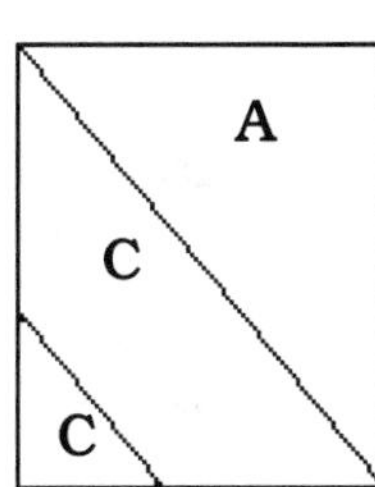

Alternate Layout

If you wish to make smaller groups, this alternate layout is designed for groups of 4

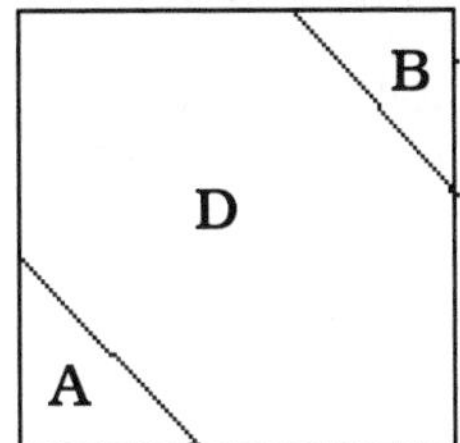

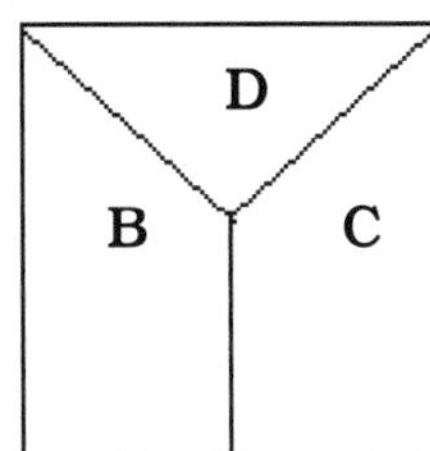

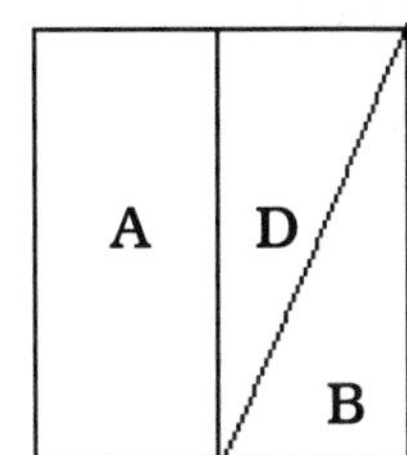

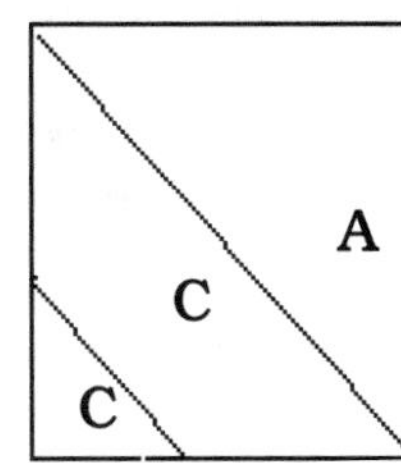

Honey From the Rock

Lawrence Kushner

Distribute and read after the
Broken Squares Exercise

Each lifetime is the pieces of a jigsaw puzzle.
For some there are more pieces.
For others the puzzle is more difficult to assemble.
Some seem to be born with a
nearly completed puzzle.
And so it goes.
Souls going this way and that
Trying to assemble the myriad pieces.

But know this. *No one has within themselves*
All the pieces to their puzzle.
Like before the days
When they used to seal jigsaw puzzles in cellophane
Insuring that all the pieces are there.

Everyone carries with them at least one
And probably many pieces to someone's puzzle
Sometimes they know it.
Sometimes they don't.

And when you present your piece
Which is worthless to you,
To another, whether you know it or not,
Whether they know it or not,
You are a messenger from the Most High.

Honey From the Rock

Lawrence Kushner

Distribute and read after the
Broken Squares Exercise

Each lifetime is the pieces of a jigsaw puzzle.
For some there are more pieces.
For others the puzzle is more difficult to assemble.
Some seem to be born with a
nearly completed puzzle.
And so it goes.
Souls going this way and that
Trying to assemble the myriad pieces.

But know this. *No one has within themselves*
All the pieces to their puzzle.
Like before the days
When they used to seal jigsaw puzzles in cellophane
Insuring that all the pieces are there.

Everyone carries with them at least one
And probably many pieces to someone's puzzle
Sometimes they know it.
Sometimes they don't.

And when you present your piece
Which is worthless to you,
To another, whether you know it or not,
Whether they know it or not,
You are a messenger from the Most High.

Honey From the Rock

Lawrence Kushner

Distribute and read after the
Broken Squares Exercise

Each lifetime is the pieces of a jigsaw puzzle.
For some there are more pieces.
For others the puzzle is more difficult to assemble.
Some seem to be born with a
nearly completed puzzle.
And so it goes.
Souls going this way and that
Trying to assemble the myriad pieces.

But know this. *No one has within themselves*
All the pieces to their puzzle.
Like before the days
When they used to seal jigsaw puzzles in cellophane
Insuring that all the pieces are there.

Everyone carries with them at least one
And probably many pieces to someone's puzzle
Sometimes they know it.
Sometimes they don't.

And when you present your piece
Which is worthless to you,
To another, whether you know it or not,
Whether they know it or not,
You are a messenger from the Most High.

Honey From the Rock

Lawrence Kushner

Distribute and read after the
Broken Squares Exercise

Each lifetime is the pieces of a jigsaw puzzle.
For some there are more pieces.
For others the puzzle is more difficult to assemble.
Some seem to be born with a
nearly completed puzzle.
And so it goes.
Souls going this way and that
Trying to assemble the myriad pieces.

But know this. *No one has within themselves*
All the pieces to their puzzle.
Like before the days
When they used to seal jigsaw puzzles in cellophane
Insuring that all the pieces are there.

Everyone carries with them at least one
And probably many pieces to someone's puzzle
Sometimes they know it.
Sometimes they don't.

And when you present your piece
Which is worthless to you,
To another, whether you know it or not,
Whether they know it or not,
You are a messenger from the Most High.

BUTTONS

Purpose: To become more aware of why certain situations "push our buttons" so that sometimes we "lose our cool" - to consider how we might calm ourselves in such situations and to practice doing just that.

Time: 30 - 40 minutes.
(This exercise can be split: first, steps #1 - #5, later steps #6 and #7.)

Materials: Button Circle Poster (next page)

Procedure: Set Up

1. Explain that sometimes certain situations "push our buttons" so that we may "lose our cool." In trios we're going to consider why this might be so.

2. Form trios, in or near the circle. Ask everyone to share a situation that often "pushes their buttons." Allow about 5 to 10 minutes for this.

3. Point out the Button Circle poster. Mention that probably most people mentioned a situation and a feeling connected with it. For example, "If people start to tell me what a great time they had getting drunk, I get angry."

4. But why? What lies between the situation and my anger? It's my "point of view." I value not getting wasted myself. Also, my brother's an alcoholic and I hate it when he tells supposedly funny "war stories." It's my old experiences. Under my anger, I'm sure there's hurt and fear.

5. Back in trios, have people consider what in their "point of view" comes between their situation and their feelings. Allow about 10 minutes.

6. In the big circle brainstorm possible ways to calm or cool our "buttons." If "self talk" isn't mentioned, ask if anyone has ever tried it.

7. Go back to trios to practice calming our "buttons.." First have A and B role play. Have B try to push A's "buttons," using the situation A had described. A will try to "keep cool." C will observe and give feed-back. Repeat two times, switching roles. (You may want to do a demo skit.)

Processing:

- Did anyone gain any insights?
- Might you be able to use your calming method(s) in real life?

Note: Having co-facilitators participating or observing is helpful. This exercise is particularly useful before or after any Feeling exercise.

You may wish to give everyone a button as a calming keepsake.

Buttons Circle

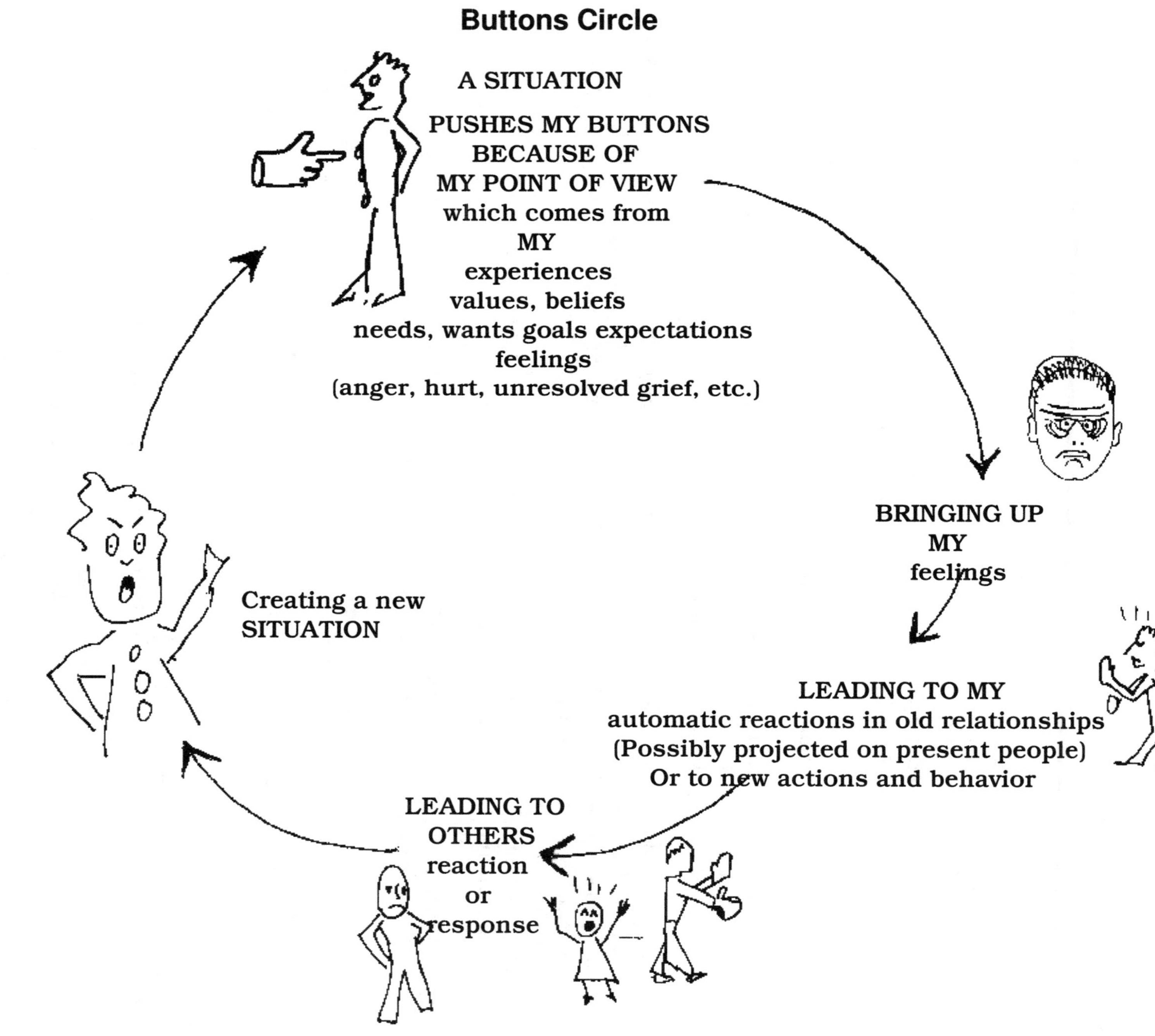
A SITUATION
PUSHES MY BUTTONS
BECAUSE OF
MY POINT OF VIEW
which comes from
MY
experiences
values, beliefs
needs, wants goals expectations
feelings
(anger, hurt, unresolved grief, etc.)
BRINGING UP
MY
feelings
LEADING TO MY
automatic reactions in old relationships
(Possibly projected on present people)
Or to new actions and behavior
LEADING TO
OTHERS
reaction
or
response
Creating a new
SITUATION

CANDY KISSES

Purpose: To explore how we often respond competitively even when that is not the stated task.

Time: 15 minutes

Materials: Candy Kisses, M&M's, Tic Tacs, or other small candy

Procedure: **Set Up:**

1. Have participants seated in pairs facing each other across a table or desk, or lying on a clean floor. Move them quickly into position, with concise, brief instructions. No talking once participants are in pairs. Do not explain or answer questions.

2. Everyone put right elbow on table with arm straight up, and clasp hands.

3. Facilitator says "You get one point each time you touch the back of the other person's hand to the table. You have 15 seconds to score. Now begin." (If asked, say this is not "arm wrestling" although it looks similar).

4. "The object of each individual is to get as many points as possible in 15 seconds." (This is key. Do not refer to "opponent," "partner," or "your team"). Everyone keeps track of his/her points.

5. Ask for scores and hand out candy. (How many is irrelevant, but do have some overall "reward" pattern in mind).
   _____ To the pair(s) which had the highest and equal number of points. (Don't explain yet, but this shows there was probably cooperation)
   _____ Could give out lesser amounts of candy to any other pair with somewhat equal number of points. (Some cooperation)
   _____ If one or both members of any pair had zero points, that team gets no candy. (No cooperation, "lose/lose" situation).

Processing:

- What happened? What do you think this was about?
- Do you feel cheated? What do you think the scoring rules were?
- Would your behavior be different if it had been explained before we started?
- Do you always "lose" something when the other person gains something? (Not necessarily, although it sometimes does happen, e.g., one job, ten applicants)

Note: This is an opportunity to introduce concept of "Win/win."

CHANGES 1,2,3

Purpose: To be more aware of other people; to consider how aware we usually are and to think about how our awareness or lack of awareness might relate to conflict

Time: About 20 minutes

Materials: None

Procedure: **Set Up:**

1. Explain that in this exercise everyone is going to have a chance to test how aware they are of others and how observant they are.

2. Count off by half the number of participants. Have everyone stand opposite their like number on either side of an imaginary line that you designate. Say that those on one side of the line will be the A's. Those on the other side of the line will be the B's.

3. First have the A's observe the B's carefully for about a minute. Then have the A's turn their backs toward the B's. When the A's back is turned ask the B's to change three fairly obvious things about themselves e.g., taking off their glasses, rolling up a sleeve, adopting an attitude.

4. Give the B's only a minute or so to make the changes. Then have the A's turn backs towards the B's and try to determine what changes were made.

5. Next have an A at the "top" end of the line walk down to the "bottom" end of the A line. Have all the other A's move up one place. Hence everyone gets a new partner.

6. Now have the B's be the "observers" and the A's be the "changers." Repeat steps 3,4, and 5 three times switching roles alternately, (for a total of four changes - 2 changes for each person). Then have everyone return to the circle.

Processing:

- Was this easy, difficult or frustrating for the observers?
- Would we become more aware of the changes in others if we practiced?
- Can being aware of others help us resolve conflicts? avoid conflicts? How?
- What might we notice about our friends or parents or teachers that would help us understand how they're feeling?
- How might we show our understanding of one another's feelings?

This was adapted from Creative Conflict Resolution

CHECKERBOARD DESIGN

Purpose: For the group to experiment with cooperation. Especially good for young students.

Time: 20 minutes

Materials: Two pieces of contrasting color construction paper per group (no scissors, paste etc.).

Procedure: **Set Up:**

1. Divide into groups, about four per group.
2. Ask people not to talk. Have them look at the material, and think about what a checkerboard design looks like. (About one minute).
3. Then, ask groups to discuss and plan together about how they will make a checkerboard design out of the two pieces of paper. (About 3 minutes).
4. All groups stop talking. Each group has about 5 minutes to make the checkerboard design.

Processing:

- Was everyone involved in the decision making process?
- Were everyone's ideas equally considered?
- Did anyone play a particularly helpful role in getting the group to accomplish the task?

CHOICES I

Purpose: To begin thinking about the choices we can make, including how we live our lives; to begin to realize that the ability to choose is a central belief in AVP; to become aware that we can even choose to change.

Time: 15 - 20 minutes

Materials: None

Procedure: **Set Up**

1. Ask everyone to imagine that the floor is divided into four sections. Each section will represent a different choice. You will describe various choices and everyone will stand where they choose.
2. People's first choice will be their favorite season. Designate one season per section of the floor and ask people to stand in the season they like.
3. Then let each section stand for one of four "fast food" restaurants and ask everyone to stand in their choice. Repeat using four sports.
4. Next, ask people to place themselves along an imaginary line based on how they would handle the following situation: They are in a cafeteria line and someone knocks their tray out of their hands. Indicate that one end of the line is "walk away" and the other end is "get into a fight."
5. After people have placed themselves along the line, ask volunteers to tell why they put themselves where they did. Is the choice less clear-cut in this type of situation? Might it depend on circumstances such as
   a) the size of the person with whom we're dealing?
   b) whether or not we know the person?
   c) our own mood? our own experience? (etc.)

Processing: (After having group return to the circle of seats.)

- How important are the choices we make?
- Are some choices easier to make than others?
- Is it possible to change our choices? Is this easy or difficult?
- Do we have a choice about how we act when we're angry?

6. Ask the group for four ways that they respond to anger. Responses might be:
   a) go for a walk;
   b) get into an argument;
   c) go to one's room and listen to music;
   d) try to talk about the problem.
7. Designate a section of the floor for each of the four responses. Ask everyone to stand in the section they would choose. Ask if it would be hard to make that choice in real life.

Note: You may want to mention that we're not trying to come to any monumental conclusions here; we're just starting to think about some important things, such as anger. We'll be looking at positive ways to deal with anger as the workshop continues.

CHOICES II

Purpose: To make some choices and to consider a central belief in AVP that we often have more choices than we think we have. (We may even choose to change.)

Time: 20 minutes

Materials: Four large posters taped in four corners of the room and folded so that, initially, only the word, "Choices" shows. As the category of choice is announced, facilitators or others will uncover one line at a time. The posters read as follows:

CHOICES	CHOICES	CHOICES	CHOICES
McDonalds	Wendy's	Kentucky FC	Burger King
Basketball	Ice Hockey	Volleyball	Football
Bottle it up	Get physical	Break something	Talk
Try something new	Ask for help	Give up	Pout

Procedure: Set Up

1. Put up the posters before the session or at "break." Alert teammates about uncovering lines as you mention categories.

2. While everyone is seated, explain that you will mention some categories in which choices can be made. After you mention a category, people will place themselves near a "choice" you'll read. Then you'll ask some other questions.

3. The questions indicating the categories are:
   If you were hungry which fast food restaurant would you choose?
   Which sport would you choose to play or watch?
   If you were angry at someone or with a situation, what might you do?
   If you were frustrated trying to finish a task, how might you respond?

4. After each category, while people are standing in place, ask questions such as:
   Would someone like to say why they put themselves where they did?
   Does anyone feel uncomfortable where they are?
   Is there anyone who didn't like any of the choices? If so, how might they show this? Might an area be designated for "none of the above"?
   Is anyone torn between two or more choices? Can they show this physically?

Processing:
- How important are the choices we make?
- Can we choose to change the choices we make? Is this easy or difficult?

Note: It's important to keep this moving so people don't get tired standing.

CHOICES AND CONSEQUENCES

Purpose: To develop decision making skills, particularly around moral dilemmas

Time: 45 minutes

Materials: Flip chart or handout

Procedure: **Set Up:**

1. Post the following on a flip chart and/or hand out copies.
   1. Define the problem
      - Whose problem is it?
      - Who does it affect?
      - Who is concerned?
   2. What are the choices?
      - List all possible choices, including doing nothing or not choosing
   3. What are the consequences of each choice?
      - Long term consequences
      - Short term consequences
      - Secondary consequences
      - Positive and negative consequences
   4. Weigh the choices
   5. Choose
   6. See what happens
   7. Perhaps reconsider
2. Divide participants into groups of four. As time allows, have each group consider each of the following problems below and come up with a decision for the group.
3. Have each group report on their decision before moving on to the next problem.

Processing:

- Was your group able to come up with a solution that people agreed to?
- What was it like to go through this process to solve a problem?
- Is talking through a problem like this with other people helpful? Confusing?

Sample problems:

1. You need to study for an important test tomorrow that you HAVE to pass. A boy/girl who you really want to get to know better calls. You talk for a while and then s/he asks you to go tonight to a movie you've been wanting to see.
2. You and a friend are driving in your parents' car. Your friend pulls out a bottle of alcohol and offers you a drink.
3. You are shopping with a friend and you see him/her secretly slip some items into a bag.
4. You need to pass a test in your hardest subject. A friend offers to allow you to cheat off his/her test.
5. You have recently gotten a part-time job in a retail store. The manager tells you that whenever young people of a certain ethnic origin come into the store, it is your job to follow them around and make sure they don't steal anything.

CHOICES FOR ADVANCED

Purpose: To explore the idea that no matter where we are and how helpless we may feel we still can make choices; to consider which choices will enhance (increase) and which will diminish our freedom to live our lives the way we want to live.

Time: 30 minutes or more

Materials: Newsprint and markers enough for 4 or 5 groups; a poster as follows:

CHOICES

Some Diminish Freedom	Some Enhance Freedom
and can lead to	and can lead to
prison, death, addiction,	health, good jobs, long life
illness, loss of options	family ties, peace of mind

Procedure: Set Up:

1. Explain the purpose as stated above. Show the poster and ask for volunteers to read the different sides.

2. Say that in small groups people will brainstorm choices that might diminish their freedom and choices that will enhance their freedom. Encourage them to think of choices that they can make in the present — right now! You might ask for one example of a choice that would diminish freedom, e.g., trying drugs, and one that would enhance freedom, e.g., getting an education.

3. If there are no questions, form groups, assign work places, distribute materials and have them begin. Let them know that they'll have about 10 minutes.

4. When each group has some things on both lists have people return to the circle staying with their groups. Post the lists and have volunteers read them.

Processing:

- What do people think about the choices listed?
- Are some of the choices difficult to follow? Which ones? Why?
- Do we always have choices? What about the, "I didn't have a choice" line?
- Might difficult situations arise because of unwise choices made in the past?
- What can we do to help us stick to wise choices?

Note: The idea that we have choices is a key concept of AVP. Freedom is an integral part of the picture because freedom of choice is what it's all about.

Before Step 1 above, you may wish to brainstorm how people would like to be living in four or five years. They probably dream of family ties, good job,peace of mind etc. Then you can proceed as above.

CIRCLE GAME

Purpose: To provide an active way for the group to get acquainted

Time: About 10 minutes

Materials: List of categories that can be varied according to the group (see *Note)*; (a sample list that seems to work for 12 year-olds is attached)

Procedure: Set Up:

1. Have everyone stand in a large circle.

2. Explain that you'll call out different descriptions that might be true of some of the members of the group.

3. Anyone who thinks the description fits, steps into the middle of the circle for just a few moments and then steps back. For example, "Everyone who has ever climbed a tree, step into the circle."

4. Thank those who stepped into the circle and invite them to step back out. Then continue with other categories. (see list next page) Keep it lively!

Processing:

- How did that go?
- Did you have anything in common with others?
- Did any of these things that we have in common surprise anyone? Why?

Note: This can be used at the beginning of an Advanced Workshop for older students by using age-appropriate categories.

Instead of stepping, you might have people "leap" into the circle and then "jump" back out.

You might ask the participants to suggest some categories after you've done five or six.

Keep this moving and lively!!

Suggested Categories For Circle Game (For 12 Year Olds)

Everyone who:

- comes from a large family
- plays a musical instrument
- was born in ________________(choose an appropriate place)
- is an only child
- has ridden a pig
- gets nervous trying something new
- has a body piercing
- likes camping
- has fallen out of a tree
- has traveled out of ___________(choose an appropriate place)
- has ever dyed his/her hair
- feels good after finishing a job
- has been in a fight, either verbal or physical
- has a close relative born in another country
- has milked a cow
- would like to try sky diving
- has written a poem
- has experienced divorce in his/her close family
- can really speak a language other than ________(you choose)
- has been in a play
- belongs to the human race (*use this one last)*

CLIQUE CLASH

Purpose: To develop an understanding of the desire for and the effects of belonging to groups.

Time: 15 minutes

Materials: Index cards with "zappers" (see below)

Procedure: **Set Up:**

1. Randomly divide participants into four social groups (clubs or cliques).

2. List on newsprint attributes with which people may identify, e.g., "help others," "great dressers," "very smart," "good athletes," "throw great parties," "very popular, very cool."

3. Have each group chose ONE of these attributes as its identity. Also, ask them to develop a signal, special handshake or gesture to greet each other with. (No more than 5 minutes for both tasks).

4. Ask them to get up and mingle for three minutes, greeting everyone (including those in their own group) with their group's signal.

5. Have them get back into their groups, and give each group an index card with a "zapper." Examples might be : "You are a mess!," "What's wrong with you?," "Your hair looks like a mop!," "You smell bad!," "Your clothes are wrinkled!," "Your zipper is down!". Have everyone mingle for three minutes and greet each other with the zapper.

Processing:

- Does it feel different if someone from another group zaps you?
- Does it matter who in your own group zaps you?
- Does it matter what time of day or on what day someone zaps you?
- How is this like real life cliques?
- What are some good things about hanging out with groups or cliques? What are some bad things?

CONCENTRIC CIRCLES (AKA TALKING CIRCLES)

Purpose: To help people begin sharing one-on-one with half the people in the group in a comfortable setting; to experience commonalities and hence build community

Time: About 40 - 60 minutes for a group of 20

Materials: A list of topics numbering half the number of those who will participate (see samples on page G-35).

Procedure: **Set Up:**

1. Explain that in this exercise everyone will have a chance to talk briefly on some given topics with about half the people in the group.
2. To do this, we'll form two circles, one facing in and the other facing out. Ask everyone to count off by two's, with as many facilitators as possible taking part.
3. Ask all the "one's" to pick up their chairs, step into the circle, turn around and sit opposite the "two" to their right. (If several co-facilitators do this as it is said everyone will get the idea.)
4. When everyone is arranged, (and don't worry if some get a little confused), say that in a moment you'll ask the people in the outer circle to speak on a topic you'll give them. They'll speak for about a minute or so. You'll time them and when time is up you'll raise your hand. Ask everyone to finish their thought when they see hands being raised. Explain that then the inner circle will speak on the same topic.
5. Ask that as listeners all listen carefully, without interrupting, asking only clarifying questions.
6. If there are no questions, read Topic 1 and ask the outer circle to begin and proceed as in #4. above.
7. When both circles have talked, ask those in the outer circle to move one chair to their right.
8. For Topic 2, ask the inner circle to speak first. (This avoids having the same people being put on the spot to speak first every time.)
9. After both circles have spoken on Topic 2, ask the inner circle to move one chair to their right. (This gives each circle a chance to move every other time). Note that having both circles move in the same direction gives people a new partner with each move.

Processing:

- Were there any favorite topics?
- Were any topics difficult?
- Did anyone find something s/he had in common with someone else?
- Were there any surprises?

Note: It's good to start with the least personal topics. The sample topics take that in mind. They work well particularly in a Basic when participants may be hesitant about speaking. Topics more suitable for an Advanced and a T4F may be found among the "Gatherings" in Section I.

Rather than timing strictly by the clock, listen to noise level to determine when to cut off conversation.

Ending on a positive, light note is wise.

This exercise is conducive to co-facilitation. One person could manage the movement; the other could state the topics and keep track of time. Both, standing outside and at opposite sides of the circles, would raise their hands.

Two topics that have proved meaty enough for Reflective Listening are: "My idea of a good friend is..." and "Something I hope to do in the future is... ." These topics are therefore not included in the accompanying list of topics though they are often on other lists for Concentric Circles.

Concentric Circles

Topic	1	2	3	4	5	6	7	8	9	10	11
Speaks 1st	Out	In	Out	In	Out	In	Out	In	Out	In	Out
Speaks 2nd	In	Out	In	Out	In	Out	In	Out	In	Out	In
Moves	Out	In	Out	In	Out	In	Out	In	Out	In	Out

Sample Topics

A time of year I really enjoy is...... because...

A sport or pastime I think is great is... because..

Some foods that I find delicious are...because..

Given an opportunity to travel, I would go to...because ...

A type of music I love to listen to is.... because.

A favorite possession of mine is ... because....

A good thing I remember about my childhood is...

Something I've done that I'm proud of is....because...

A value that is important to me is....because...

An important person in my life is... because...

A time I made someone happy was....

A good quality of mine that I'd like to strengthen is....

A person I really admire is....because....

My idea of a good time is...because...

CONSTRUCTION CREW

Purpose: To consider what's involved in giving and receiving instructions; to think about how trust and respect relate to authority figures.

Time: About 20 -30 minutes

Materials: A "model" to be copied (made of legos, tinker toys etc.); a supply of the same materials for each group so that each group can reproduce the model.

Procedure: **Set Up:**

1. Explain that in the hall (or somewhere) there is a model made of, for example, legos. In small groups, people will try to construct a copy of this hidden model.

2. To do this each group will choose an observer. This person will be the only one in a particular group who will observe or see the model. The observer will look at the model and come back to her/his group and explain to the group how to make the model.

3. The observer may go back and forth to see the model as often as s/he wishes. The observer may point to the materials but may not touch the materials.

4. Each group will choose its own observer. It is important to choose someone who has an eye for details and who can give instructions clearly. Encourage groups to choose carefully because it will not be permissible to change observers in mid-stream. Groups may wish to have members describe something they can all see, to get an idea of whom they wish to choose.

5. If there are no questions, divide everyone into groups of 4 or 5. Assign work areas as far apart as possible and have each group choose its observer. Allow 4-5 minutes for this.

6. After all groups have chosen an observer, let the process begin. You can limit building to 15 minutes or allow it to continue until all groups are finished. Decide with your co-facilitators, depending on how things are going.

7. At the end of building, have groups return to the circle with their construction and bring the model into the room as well.

Processing:

- Was this easy, difficult or frustrating for observers? Group members?
- Did people feel rushed? in a race with other groups? Why might this be?
- Did the observers feel their groups listened to them?
- How do people feel about giving instructions? Taking instructions?
- Is it sometimes difficult to trust/respect people giving instructions? Why?
- Does this apply to authority figures in real life, too? How?

COOPERATIVE DRAWING

Purpose: To experience making a cooperative decision, and working together to carry out the decision.

Time: About 15 minutes

Materials: Large sheets of paper and a huge supply of brightly colored markers

Procedure: **Set Up:**

1. Explain that in a minute you will have the participants form groups of 3.

2. Each group will talk about what they'd like to draw and then work cooperatively to complete the drawing. They'll have about 15 minutes for the whole project.

3. Suggest that in their groups they use a "go-around" to help them decide what to draw and to decide who will do which part of the drawing.

4. Model a "go-around" with two co-facilitators. The first person may want to draw the Empire State Building; the second may want to draw a giraffe; the third may want to draw a flower. Discuss how this might be put on paper, that is, what will go where. (If you have only one co-facilitator ask for a volunteer to model a "go-around." In this case let the volunteer be the first to say what s/he would like to draw.)

5. When people see that any combination of things might go together divide the group into trios, assign each trio working space, hand out materials and have them begin.

6. Have the trios bring their drawings to the large circle when they are finished. Ask volunteers from each trio to talk about what their trio drew.

Processing:

- Is it easy or difficult to do something creative in a group?
- Did the "go-around" help in making decisions?
- Might they be able to use "go-arounds" in other situations?
- Did everyone get a chance to say what s/he wanted?

Note: You might want to display a couple of modern art works which involve a variety of subjects in one work.

This is an exercise which works especially well with younger students, such as 10 year-olds.

CO-OP MONSTERS

Purpose: To experience cooperation, affirmation and creativity in small groups.

Time: About 20 minutes, depending on the amount of discussion that occurs.

Materials: Newsprint, colored construction paper, markers, scissors, masking tape.

Procedure: Set Up:

1. Say that in this exercise, participants, working in small groups, will create monsters in a cooperative way. The monsters can be anything the group decides. They might be creatures from outer space, animals that didn't make it on the ark — whatever!

2. In their groups, they'll decide what type of monster they'd like to draw. They will also decide which part(s) each would like to draw. Suggest that the groups use "go-arounds" to get everybody's ideas. Remember, since it's monsters that are being made, it's fine to have 2 heads, one long leg and another that's short, etc. People may wish to work privately on their particular part(s) and later join it (them) to the rest of the monster.

3. If there are no questions, form groups of 4 or 5 and assign each a work space. Distribute materials and tell the groups that they'll have about 15 minutes.

4. When you come back to the circle, invite each group to say a little bit about its monster. As many members of the group as would like, can say something. Affirm each group's monster before processing.

Processing:

- How did the groups decide what type of monster they would create?
- How did groups decide who would draw the various monster parts?
- Did everyone think they had enough of a say?
- Is the "go-around" a useful tool in giving everyone a say?

Note: Masking tape works well for putting the parts together.

This was adapted from The Friendly Classroom for a Small Planet

CO-OP POSTERS (AKA TOOL BOX)

Purpose: This exercise gives everyone a chance to cooperate while creating a poster about AVP that they can bring back to their class or school.

Time: About 20 minutes

Materials: Newsprint or poster board and markers (3 sheets and 15 markers for 3 groups of five.)

Procedure: **Set Up:**

1. Explain that at this time everyone is going to have a chance to help create a poster that they can put up in the school to remind them of AVP. They'll make the posters in small groups.
2. Each group will decide what they'd like to put on the poster. They might have a "go-around" before they start making the poster so that everyone has a chance to express his/her ideas.
3. Have the group count off by 3's, to end up with 3 groups of five (assuming there are 15 participants). Assign a work area for each group. Have your co-facilitators help you distribute materials and be available if there are any questions.
4. When the posters are complete, ask everyone to return to the circle and ask for a volunteer(s) from each group to speak about the group's poster.

Processing:

- How did that go?
- Is it easy or difficult to do creative things in a group?

Note: Co-op Posters is often used in a mini program with eleven year-olds. If it is done after Intro to Win/Win, you might ask that they include some ways to 'Cool off' in their poster.

In a Basic workshop this activity is called Tool Box. Participants are asked to create a Tool Box of ideas from AVP that they might use in school, at home or in their community. Naturally, the number and size of the groups would depend on the number of participants.

If time is short, a large group brainstorm called "Tool Box" might be done just before Role Plays as a reminder of the tools that might be used during the Role Plays, as well as in real life. Individual "Tool Box" sheets might be used as handouts at the end of the workshop.

CREATIVE CONSTRUCTION

Purpose: To come to an agreement on a project to be built and to cooperate in the construction.

Time: About 25 minutes

Materials: 10 sheets of newspaper or newsprint and 3 yards of masking tape for each small group of four or five participants; a poster:

> WHAT do you want to build?
> HOW will you build it?
> WHO will do what?

Procedure: Set Up:

1. Explain that in this exercise people will work in small groups to build or construct something. The materials that each group will use are 10 sheets of newspaper (or newsprint) and 3 yards of masking tape.

2. Point to the poster and say that first each group will talk for five minutes to decide **WHAT** they'd like to build, **HOW** they're going to build it, and **WHO** will do what. Suggest that they have a 'go-around' to help them decide **WHAT** they'd like to build.

3. After the five minutes is up, the group will work in silence for ten minutes to actually do the building.

4. If there are no questions, form small groups and have them begin discussion. Remind them about having a "go-around." You and some co-facilitators can distribute the material near each group. Remind them that they're not to work with the material until the discussion period is up.

5. When five minutes is up, signal that they may start working in silence.

6. When building time is up, have people stay with their group and return to the circle, with their construction if possible.

Processing:

- How did that go?
- Did things go according to plan?
- Is it easy or difficult to do creative things in a group?
- Did everyone feel that they participated in both the planning and building?

Variation: Have participants create an "egg drop" landing device using 8 bendable plastic sipping straws and masking tape. Each group should be able to drop the egg in its created landing craft from a height of 6 feet without breaking the egg.

Note: It's sometimes fun to take pictures during this activity.

CROSSOVER

Purpose: To look at similarities and differences in our life experiences and the prejudices/stereotypes we may have about the categories mentioned. (Can be a community builder, but watch out for emotional reactions to sensitive questions.)

Time: 30 minutes (take less time for reflection for a young group)

Materials: A list of 10 - 12 descriptions that are appropriate for your group (suggestions below)

Procedure: **Set Up:**

1. Have the group stand in a row across one wall. Have enough space for some to cross to the other side of the room and feel separated from the initial group.

2. Say: I will read a number of descriptions. If the description is true for you as you define it, please cross over to the other side of the room. Even though the description is true, you may, at any time, choose not to move. Simply stay where you are, but think about that decision and what it means to you. Please keep a respectful silence during the exercise.

3. Start describing: Please cross over if you were....... After people have crossed say: Look carefully at who is in your group, those who share this experience with you. Consider quietly, any surprises?

4. Say to those who did not move: Observe who crossed over and who is left on your side. While keeping a respectful silence, consider how it feels to be on your side with these particular people.

5. To those who moved: Look across the room at those who did not cross over. Who is still there? Where are most of the people? Just think about it.

6. Say: "Take a moment to get a good sense of what this (description) or (group) means to you in your life. Would you change things if you could?"

7. Is anyone alone? What is it like to be the only one of your group?

8. Ask the first group to please cross back over.

9. Continue to consider categories as above, working from easy to difficult.

Processing:

- What happened? What feelings came up?
- Any particular reactions about either moving or staying?
- Did you learn something new about anyone? Were you surprised (without pinpointing any individual)?
- Did you choose not to move any time? Can you say what feelings came up about that decision?
- Did you notice anything about the categories, a common thread?

Note: Be sensitive to the group. Remind everyone of the importance of confidentiality.

When using many of the categories relating to fights and weapons, it is wise to end with some of the positive categories involving nonviolence. This is particularly true for younger participants.

It is possible that some participants may wish to respond to some of the questions asked in the course of doing the exercise. Try to go with the flow and do what you think best meets the needs of the participants. If you have people respond, you may have to remind others to be mindful of keeping a respectful silence when someone is responding.

Possible General Descriptions:
Please cross over if you

were an only/oldest/youngest/middle child
had 5 (6) or more children in your family
had no siblings of the same sex as you
were born/raised in the South
were born outside the United States
were raised in a rural area
were raised on a farm
were raised in a working class environment
were raised in a family with ample economic resources
were raised in a family where money caused you stress
were raised as Polish, or other Eastern European
were raised as African, African-American, or Caribbean
were raised as European (Italian/French/German/Irish/English)
were raised as Latino/Latina
were raised as Asian
were raised as indigenous/native person/Native American
were raised as Jewish
were raised as WASP (white Anglo-Saxon Protestant)
were raised as a minority of any kind
were raised by one parent
were raised by a family member other than a parent, e.g., a grandparent
are or have been a single parent
lived in a home where there was a problem with alcohol or drugs
lived in a home where there was physical, verbal or sexual harassment
lived in a foster home
at one time had or now have a physical, emotional or psychological disability
are a person who ran away from home
are not or have not been on speaking terms with a family member
were ever labeled or assumed to be gay

Possible Description Pertaining to Fights and Weapons
("seen" means "seen with your own two eyes" [no hype])

have seen a fight
have seen a fight where blood was drawn/ someone was stabbed/shot
have been in a fight
have been in a fight where blood was drawn/ someone was stabbed/shot
have started a fight
have been goaded (persuaded) to fight by someone else
have stabbed someone
have shot someone
have had a friend or family member hurt by physical violence
have been hurt by physical violence
have hurt someone else physically

Possible Descriptions Pertaining to Nonviolence

have been tempted to fight but didn't
have talked someone else out of fighting
have been talked out of fighting
wish someone had talked you out of fighting

ESCALATOR

Purpose: To examine the process of conflict and to pinpoint opportunities for change. May be used instead of role plays in an advanced workshop.

Time: One hour for Part I and one hour for Part II.

Materials: Newsprint and markers.

PART I - Analysis of Conflict Situation

Procedure: Set Up:

1. Give a role play or "story." An example is included below.
2. Have the audience explain the steps (events) in the "plot" where the escalation occurred. Write these events on the tops of the "steps." See Steps in Escalation.
3. Underneath each "step" write what the audience thinks the feelings of the participants were when the event happened. See Feelings of Participants.
4. Discuss at what points a change in behavior could have sent the parties down the escalator. See Possibilities of De-escalation.

Escalator Story

Dave and Jim are sitting in English class at a time the class is supposed to be reading their assignment silently. Dave is co-captain of the football team, which had finished with a winning season. Dave is not doing a spring sport, although he works out regularly in the weight training room in preparation for spring football practice. Jim is co-captain of the baseball team, which so far this spring has a 2 and 8 losing season. Jim is the starting catcher and sometimes pitches. His hitting has been poor this season, far behind his record last year as a junior.

Dave, who is sitting behind Jim, begins to kick Jim's chair. Jim turns around and says in an irritated tone "Cut it out!" Dave kicks the chair again. Jim turns around and says "I said cut it out, A-hole!" Dave retorts, "F-you, A-hole, you can't even hit a baseball." Jim does not respond but pretends to read as he notices the teacher get up. Dave mutters loudly enough for everyone to hear, "Call me an A-hole and I'll kick your ass!" Jim, red faced and furious, gets up, turns around to face Dave, and says "You got something to say to me, you say it to my face!"

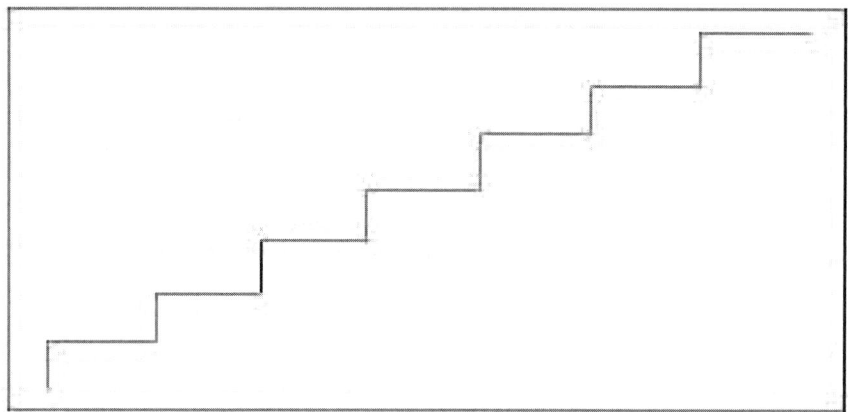

Steps In Escalation

The "steps" in the escalation are what happened and not the listeners' evaluations of what happened. The steps in the story are:

1. Dave kicks the chair.
2. Jim says "Cut it out!"
3. Dave kicks again.
4. Jim name-calls.
5. Dave name-calls and insults Jim's skill.
6. Dave threatens Jim.
7. Jim confronts Dave with a dare.

You may need to read parts of the story over again to make certain the steps in the acceleration are given in order. Write these above the line on each step of the escalator.

Feelings of Participants

Then, have people decide what Dave and Jim felt at various points and write the feelings beneath the line on each step.

Possibilities of De-escalation

Then ask the audience to look at the escalator and decide at what point(s) different responses might have de-escalated the conflict and/or at what points someone other than Dave or Jim (other students or the teacher) might have intervened. Remind the audience that in this case the teacher's goal is not to punish the two, but to resolve the conflict so that there is no fight in the classroom or later. You might ask if suspending the two boys would resolve the conflict; most people realize that it would just send the conflict out of the classroom,

Write all of these suggestions on a large sheet. Then ask which, if any, of the suggestions are practicing Transforming Power. You may ask them to refer to their guidelines.

Note: Having two facilitators do a carefully rehearsed skit of the second paragraph of the story really catches people's attention. It can be repeated in slow motion to help the group see the steps.
This exercise can be very helpful as a preparation for both "Feeling Messages" and Role Plays.

PART II - Analyzing Personal Stories in Small Groups

Procedure: Set Up:

1. Divide into groups of 3-4 (any larger groups means more time to tell stories and less time for analysis) and give each group a pencil and paper for the recorder.
2. Explain that each group is to do the following:
    1. Share stories of conflict situations
    2. Choose a story that the group decides would be helpful to analyze. It is important to choose a simple story. Stories involving only two individuals are usually best.
    3. Choose a recorder, someone who will write down the steps as the group describes the steps in the conflict.
    4. Decide what steps (or behaviors) escalated the conflict and which ones de-escalated the conflict. Explain at this point that the steps may go up or down depending on the story.
    5. After these decisions have been made, draw a large escalator in the shape that will illustrate the escalation/de-escalation, and label each step.
    6. Select someone to:
        a. Tell the story to the large group, using the escalator diagram that has been made.
        b. Lead the audience in analyzing the conflict (asking for the feelings/needs of the individuals in the conflict at each step).
        c. Write down the audience's responses on the large escalator below each step.
        d. Lead the audience in discussing where and what one of the participants in the conflict might have done to de-escalate the conflict at any point if that participant had understood the other person's interests, feelings or needs.
    7. If you have time left in your small group, discuss part (b) analyzing the conflict among yourselves but do not write your group's response on the large escalator.

Note: If some small groups finish steps 1 through 6 before others, they might discuss and analyze the conflict as in 6.b., within their groups *<u>without writing</u>* *any responses on the big escalator.*

After each group has presented, you might ask if any de-escalation suggestions involved Transforming Power. At the same time, do not let the discussion drag.

You may need to insert a Light and Lively between group presentations, just as is done for role plays. This exercise is an excellent substitute for role plays in Advanced Workshops.

FACTS AND FEELINGS

Purpose: To help people begin to get in touch with different layers of their various feelings.

Time: About 20 minutes

Materials: Copies of the Facts and Feelings Person for each person (see next page); pencils; markers; and newsprint with a large copy of the Facts and Feelings Person.

Procedure: **Set Up:**

1. Explain that there are hundreds of things that happen to us throughout our lives. Let's call these happenings, "Facts." Let's call the first fact "birth." (write "birth" on the newsprint, above the person's head).

2. Ask the group for some other facts that may have occurred in a person's life. e.g., "birth of a sibling," "going to day-care," "first day at school." Try to get about six or seven suggestions recorded.

3. Mention that all of the "Facts" have "Feelings" that relate to them. Give an example from your own life. Perhaps on your "first day at school" you were both "excited" and "nervous." Write these feelings inside the person's body and connect these "Feelings" with the "Fact" to which they relate.

4. Ask the group for "Feelings" that might relate to some of the "Facts" that are already recorded on the newsprint. Might different people have different "Feelings" relating to the same "Fact"?

5. In order to know ourselves a little better, each person will work privately for five or ten minutes and record some of the "Facts and Feelings" of her/his life on individual person sheets. No one will have to share what they write.

6. If there are no questions, hand out the "Facts and Feelings Person" sheets and pencils and suggest they find some space and start to work.

Processing:

- Did you find this easy or difficult?
- Do people's "Facts and Feelings" influence their "points of view"?

Note: Some people may get stuck. Urge them to try but be prepared to cut the time. You might encourage people to work on this further by themselves.

Facts and Feelings Person

BIRTH

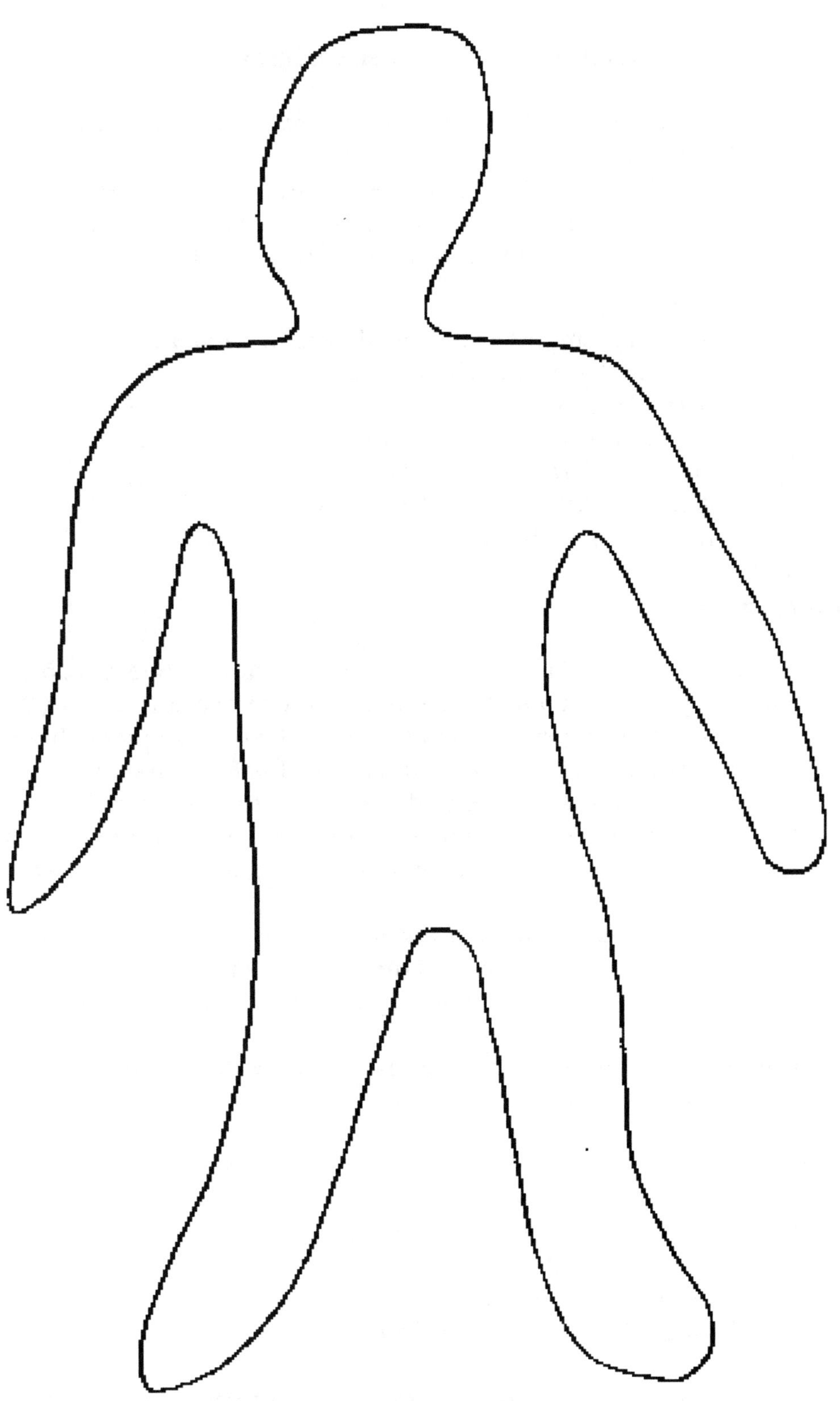

FAIRY TALE THEATER

Purpose: On perspective-taking and stereotyping; practice in creative thinking.

Time: 30-40 minutes, depending on size of group

Materials: Copy of *The Old Woman in the Forest (Hansel and Gretel* as told by the witch)
Names of very familiar fairy tales or children's rhymes on slips of paper. They must be stories with a "bad guy," a character who could be considered maligned by the way in which the story is told.

Examples:
wicked stepmother or stepsisters in *Cinderella*
troll in *Three Billy Goats Gruff*
Rumplestiltskin
wolf in *Little Red Riding Hood*
spider in *Little Miss Muffet*
giant in *Jack and the Beanstalk*
wolf in *Three Little Pigs*

Procedure: Set Up:

1. Read or tell *The Old Woman in the Forest* story. (See next page)
   How did you feel about the witch before you heard this story?
   Now that you've heard the witch's story, how do you feel about her?
   How did you feel about Hansel and Gretel before this story?
   Do you think about Hansel and Gretel any differently now?
   Have you ever looked at some situation in your own life one way but changed your mind after you listened to another person tell his/her side of the story?

2. Divide into small groups of four or five. Have each group draw a story slip from a hat and rewrite how the maligned character would tell the story from his/her point of view (allow approximately ten minutes).

3. Come together in full circle and have each group share its revised version. They may read it, act it out or even sing it.

Processing:
- Does this relate to real life?
- Is it difficult to change one's image?
- How do I see myself?
- How do I think others see me?
- How would I like others to see me?

Note: The last three questions may be done privately on paper. Also see exercise "Who, Me?"

The Old Woman in The Forest

The people in the village say that I am a witch. I don't even know what a witch is! Well, there is nothing I can do about people's opinion of me. I came out here to the forest to live alone. I was so tired of everyone laughing at me and little children making fun of me in the street. I guess I do look kind of odd with my big nose and pointy chin, but I didn't chose to look this way; it's just the way I am. No one seems to want to get to know what I am really like.

It is peaceful and quiet here in the forest with no one to bother me most of the time. Sometimes some of the children from the village come all the way out here just to call me names and peek in my windows. I get mad and yell at them to go away. I've heard that they go back with stories about how I said I would kill them. Well, maybe I should control my temper better and not say things like that. I would never do something so awful. I can't understand why anyone would take that seriously.

There were even rumors about me when those children went into the forest and were never heard from again. Personally, I think they must have wanted to leave that little village and go somewhere more interesting. But people said I might have done something to them like cooked them in my big cooking pot. Really! Sometimes people have very creative imaginations.

Then that new pair, Hansel and Gretel, showed up the other day. They certainly weren't too smart about the forest. Imagine leaving a trail of breadcrumbs to find your way back! Don't they realize the woods are full of birds and animals looking for a little extra food?

I felt sorry for them. I guess their new stepmother is pretty mean and kicked them out of the house. They seemed so lost and scared, I had pity on them and invited them in to give them something to eat before I showed them the way home. Well, were they ever rude! They acted scared of me and I even heard Hansel whisper to his sister that I was trying to fatten them up to cook them! And after I gave them my best cookies. Then they ran away while I was getting them some refills on milk. If they do find their way home, I can't imagine what stories they will spread about me now.

FISHBOWL INTERVENTION STRATEGY

Purpose: To give the group a means of addressing an individual's problems collectively. It is also a means of using the group as a support system for individuals when they need assistance in working out problems.

Time: 60 minutes – make sure this doesn't run too long.

Materials: Writing paper, writing tools, scrap paper.

Procedure: **Set Up:**

1. Explain to the group that we are now going to work with a process that will help us to draw on the collective knowledge and understanding of the group to address individual problems.
2. Ask the group to take a moment to reflect silently on the week's experience at school, work, community/neighborhood or home. Was it what they were expecting? Did they make any meaningful connections? Ask them to recall an incident which they wished they had handled more effectively, or one they can foresee developing into a problem. It could be an incident with another person, or an individual one, such as being late. It should be a situation that they think could have gone better and where they would like to make some progress.
3. Pass out paper, and have participants write the specifics of the situation, without using names or identifying information. Include brief details, parties involved, and any lingering feelings. Give about 10 minutes to complete. Facilitators may share a scenario of their own as a example. Explain that the scenarios will be collected, and a few chosen to be worked on by the group.
4. Collect the scenarios, and regroup participants in a seated circle. In the center of the circle, place two chairs facing each other. Explain, this is called a "fishbowl." The chairs of the circle are the sides of the "fishbowl" and you, the people sitting in the chairs are "viewers." Designate one center chair as "counselor," and the other as "client." Ask for two volunteers to sit in the chairs.
5. Explain the roles to the volunteers. The "client" selects a scenario from those collected, and presents it as his/her own. Clients must not chose their own scenario to present; ask them to chose another if they do. After reading it, the client remains silent. The "counselor's " role is to suggest possible strategies to address the concerns in the scenario. Viewers simply observe, listen and do not speak.
6. If a viewer thinks of another strategy to offer, s/he can enter the fishbowl by tapping the present counselor's shoulder after he or she has given ideas. Once tapped, the counselor should yield the chair.
7. The group works on the problem until there are no more strategies to suggest. At that point, the client thanks the group for its attention and leaves; the seated counselor becomes the new client and selects the next scenario. A new person can volunteer to be "counselor" and the counseling process begins again.
8. Depending on time restraints and the size of the group, the facilitator may want to limit the group to two or three strategies per scenario, or limit the number of scenarios to be worked on.

Processing:

- What was useful about this process?
- Did you learn anything new about how to address these concerns?

Note: In Step 7, you might ask for two new volunteers to involve more people.

FISH BOWL MODIFIED

Purpose: To provide a safe manner for discussing "hot" issues or Unanswered Questions.

Time: About 30 minutes

Materials: A timer and four empty chairs labeled A, B, C and V, positioned at the empty end of a "horseshoe" arrangement of everyone's chairs.

Procedure: Set Up:

1. Explain that this exercise will give people a chance to speak on issue "X."

2. In a minute, three people who would like to speak about issue "X" may take chairs A, B or C. Chair V will remain empty. It stands for a view that no one expresses today.

3. The person who sits in Chair A will be the speaker. When finished, s/he will return to the circle. The people in chairs B and C will move over a chair and there will be a new speaker in chair A. Another person can come up and take Chair C.

4. The person in Chair A may speak for a minute or less. Someone will time each speaker. When a minute is up or when they finish speaking, speakers will return to the circle. They may speak again by taking Chair C when it becomes empty.

5. The Fish Bowl will last about twenty minutes.

6. If there are no questions, tell people they may go up to speak if they wish and begin.

Note: There's no need to process this exercise, unless someone in the group wants to comment about it as a process

Fish Bowl Modified allows people to state their position without arguments.

FOCUSING ON VIOLENCE/NONVIOLENCE

Purpose: To connect the Advanced Workshop with the Basic Workshop and to begin the process of Goal Setting in an Advanced Workshop.

Time: 15 - 20 minutes

Materials: Old brainstorms of Violence and Nonviolence (preferably one done by the same group in a Basic); magic markers.

Procedure: **Set Up**

1. Before a break or meal, point out the old brainstorms for Violence and Nonviolence. If the team prefers and there is time, brainstorm new lists.

2. Ask people to choose a word from each list that is significant for them.

3. People may add to the lists if there's something missing for them.

4. Ask people to circle the words they choose. The same word may be chosen by more than one person.

5. After the break, form pairs. Have one person speak for a minute about a word from the Violence List that is significant for her/him. That person's partner listens and reflects back what s/he heard. Then, switch roles.

6. Change partners and repeat #5 using a word from the Nonviolence list.

7. Change partners again and have people speak about what they'd like to get out of the Advanced workshop.

Processing:
- Did reflective listening help you clarify your thoughts?
- Did revisiting the Violence/Nonviolence lists help you choose goals?

Note: You may wish to give an example of what is significant for you to make "significant" clear.

Facilitators may wish to remove themselves from the last question, or at least explain that the workshop will focus on the goals of the participants.

GARBAGE BAGS

Purpose: To provide a lively cooperation game with a lot of versatility; to explore ways to use what's at hand and perhaps change a situation from useless to positive.

Time: About 30 minutes

Materials: 4 or 5 paper bags, each containing a variety of 4 or 5 small odds and ends; e.g. a group of 5 will need one bag containing 5 objects (one for each member of the group). Suggestions: empty toilet paper roll, three prong electrical adapter, a toy hammer, a small doll, a colorful scarf, rubber band, balloon, toy boat or car, harmonica, whistle, a mask, etc.

Procedure: Set Up:

1. Explain that people will work in groups of 4 or 5. Each group will get a bag of "garbage" with which to work. The task of each group is to work together to create something positive out of this "garbage."

2. They might perform a skit using the objects; they might create a special arrangement (collage) of the "garbage" that is exciting; they might tell a story about the objects.

3. You might give an example of what one or two things might become. For example, the empty toilet paper roll might really be a spy glass or an old drain pipe where a family of field mice lives. Ask the group for other suggestions.

4. Say that when each group gets its bag each person in the group, <u>without</u> <u>looking</u>, will reach into the bag and pull out one object. Since each has an object, each will take part in what the group creates.

5. If there are no questions divide everyone into groups of 4 or 5. Assign work areas as far apart as possible. Say that they'll have about ten minutes to plan their creations. Encourage them to be extravagant. Just create something positive. Suggest that they have a "go-around" to get everyone's input.

6. When the groups are ready (don't let planning go on too long), have them come back to the circle to display their creations, act out their skits or tell their stories.

Processing:

- Was it easy, difficult, or frustrating to cooperate while being creative?
- Might one person's ideas have inspired others' ideas?
- Do we ever use the garbage we collect in our lives like this?
- What kinds of garbage might we pick up as we go through our lives?
- Is our garbage always physical? Are we ever handed other people's garbage?
- Do we have to carry our garbage forever? How might we cope with it?

GOAL SETTING PART I

Purpose: To begin having the group set goals for an Advanced Workshop.

Time: 15 minutes

Materials: 20 - 30 sheets of 8x10 paper - it could be scrap paper - only one side will be used.

Procedure: **Set Up:**

1. Explain that in this exercise they'll be working in three groups. The first task for each group is to have a go-around. Each person will state her/his goals for the workshop.

2. Some goals may be similar; some may be unique. The second task for the group is to record the goals of the group, putting one goal on each piece of paper. Similar goals might be combined, if everyone agrees to this. Ask them to print each goal on one sheet of paper, printing as big as possible.

3. If there are no questions regarding the task, form three groups and assign them space to work. Give each group paper and several markers of the same color. Tell them they'll have about 10 minutes.

4. When they return to the circle have each group read its goals. Explain that the goals will be discussed further in Goal Setting Part II.

Processing:

- How did that go?
- Did each person have a say?

Note: This exercise would follow Focusing On Violence/Nonviolence; hence everyone has had a chance to speak about her or his goals in pairs.

It is helpful to have a team member with each group to facilitate the process. The team member would not state any goals.

Breaking Goal Setting into two parts has two advantages. First, it makes it less heavy, especially if Goal Setting 1 is followed by a L&L and a Break. Second, if Triangles is done before Goal Setting Part II it gives everyone a chance to experience consensus in a somewhat physical way.

GOAL SETTING PART II

Purpose: To continue having the group set goals for an Advanced Workshop. To experience the process of making decisions by consensus.

Time: About 20 minutes

Materials: Goals on 8x10 paper that the three groups made during Goal Setting I, and masking tape.

Procedure: Set Up:

1. Place all the "paper" goals on the floor in the middle of the circle.

2. Ask everyone to walk around the goals in silence looking for similarities. After everyone has had a chance to go all the way around the circle, ask if anyone sees any similarities.

3. If someone sees a similarity, ask if all agree and put similar goals together. Combine as much as possible and have one area for unique goals. When all the goals have been sorted, tape similar goals to one sheet of newsprint, or masking tape them in groups directly onto a wall.

4. Explain that for the rest of the workshop, if it is agreeable, everyone will try to work on these goals. The facilitators will try to present exercises that deal with these goals. The participants will check their goals periodically to see if they're being addressed. It is important to have consensus on this - to be sure that everyone is satisfied with this approach.

5. Each person has a say in consensus decision making. They may say one of three things:
   1) I'm satisfied,
   2) I'm not entirely satisfied but I can live with it/them, or,
   3) I'm not satisfied and I think we need more discussion.

6. If there are no questions, have a "go-around," so that everyone has a chance to respond as above.

7. When consensus is reached, thank the group and remind the participants that as the workshop continues, if anyone thinks some goal isn't being addressed, it is important to speak up.

Processing:

- Have you ever tried consensus decision making before?
- What do you think of it?
- Might it be useful in ordinary life?

GUIDED REFLECTION

Purpose: To imagine offering forgiveness to someone with whom we have unfinished business.

Time: About 15 minutes

Materials: The reflection, which follows; 8x10 paper and crayons or markers for everyone

Procedure: **Set Up:**

1. Explain that this exercise will be done in silence with eyes closed. It involves the imagination. Some may find this type of activity unusual. If after starting, some wish to pass, that's fine. Say: "If you choose to pass, please just relax and remain in your seat, keeping a respectful silence so you don't disturb others."

2. If there are no questions, begin reading the attached reflection. Read slowly and thoughtfully. Try to imagine what the reading suggests yourself, so that you give others enough time to picture what is being suggested.

3. As people are "returning to the room" after the reflection, explain that you and a few teammates are going to distribute some drawing materials to everyone. Do so as quietly as possible.

4. After most people have opened their eyes, invite everyone, in silence, to make a sketch of what they imagined. The sketches will be shared only if people wish to show them. Say that they'll have just a couple of minutes for this.

5. After a few minutes ask if anyone would like to talk about the picture s/he has drawn.

Processing:

- Would anyone like to make any comments on this activity?

Note: You may wish to dim the lights during the course of the reflection.

Reflection on Forgiveness

All, right. Let's begin. Please relax in your chair and close your eyes. Adjust your body so you feel comfortable. Take several deep breaths. As you inhale think of breathing in the positive, and, as you exhale, think of getting rid of the negative.

Imagine that you are some kind of land animal - see yourself and feel yourself as this animal. Breathe deeply as this animal.

Now imagine that some person, this individual with whom you have some unfinished business, is also a land animal. Try to picture them as animal as clearly as possible.

Next, see yourself as animal, at the edge of a beautiful green meadow. It's a lovely day - warm but not too hot - one might call it a soft day. You're enjoying the day immensely.

But then, on the other side of the meadow, you suddenly see the animal with whom you have unfinished business. What feelings well up inside of you? Are you angry? - or scared? Might hurt lie beneath this anger or fear? Try to breath deeply, even with these difficult feelings.

Now look across the field and see the other animal approaching. The other animal is not yet aware of your presence. Can you look at this animal with new eyes? Can you see any good in this animal? Is he or she also vulnerable? Has he or she any unmet needs? What might these needs be?

Slowly approach this animal with respect - being open to the positive. Suggest that you both rest beneath a shady tree. Ask if you can both talk about how you feel.

Ask this animal to try to tell you where he or she is coming from - what his or her point of view is. Listen carefully. Perhaps, even if nothing is said the silence may speak to you.

Now speak about how you feel. Say if you've been angry, or scared, or hurt. Perhaps this other has never fully realized your pain. Perhaps, just perhaps, he or she may ask for forgiveness. But maybe he or she has trouble speaking. Asking for forgiveness is not easy. But at least you've expressed your feelings. Perhaps you can offer forgiveness regardless of how the other responded.

Quietly leave the other and come back to the edge of the meadow. And, whenever you're ready, come back to the room. When you're back in the room, slowly open your eyes but remain quiet.

HAND PUSH

Purpose: To consider a usual reaction when a person is pushed, physically or verbally.

Time: 5 minutes

Materials: None

Procedure: **Set Up**

1. Ask the group to stand and count off by 2's. Ask the 1's to turn and stand, face to face, with the 2 on their right.

2. When everyone is arranged, ask the 2's to place their hands together palm to palm with the 1's.

3. Next ask the 2's to push against their partners' hands. (Notice how the 1's react).

4. Call "cut" after a few seconds. Ask the l's what happened when the 2's pushed them. Probably a good number will push back. Question if this is a natural reaction.

5. Have people sit down. Have them consider if people react in kind when they're "pushed" verbally as well. For example, if A says to B, "You are so stupid." B is likely to reply, "You're no genius either!" Ask the group for a couple of other examples.

Processing:

- How do people generally react if they are judged or blamed or called names.?
- Do these kinds of "pushes" escalate/worsen or defuse/calm conflicts?

Note: This might be a good introduction to one of the Feeling Statements exercises. It might also be used between segments of a Feeling Statement exercise, or if you want to emphasize avoiding the use of the word "you" in Feeling Statements.

After introducing Feeling Statements you may wish to do another demonstration of "hand push." This time ask for a volunteer to be a 2 pushing against your hands. When the person pushes, open your arms and embrace her/him. (However, some might interpret the embrace as a grab. You could do this demonstration with a teammate.)

HASSLE HELPS

Purpose: To practice using the skills suggested in Red Yellow Green and Win/Win.

Time: 15 - 20 minutes

Materials: Sample scenarios (which follow); Red Yellow Green and Win/Win posters.

Procedure: Set Up

1. Review the skills used in the Red Yellow Green and Win/Win processes. Explain that this activity will give us a chance to practice such skills.

2. Form pairs by counting off by half the number of people. Have like numbers arrange themselves on either side of an imaginary line.

3. Call one side of the line the A's, and the other side the B's. In the first and third scenarios the A's will practice their skills as they're hassled by the B's. In the second and fourth scenarios the B's will practice their skills as they're hassled by the A's. Say that you'll call "freeze" to stop action.

4. Read one of the "Type X Scenarios" so the A's are the "you's" and the B's are the hasslers. If there are no questions, read the scenario a second time and tell them to begin.

5. Call "freeze" and ask if any of the A's were able to use their skills. Have a couple of demonstrations.

6. Read another of the "Type X Scenarios" so the B's are the "you's"and the A's are the hasslers. Read it a second time and have them start.

7. Continue as in step #5, this time focusing on the B's.

8. Have everyone change partners, while remaining an A or B.

9. Repeat steps #4 through #7 using the "Type Y Scenarios."

Processing:

- Is it difficult/possible to "keep your cool" when being hassled?
- Does responsibility or lack of responsibility make a difference?

Note: Having co-facilitators along the line as participants or observers is helpful.

Scenarios for Hassle Helps

Type X Scenarios - The "you" bears no responsibility.

Spaghetti Scenario: You are an assistant cook working in a summer camp. You and your partner are getting spaghetti out of a large pot. Your partner drops the spaghetti on the floor and immediately runs out of the kitchen. It's 10 minutes before the campers are due to arrive for dinner. The chief cook comes along, sees the spaghetti on the floor and starts to yell at you.

Accusation by a Friend: You and three friends were out last Saturday night and one friend did something that wasn't wise. Monday morning that friend comes up and starts yelling, "Where do you get off telling everybody about what happened Saturday?" In fact, you didn't tell anyone anything!

AVP Completed Scenario: You just finish an AVP workshop and a peer (fellow student, co-worker) comes up to you and says, "I hear you did that AVP thing. What a crock!"

Type Y Scenarios - The "you" does bear responsibility.

Unfilled Car Scenario: You used the car last night and brought it home on "empty." This morning another house member wants to get to a special meeting. When s/he sees the gauge on "empty" s/he starts yelling at you.

Unkept Promise Scenario: You promised your parents you were going to work harder at school. Somehow time slipped by and you never got in a major report for History. You failed the quarter. Now your parent sees your report and starts yelling, "That's it! You're grounded!"

Loose Dog Scenario: You have a lovely dog but it sometimes get loose, runs over to your neighbor's yard, and leaves a load. Your neighbor has complained in the past. This time your neighbor is chasing your dog and yelling at it and you.

Note: If "Brainstorm for Role Plays" is done before Hassle Helps you might write a scenario based on one of the groups suggestions.

HEARTBROKEN CHRIS (OR PAT)

Purpose: To look at the way "put-downs" can affect us. (For eleven year-olds)

Time: 20 minutes

Materials: Large oaktag gingerbread person, Chris; construction paper heart taped in place; paper and pencils for small groups; set of lines for the 5 people Chris meets:

Mother:	You're not going to wear THAT to school!
Sister or Brother:	You'll never be beautiful/handsome. Give up the bathroom. I need it.
Bus driver:	Sit down and shut up.
Friend:	How come you've been talking about me behind my back?
Teacher:	Why aren't you more like your sister?

Procedure: Set Up:

1. Explain that Chris is a student just waking up in the morning, feeling good. We're going to hear some comments people make to Chris.

2. Ask for volunteers to be characters in Chris' life, namely, Mother, Sister or Brother, Bus driver, Friend, Teacher.

3. Give each volunteer a "script" and "clinic" with them telling them that after they read their line they will tear off a piece of Chris' heart and keep it.

4. Narrate the story:
   One day when Chris came to breakfast his mother said........;
   Shortly after, when he was in the bathroom his sister/brother said.....................;
   When he got on the bus, the Bus Driver said...................;
   When he went into school his friend said........................;
   In class his teacher said.........................

5. Divide into 3 or 4 small groups. Have each small group write a new line for each character. Try to say the same thing in a positive way.

6. When the groups are ready, have everyone come back to the circle with their group. Have each group read a new Mother's line. Put back the piece of heart "Mother" had broken off. Have each group read a new Sister/Brother's line. Put back the piece of heart s/he had broken off, etc.

Processing:

- How does Chris' heart look now?
- How do you feel when people put you down?
- Is it a joke to put people down?
- Does the person who's put down think it's funny?

ICE CREAM

Purpose: To check out an alternative to grabbing power (This is often done following Power Trip) To introduce the idea of consensus as the power of agreement.

Time: 15 minutes, depending on the amount of discussion that occurs.

Materials: None.

Procedure: **Set Up:**

1. Divide the participants into 3 or 4 groups. They needn't be equal groups.

2. Explain that each group signed a raffle ticket at a grocery store and won a big tub of ice cream. Their task is to decide on one kind of ice cream that will satisfy all the members of the group - a kind that each will really enjoy. (Really agreeing and not just going along is the important thing). (The only kind that's not OK is the "Neapolitan" style with vanilla, chocolate and strawberry all in one tub.)

3. Give them about five minutes to make a decision. In the big circle have the groups report what happened — what they decided and how they came to their decision.

Processing:

- Did they find this different from Power Trip?
- Did anyone take over the decision making?
- Which process takes more time?
- Which process is easier?
- Which activity satisfies more people?
- What happens if a group can't decide on one thing?
- Does this happen in real life?

IN COMMON

Purpose: To get used to talking to people we may not know well. To begin building community.

Time: 15 - 20 minutes

Materials: Paper and pencils for each pair; a poster with a few ideas of things people might have in common, e.g. hair and eye color, pets, pastimes (for younger participants a poster made with bright colors is particularly appropriate); newsprint or poster paper and magic markers for each group of 4 (or 6).

Procedure: Set Up

1. Explain that this exercise will be done in 2 parts, first in pairs and then in groups of 4 (or 6). The task is to find as many things as possible that they have in common. Mention the things on the poster as examples.

2. Divide the group into pairs by counting off by ½ the number of the group. One facilitator may have to sit out to have the number come out even. Partners are people who have numbers "in common" or the same.

3. Give the pairs paper and a pencil and ask them to make a list of things they have in common. Tell them they'll have about 3 or 4 minutes.

4. Next move the pairs into groups of 4 (or 6). Give them newsprint or poster paper and a couple of bright markers. Ask them to compare their lists. Put those things that all share in common on the newsprint. Perhaps they'll find things that weren't on their first lists. Again, give about 3 or 4 minutes.

5. Ask people to come back to the big circle with their group. Ask each group to read those things which its members have in common.

Processing:

- Were they surprised at the number of things they had in common with others?
- Does it make a difference if we have things in common with someone else?

Note: This exercise can be used to build community at the beginning of a mini-session with middle school children or at the beginning of an Advanced to incorporate new people into a group in a relaxed manner.

For younger people, for example eleven year olds at the beginning of the school year, it may be scary to talk to people who aren't their "best friends." The colorful poster may help them look on this activity as less frightening.

IT'S HOW YOU SAY IT!

Purpose: To develop an understanding of body language, tone and inflection, and the effects of insults, building on the saying, "It's not what you say, its how you say it!"

Time: 15 minutes

Materials: None

Procedure: **Set Up:**

1. Tell the group that we will be experimenting with how people say and react to comments. Ask the group to imagine that someone is acting silly at a time most people are serious (like at a funeral).

2. Demonstrate how you might respond to this person with different tones and meanings by saying "You're crazy!" in a teasing and fun-loving way, or an angry and disgusted manner.

3. Go around the circle saying "You're sick!" halfway, then "You're stupid!" the rest of the way, getting interpretations for the meaning from the group. (If the group thinks of other possible insults, this should be addressed in the debriefing).

4. Ask the group to pair up, identifying A's and B's. A's say to B's "You're a nut!". B's tell A's how it felt. Reverse, using "You're so gay!".

Processing:

- What was this like?
- Who can you say certain things to, without worrying about how they will be taken?
- Is it easy to have our intention be misinterpreted? How?
- (If additional insults were suggested by the group) Do we compete about insulting people, even if we think we are good natured about it?
- Do we try to be more clever in our insults than the other person?

I WANT / I WANT

Purpose: To help to clarify the underlying concerns and issues of each person in a conflict situation; to move us to real understanding of "I Messages," by owning our own fears; to develop empathy; to experience unity beneath our concerns.

Time: 30-60 minutes (2-4 scenes) Allow about ten minutes for each scenario (2 minutes for each person, 4-6 minutes for processing). Exercise **must** be done in **pairs of scenarios** to allow participants to experience different roles.

Materials: None

Procedure: Set Up:

1. Divide groups into pairs, with an A and B partner.
2. Read prepared scenarios, (or if time allows, participants may offer suggestions for scenes) with A and B roles.
3. A begins, completing the sentence, "I want....." with respect to their position in the conflict. Allow two minutes. This should be a series of simple, quick, top-of-the-head sentences, "I want...I want...I want..." No lengthy explanations. B listens attentively without interrupting. **This is not a dialogue. The purpose is not to persuade, but to clarify issues and offer insights into the other person's concerns and needs or feelings.**
4. B completes "I want...I want..." sentences, while A listens.
5. Allow participants to share quick discoveries with the group. Save thorough debriefing until the end of the exercise.
6. Read a second scenario, making sure to switch power/authority position of A and B. Repeat exercise and brief sharing/ ventilating.
7. Sequence may be repeated with two more scenes at this point.

Processing: Have group form circle, staying seated next to partners.

- What happened in your pairs?
- Were there any surprises/"a ha!" experiences?
- What was it like to have to stick to "I want..." statements?
- What insights did you gain from your partner's sharing/
- What did you learn about the other's issues/position?
- What did you learn about your own issues/position?
- Did you feel more understanding of your partner's position listening to "I wants..."?

Sample Scenarios:

1. A fifteen year old wants to go to an all night, unchaperoned party. The parent wants the youth home by midnight.
2. A young driver wants to borrow his/her parent's car. Young driver is not allowed to borrow car due to previously unsafe driving, resulting in damage to the car.
3. Parent wants youth to stay home and do chores. Youth wants to go out with friends.
4. Parent is concerned about youth's new friend who has a reputation for drug use. Parent wants to discourage youth from hanging out with friend.

LABELS

Purpose: To experience being labeled; to see if being labeled influences our attitudes towards ourselves; to develop empathy towards others who are labeled

Time: 30 minutes or more (See Notes following the exercise)

Materials: sets of stick-ons with the following: "Ignore me"; "Tell me I'm right"; "Tell me I'm wrong"; "Encourage me"; "Listen to me." (4 sets for a group of 20); paper and pencils for the recorders; a poster with the task: Brainstorm a list of oppressed people in our society.

Procedure: Set Up:

1. Explain that people will be working in groups of 5. Each group's task will be to brainstorm a list of oppressed people in our society (point out the poster). Each group will need a recorder to write the brainstorm list.
2. The challenge is this: The 5 people in each group will each have a "label" placed on his/her forehead. People won't know what their label is. Everyone will try to treat others according to the instructions on the labels.
3. You may wish to model this with a teammate, e.g., put a label on your teammate that says, "I'm a clown." (Explain that this is not one of the labels the groups will be using). Have your teammate suggest that: "Farmers are an oppressed group." You might reply, "Are you serious? Farmers? You're always joking. Get serious."
4. If there are no questions, form groups of 5, arranged in semi-circles facing away from other groups (so no one sees the labels of other groups). With the help of teammates give paper and a pencil to each group and place the stick-ons on people's foreheads. Then have each group choose a recorder and begin.
5. Allow about 10-15 minutes for group dynamics to develop. (You may wish to have teammates act as observers in each group.) After each group has a few things on its list, have everyone return to the circle, staying with their groups.

Processing:

- Was this a difficult challenge? If so, why?
- What has this got to do with AVP?
- Has anyone ever felt labeled?
- What happens to us if we're ignored (or told we're wrong, etc.) all the time?
- What happens if we are encouraged? Listened to?
- Do we ever respond to others as if they had labels?

Note: This may stir up some deep emotions. If so, you may wish to have everyone take several deep breaths for a calming effect. Have people slowly breathe in the positive and then have them exhale, getting rid of the negative.

Another option for a task to accomplish: Give each group a set of tinker toys and have them discuss and agree on what to build and how to build it, following their labels. They must come to agreement before they open the box of toys.

Some people choose to do this exercise with all labels being negative. Other options are "Ignore me," "Laugh at everything I say," "Humor me," "Disagree with everything I say," "Don't make eye contact with me."

LET'S GO SWIMMING

Purpose: To demonstrate stereotyping of others and to investigate typical responses. To increase awareness of self stereotyping

Time: 45 minutes

Materials: Three sheets of newsprint and markers; three labels (TESTERS, WADERS, PLUNGERS) posted at different areas in the room; a poster with the questions:
1) How does your group describe each of the other groups?
2) How does your group describe itself?

Procedure: **Set Up:**

1. Explain that our approach to life may be similar to the way we enter a cold pond for swimming. Describe the three approaches. Be sure **WADER** is clear, (not **waiter**).

2. Ask people to choose the most appropriate group (as they see themselves) and move to the area marked with that particular label.

3. Give poster paper and markers to each group and ask each group to brainstorm answers to the questions above (see "Materials").

4. You may need to mention that they are to describe their understanding of the other categories (as experienced in their own lives). They are not describing the individuals who happen to be in the group at that moment. Give about 5 minutes for this.

5. When finished, have everyone return to the circle, staying with their group. Ask that all descriptions of one group (e.g., PLUNGERS) be read. (This puts focus on how differently one group is seen by different people. If the PLUNGERS read all three of their lists, the focus would be on how the PLUNGERS alone view folks.)

6. Ask: Are there differences? How do we know which descriptions are correct? How does it feel to hear yourself described in ways you agree with? Disagree with?

7. Repeat steps #5 and #6 with the other two groups.

8. Ask: Does anyone want to change to a different group. Are you surprised at the choice any one person made?

Processing:

- What did you hear in the lists? - superiority? kindness? insults?
- Can we agree on one or two outstanding characteristics for each group? How might they be said negatively? positively? (e.g., Speed of mental processing could be "reckless" or "quick" for PLUNGERS and "slow" or "careful" for TESTERS.)
- Did you find yourself taking other groups' comments personally? You may not know anyone in this workshop well enough to care what they think of you, but how would you feel if someone from your own life described you with one of the words you found offensive?
- What does this activity have to do with real life?

Note: This activity may bring up some strong emotions. Be prepared to allow time to diffuse same.

LIFE BELIEFS

Purpose: Community building; to develop self-awareness

Time: 20 minutes

Materials: None

Procedure: **Set Up:**

1. Have the group stand and move chairs out of the way. Draw an imaginary line down the middle of the room. Explain that the line is a continuum, and that the ends are extreme positions on each of the questions which will be asked. (For example, in the first question, you might say "This end of the line represents that you believe that people are basically good, and this other end of the line represents that you believe that people are basically evil. Exactly in the middle means you believe that people are about equally good and evil. Arrange yourselves along the line to represent the position which seems most true to you").

2. The facilitator will read each question, and ask participants to line themselves up according to how they believe on that question. Participants can be at any place along the line, depending on how strongly they feel about the question. After each question, ask a few volunteers to explain why they answered the question the way they did.

The Questions:

1. Do you believe humanity is basically good OR evil?
2. Do you believe in a higher power (however you define it)? YES OR NO?
3. Which is more important: "Who you are" OR "What you do"?
4. Is your fate or destiny predetermined (decided in advance without your input) OR are you free to make your own choices?
5. Which is more important: Individuals OR the community?
6. Do you believe that society should help its members who are unable to help themselves? YES OR NO?
7. Do you believe that some people are entitled to special consideration under the law? YES OR NO?
8. Do you believe that people should be allowed to make their own choices regardless of harm to themselves? YES OR NO?

Processing:

- Were you surprised at the different positions that people took on the line?
- Are there any of these questions where you were not sure what you believe?
- Do you think you might have answered any of these questions differently at some other time in your life?

Note: Sometimes we break this exercise into two segments and do four topics early in the workshop and four later on.

Some facilitators prefer to simplify this by making all the questions statements, as in "Here is a statement - 'People are basically good'. If you agree, stand at this end of the line; if you disagree, stand at this end."

LISTENING AND BRAINSTORMING DO'S AND DON'TS

Purpose: To provide a light-hearted, active way for people to consider listening skills

Time 10 minutes to speak and process pairs and 5 minutes to Brainstorm Do's and Don'ts

Materials: List of optional topics if desired; newsprint and markers for brainstorm

Procedure: Set Up:

1. Explain that in this exercise everyone will get a chance to speak and listen to three different people about three different topics. The challenge will be that they will do this standing in three different positions.

2. Have people pair off and stand by their partner, shoulder to shoulder.

3. Ask them to decide between them who will speak first. Tell them that you will signal when the first person's speaking turn is finished.

4. If there are no questions, say that the first topic is, "Which ground rule is most important for you, and why?" Have them begin and give each speaker about 30 seconds.

5. When they are finished, ask everyone to find a new partner. This time ask one person to stand behind the other. The person in front will speak first. The topic is, "Describe the oldest person you've ever met." After the first person has spoken, ask them both to turn around. The new person in front will now speak.

6. Ask everyone to find a new partner. Have them stand back to back and decide who will speak first. The topic is, "Describe a book or a movie you have really enjoyed." When both have spoken, have everyone return to the circle.

Processing:

- As a speaker did you feel heard?
- What was it like being the listener?
- How does this relate to real life?
- Does this suggest any do's and don'ts for good listening? (Brainstorm both)
- How do people feel about listeners giving advice or making judgments?

Note: "Reflective Listening" could follow this.

This exercise, though paraphrased, came from Playing with Fire: Creative Conflict Resolution for Young Adults.

LOTS OF DOTS

Purpose: To explore ways we choose those with whom we "hang out" and those we avoid.

Time: About 30 minutes

Materials: An assortment of stickers with a variety of designs or colors. Blank ones work well. With markers you can make your own designs and/or colors. Have one or two that are "one-of-a-kind." Have from two to five of a few other kinds. (For example, for a group of 20 you might have 5 red, 5 blue, 4 yellow, 4 green, 1 orange, and 1 blue/yellow.)

Procedure: Set Up:

1. Explain that in a minute you will ask participants to close their eyes. When all eyes are closed, you'll be placing a sticker on each person's forehead. The task will be done in silence, but people may help each other with gestures. You'll explain the task after everyone has a sticker and you say, "Open your eyes."
2. If there are no questions, ask people to close their eyes. With the help of co-facilitators distribute the stickers. (Decide before hand who is to get the "one-of-a-kind" stickers and place those stickers on first.)
3. When everyone has a sticker, say: "Open your eyes and stand up but please don't speak. The task is this: "Please arrange yourselves as you think best." Repeat this. (It is important NOT to give any further directions. Just repeat the task if people ask questions. You may remind them that people may use gestures to help each other.)
4. If there are no questions, let them begin.
5. Try to notice what happens. Look for people's reactions if they are pushed away from or pulled toward others.
6. As the milling around slows down, ask several times, "Are you comfortable where you are now?" Let them continue to shift until they seem comfortable.
7. Debrief as people have arranged themselves - either in place or with people sitting as arranged.

Processing:

- How did you decide how to arrange yourselves?
- How did you feel about the arrangement? (check with the "loners")
- What are the "dots" that divide us in real life?
- Might you like to arrange yourselves differently?

Note: It is important to state the task clearly at least twice. The key is to ***AVOID*** *using the word "group" when giving the directions.*

Try to pick strong individuals to receive the "one-of-a-kind" stickers. Ask co-facilitators for their input. Be aware of how these individuals are treated and how they feel about the arrangement.

It seems wiser for anyone who has done this exercise before to sit this one out. Then the majority can experience the choices on their own.

LOTS OF LISTENING

Purpose: To consider and evaluate different experiences of speaking and listening

Time: About 30 minutes

Materials: A "talking" object (i.e. an object that identifies a particular person as the talker); a poster of the Chinese character for the word, "listen," displayed (sample follows)

Procedure: **Set Up:**

1. Explain that in a minute you will have the participants form groups of 4 or 5.

2. In those groups, people will talk about a given topic, (e.g., what is the best movie made in the last five years?). All will try to convince the other members of their group that their movie choice is the best. And, everyone will be talking at once. (Model this with co-facilitator[s]. Don't be afraid to be loud and determined to prove the point.)

3. If there are no questions, break into groups and have the groups begin. After 2 or 3 minutes signal for silence. Ask: "How does it feel when no one pays attention to you?" "When does this happen to you?"

4. Next try the discussion again, adding one rule to the process: Only one person in each group will talk at a time. The person talking will hold a "talking" object - a tiny teddy bear might be fun. As each person finishes, s/he will pass the "talking" object to someone else. (Model this with co-facilitator[s] too.)

5. If there are no questions have the groups begin. Allow about 5 minutes. If some groups finish before others you might suggest that they ask clarifying questions of one another while waiting for other groups to finish.

6. Have everyone return to the large circle. Ask, "How did it feel when people listened?" "Might a 'talking' object be good to use in other situations?"

7. Point out the Chinese character for "listen." Explain that different parts of the character refer to the ear, eyes, heart and undivided attention.

Processing:

- Why do the different parts of this character belong to the idea of listening?
- Do they use all the parts?
- Do others in their lives use these parts? - their friends? parents? teachers?
- Would people like to "reflect back" or paraphrase what someone in their group said?
- Might another name for the character "listen" be "hearing with the heart?"

Note: Feel free to take this discussion to whatever level the students wish to go.

CHINESE CHARACTER FOR LISTEN

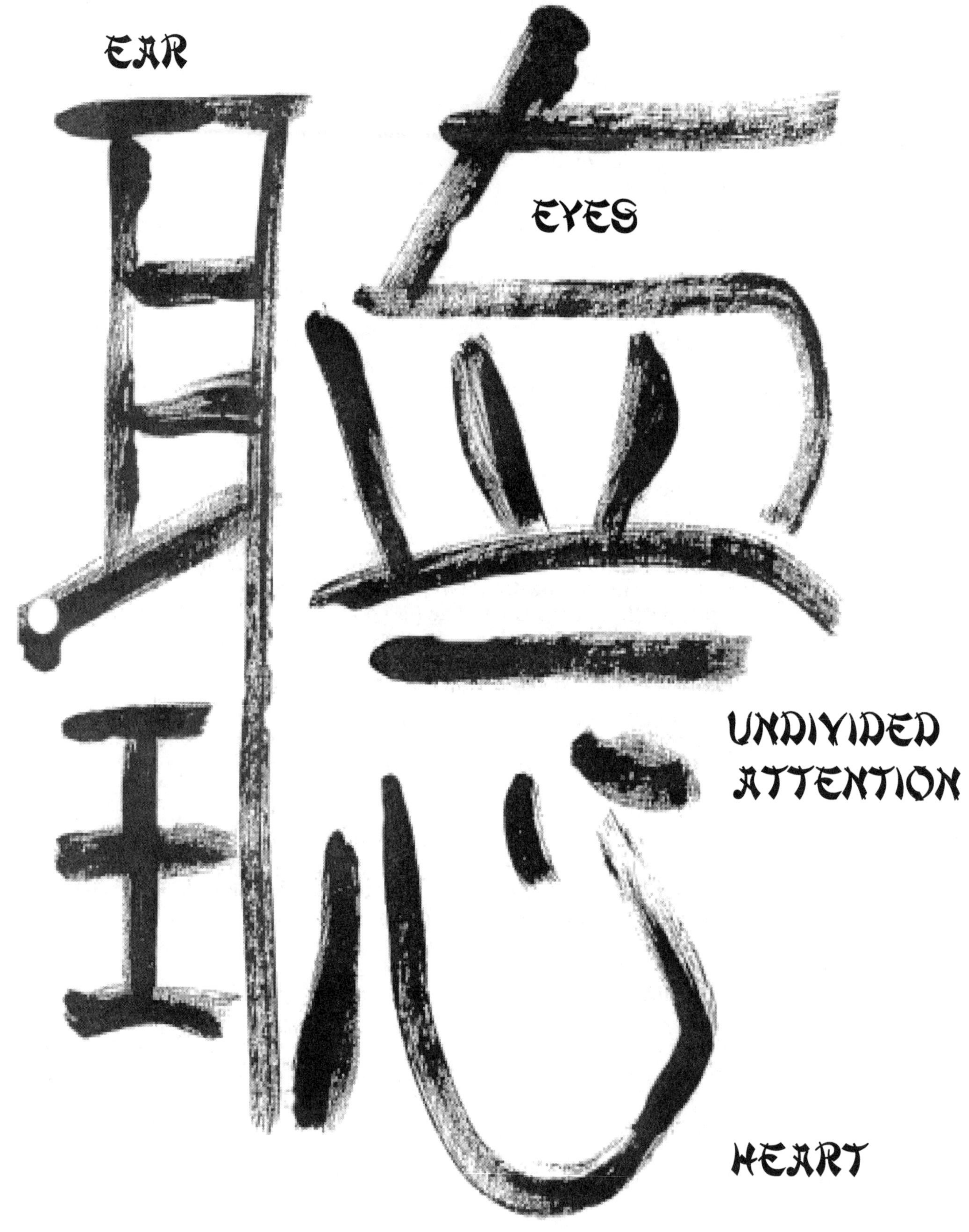

MACHINES

Purpose: To experience cooperation and affirmation in small groups.

Time: About 15 minutes, depending on the amount of discussion that occurs.

Materials: None

Procedure: **Set Up:**

1. Say that in this exercises participants, working in small groups, will demonstrate "human machines." Then others will guess what machine each group is acting out.

2. Model this with co-facilitators or a couple of volunteers. If you use volunteers you'll have to explain what you're all to do quickly and quietly. Try a washer. Two people form a circle with their arms and hands. The third squats between them and turns around shaking as if s/he were the laundry.

3. Explain that each group will choose its own machine. The groups will also plan who will do what and then "rehearse" their machines. Encourage the groups to work so that others don't hear/see what they're doing. Suggest that they use "go-arounds" so they can hear everyone's ideas.

4. Form groups of 4 or 5 and assign each a work/rehearsal space. Try to place the groups as far from each other as possible. Give them about 5 minutes.

5. When you come back to the circle have each group act out its machine and have the others guess. Affirm each group's machine before processing.

Processing:

- How did groups decide on the machine they would demonstrate?
- Did everyone think they had enough of a say?
- Is the "go-around" a useful tool in giving everyone a say?

Note: It's also possible to create a large group imaginary machine. Simply say, "I'm going to start making a large group imaginary machine. Everybody will join whenever they wish. Each will add a sound or a motion or both. Just be sure that you're connected in some way to another part of the machine." Then start.. A full group machine can be used as a closer.

Be prepared to have co-facilitators join fairly quickly.

This was adapted from The Friendly Classroom for a Small Planet.

MARSHMALLOWS

Purpose: To develop cooperation

Time: 20 minutes

Materials: Wooden blocks or carpet sections (about one per person, symbolizing "marshmallows"), two pieces of rope (to create "riverbanks" about 15 feet apart, with length depending upon the number of people).

Procedure: **Set Up:**

Tell participants:

"You are ants. Your goal is to work together to cross this river of chocolate to get to your family picnic. You can use these marshmallows as stepping stones to get across, but be careful because the river of chocolate is flowing swiftly. Remember, you have only these 'marshmallows' which have the power to hold anyone safely above this river of hot cocoa. Don't lose touch with any of the marshmallows, or they will sink into the chocolate void, never to be seen again. You must get safely from one river bank to another, and return, using the marshmallows as stepping stones."

1. Divide the group in half and situate each half at either bank of the river. Give each group a stack of marshmallows, equal to the number in their group, minus one. Tell them each group is trying to get across the river and they may begin when they are ready.

2. It is critical that there always be a point of physical contact with each marshmallow. For example, if a marshmallow is left on the floor without anyone touching it, it will quickly float down the river and be lost. The facilitators will take away the marshmallows that "sink into the chocolate."

3. Watch as they navigate, but do not offer any suggestions. Be sure the river is too wide to be crossed directly with the marshmallows of a single group. They may or may not figure out that the two sides can share marshmallows, but do not tell them this.

Processing:

- Did the groups work together and share their resources, or did they compete? Why?
- Did the groups form a plan? Was it followed through?
- Was it hard to keep touching all the marshmallows? Why?

MATCH UP

Purpose: A fun way to get people matched up in pairs. Can also be used for more serious issues such as communication or inclusion/exclusion.

Time: Ten to fifteen minutes, depending on size of group. (more time if serious debriefing is needed).

Materials: One folded slip of paper for each participant (work with even numbers so pairing works out). Each slip has a word on it. The pairs may be opposites, like HOT/COLD, or related words like SHOE/SOCK, MOON/STARS, DOROTHY/TOTO. Each word is a part of a pair of words in the collection of slips.

Procedure: **Set Up:**

1. Choose a slip of paper randomly from the pile. Make sure that everybody has one. Don't let anyone see your word.
2. Choose a one-word "clue" to your word. You may use a sound or gesture as a clue instead of a word. You may not say the word that is on your slip of paper.
3. Now, stand up and circulate and, without saying anything except your "clue" word, find the other half of your pair.
4. As each pair matches up, sit in the full circle as pairs. It is possible to have a couple of unmatched "singles" if people don't understand the clue words.
5. Then, in the big circle, find out who everybody is: ask the pairs, one at a time, what their clue words were and see if the whole group can guess the written words.
6. Ask all the "singles" for their clue words and see if they can now find their partners.

Processing:

- Did you understand your word?
- Did the choice of "clue" mislead?
- Were you concerned that you might not have a "match"?
- How did you feel being first/last to find your partner?

Note: Interpretations of the written word itself may vary (e.g., "bat" or "pop").

MIND BAG (AKA BAGGAGE)

Purpose: To remember that often we all have more than one thing on our mind.

Time: About 15 minutes

Materials: Small sheets of paper and pencils for everyone

Procedure: **Set Up:**

1. Explain that this exercise will be used as the gathering for the session.

2. Say that in a minute you'll pass out small slips of paper and pencils. Then everyone will jot down 2 or 3 things that might be on their mind just now other than the workshop.

3. No one is going to see the paper, so they needn't worry about spelling. Ask that they try to write at least one thing that they can share with the group.

4. Pass out the paper and pencils and ask everyone to begin when they have paper and a pencil.

5. Place the box for pencils in the middle of the circle. If you place your pencil in it when you're finished writing, probably others will do the same.

6. When everyone is finished writing, model what everyone will do: Say your Adjective Name and mention one of the things you've written on your paper. Then put the paper in your pocket saying that you're going to try to put this concern away for a while and focus on the workshop.

7. Invite others to say what's in their "Mind Bag," perhaps going popcorn style, (i.e. speaking out whenever they are ready rather than going around the circle).

8. Thank everyone, and encourage them to put the things on their mind "on hold" for a while so they can focus on the session.

Note: Using "Mind Bag" as a gathering before Red Yellow Green works well. If you do this you might ask participants if they see any connection between the two.

This exercise can give facilitators a rough idea of the mood of the group.

MIND SET CHAIR

Purpose: To provide a structured means of looking at difficult situations, some of which may arise suddenly in the course of a workshop; to consider varied opinions of what the "mind set" of a person such as an abuser, an addict, a sexist, a bully, etc. might be.

Time: About 20 - 30 minutes

Materials: An extra chair

Procedure: **Set Up:**

1. Place an empty chair in the middle of the circle.

2. Explain that volunteers may sit in the chair, when they so choose. When they do, they may do either of two things:
   a) "role play" the thoughts or "mind set" of a person (acting in a certain way e.g., "doing drugs"); or
   b) complete the sentence, "I think a person (acting in a certain way e.g., "doing drugs") may be doing it because....."

3. Model a) or b) yourself and ask a teammate to model the other, or ask two teammates to model one each.

4. If there are no questions, invite volunteers to go.

5. When no one new goes to sit in the chair, remove the chair and process.

Processing:
- How did you find that?
- Did it lead to any insights?
- Do you agree or disagree with anything that was said or "role-played"?

Note: This was used in a workshop which involved ten thirteen year olds and six adults. During a break, one or some of the teens, while standing on a fire escape, spat down on a mixed group of participants standing below. It was not clear who spat. Mind Set Chair provided a way to consider "where the 'spitter(s)' was coming from." In this instance, after considering the "mind set" of the 'spitter(s)', volunteers were invited to take the chair to express their feelings to the 'spitter(s)' anonymously. Both segments proved worthwhile.

MIRROR CIRCLE

Purpose: To practice communication skills, both listening and speaking; in particular, to build on the skills of paraphrasing or reflective listening. *(See other exercises that introduce these skills).*

Time: About 10 minutes, unless the sentence used is serious (see *Note*)

Materials: None

Procedure: **Set Up:**

1. Explain that this exercise is like a special "go-around." Each person, going around in the circle, will complete a sentence.

2. Everybody will say their sentence to the person to their right, as in a "go-around." Then, that person will paraphrase or say what the speaker said. In a sense, the person who paraphrases acts like a verbal mirror reflecting back what was said. After a sentence is paraphrased, the speaker may say if anything was forgotten.

3. Then the "paraphraser" becomes the speaker and says his/her own sentence. The process moves around the circle.

4. You might try an upbeat sentence like: An activity I really enjoy is .... because......... (see *Note*)

5. Ask a teammate to be at your left so you and s/he can model the process. Have your teammate start, completing the sentence you choose. You mirror back a paraphrase of what she says. Try to keep both the sentence and its paraphrase short. This will encourage everyone to get involved. It will also move it along. For example:

   Teammate: "An activity I really enjoy is hiking because it gives me a chance to be surrounded by nature."

   You: "You really like to hike because you enjoy the out of doors."

Processing:

- Was this easy, or difficult?
- How does it feel hearing what you've said paraphrased?
- Do you ever paraphrase to show people you're really listening to them?
- Why might doing this help de-escalate or calm a tense situation?

Note: Though an upbeat sentence was suggested above, this activity can be used to give everyone a chance to both speak and feel they are being heard on a more serious topic. This would probably take more like 20 minutes.

This exercise might be used to practice feeling statements, or it might be used following the exercise, Paraphrasing.

Depending on the sentence chosen, this might be used as a gathering or closing.

MY POTENTIAL

Purpose: To help participants identify the inner strengths and resources that they possess to be successful in life; to allow participants to envision themselves as people who can achieve their highest potentials; as a lead-in to later goal-setting activities.

Time: 20-30 minutes

Materials: None

Procedure: **Set Up:**

1. Explain to the group: "We are now going to do an exercise which asks us to imagine ourselves as we are when our full potential is realized. This exercise will help us to begin goal setting. Goal setting is a useful way to take direction of one's life. I am sure that many times you have set goals for yourself -- whether they are simple goals like saving money for concert tickets, or more life shaping decisions, like preparing oneself for college. No matter whether or not we have succeeded in reaching our goals, all goal setting actions involve forming a mental picture of the 'possible' and then using our inner resources to accomplish our objective."

2. Instruct participants to sit comfortably with their eyes closed, hands in their laps. Using a relaxed voice, guide participants to relax their breathing, taking slow deep breaths, about 5-6 breaths per minute. After about 10 slow breaths, say :

   "Imagine a blank space. Then, in the midst of that space, imagine a point of light that slowly fills the blankness."

   (Facilitator should pace his/her voice with the slow, deep breathing.)

3. Once they have filled up the space with light, invite the group to think of, or create, an image of the person they would like to be. Tell the group to be very free in imagining this person. Facilitator may guide the group to consider the following questions:

   "If you had freedom to be whatever way you want - what would that be?......(pause)... What are the characteristics/qualities that you already possess that could help you to become this person"?

4. The facilitator invites the group to imagine this person fully.

   "What age is this person?... Where does s/he live? ....What type of work does s/he do?.... What type of people surround this person"?

5. The facilitator asks the group to:

   "Go through the day to day life of this person;... attempt to become this fantasy person.... Once the image is fixed in your mind, hold it for a moment, and become familiar and comfortable with the picture....(long pause) ...this is the image of you at your winning best."

6. Participants open their eyes. The facilitator passes out paper and pencil for each, and instructs them to take about five minutes to write a description of their "fully realized selves" that they would share with others.

7. Facilitator asks for a volunteer to read what s/he has written. This continues until all who want to share have had an opportunity to do so.

Processing: Can focus on using fantasy to imagine one's potential, for example:

- What are the concrete steps that can be taken to move us from fantasy to reality?
- What are possible barriers we may encounter?
- What can help?

PAPER BAGS

Purpose: To present a simple example of an experiential exercise.

Time: About 5 - 10 minutes

Materials: Two brown bags, A being larger than B, - each is labeled and has a large face (neither smiling or sad) drawn on it. Both are opened and preferably set on a table.

Procedure: **Set Up:**

1. Explain that the task for this exercise is this: To place Bag A into Bag B.

2. Ask if there is a volunteer who would try to do this without asking any questions. Repeat the directions and have the volunteer do it.

3. If the volunteer does the task without a problem congratulate her/him. If the volunteer has difficulties, ask if s/he would like to ask a friend for help, or have someone else try.

Processing:

- How did you find that?
- Suppose we thought of A and B as persons; how would you find the task? That is, is it easy or difficult to know what's going on inside another person?
- Are we always sure of what's going on inside ourselves?

Note: This exercise might also be used in a facilitators' meeting to consider our own bags and how we might deal with them during a workshop - or to consider bags among participants that might make facilitating more challenging and how we might deal with them.

PAPER TIGER

Purpose: To see how our contribution to a group project affects the outcome.

Time: 15 minutes

Materials: One sheet of newsprint per group of 4

Procedure: Set Up:

1. Explain that this exercise will be done in groups of 4. Each group will have one sheet of newsprint. It will be passed around the group. People may make one or two tears in the paper each time the paper comes to them. The paper will be passed around about 3 or 4 times.

2. The task for each group is to be done WITHOUT TALKING. Say that you'll tell them the exact task after the groups are formed and each group has its paper.

3. Form groups of 4 and give out the newsprint. Then announce the task: The task is, WITHOUT TALKING, MAKE AN ANIMAL SHAPE.

4. Encourage people to not talk. Allow enough time for the animals to develop. Keep an eye on the work rather than timing it. You may wish to allow the process of tearing to go on until everyone seems satisfied.

5. As groups finish, have people come back to the circle staying with their group. When everyone is back ask each group to show its animal and report on what happened.

Processing:

- How did you decide on the animal you were making?
- Do you think everyone had a say? Can you explain?
- Did any disagreements or conflicts arise?
- How did you feel about the changes that occurred?
- How do you feel about the way the animal turned out?
- How does not talking affect working together?

PARALLEL CONSTRUCTION

Purpose: To provide an active exploration of communication skills

Time: 20 minutes

Materials: This exercise is done in parallel rows of chairs placed back to back (call them A and B). You can have as many as 8 in each row. Each row needs a cardboard work surface and a small box to hold pieces of construction paper of various colors and shapes, e.g. heart, moon, square, etc. The number of pieces will be 4 times the number of people in the row, e.g. parallel rows of 8 will need 32 pieces in each box. The 32 two pieces in Box A must match the 32 pieces in Box B.

Procedure: Set Up:

1. Ask everyone to stand. With the help of a teammate arrange two rows of chairs, back to back. Count off by A, B. Have the A's sit in one row; have the B's sit with their backs to the A's.
2. Give the first person in rows A and B a cardboard work surface and a box with the pieces of construction paper as explained above.
3. Explain that when you say, "Begin," the first person in row A will take 2 pieces from the box and start a design on the cardboard work surface. This A will then tell the first person in row B which pieces to choose and how to place them.
4. Person B will try to follow A's directions without asking any questions and without any help from her/his teammates. When s/he is finished s/he simply says, "I'm finished."
5. When B is finished, B and A pass the equipment to the next person in the row. Then the 2nd A will add two more pieces to the design and the 2nd B will try to follow directions. The design will continue through the end of each row.
6. At the end of the row, roles and directions will reverse. The last B will choose two pieces and add them to the design. S/he'll tell their A how to choose and place pieces. The design will go back to the beginning of each row.
7. When the design is finished, everyone will return to the circle to compare the completed designs. If there are no questions, begin.

Processing:

- Is this a difficult way of communicating? If so, why?
- How did it feel being the leader? the follower?
- What kind of confusion happened?
- Does this happen in real life?
- What might we do to avoid such confusion?

Note: With younger students it's wise to have fewer in each row. This cuts down on waiting time. Therefore with sixteen participants you might have 2 sets of parallel rows with 4 in each row. Call one set Rows A and B; call the other, Rows C and D.

Naturally, having 2 sets of parallel rows means you'll need 4 cardboard work surfaces and 4 small boxes. Thirty-two pieces will still be needed. Put 16 pieces in Box A to match 16 pieces in Box B. Put 16 pieces in Box C to match 16 pieces in Box D.

This exercise works well co-facilitated. Have one facilitator with each set of parallel rows.

PARAPHRASING

Purpose: To improve communication skills, both listening and speaking. To consider what part communication plays in conflict.

Time: 15 minutes

Materials: None

Procedure: **Set Up:**

1. Explain that paraphrasing is using different and fewer words to say what someone else has said. Model this with a co-facilitator. Ask your teammate to speak for about a minute about a book or a movie s/he really liked. Then you paraphrase what s/he said.

2. When you finish, ask the group if someone else would like to paraphrase what was said. After 2 or 3 people go, ask your teammate if anything important was forgotten.

3. Next, ask for a volunteer to speak about a book or a movie s/he really liked. Explain that after that volunteer speaks you'll ask for 2 or 3 other volunteers to paraphrase what the speaker said. Then the speaker can say if anything was left out.

4. If there are no questions begin. Repeat 3 - 5 times. (Consider the interest level of the entire group. Since it is a cerebral activity you may wish to call a hurricane after each time.) Say that paraphrasing is not easy. Try to encourage those who haven't tried paraphrasing to risk trying it.

Processing:

- Do you find paraphrasing easy or difficult?
- How did speakers feel hearing what they said paraphrased?
- Did speakers feel people were listening carefully?
- Do most people listen to others carefully?
- Does listening and paraphrasing have anything to do with conflict?

Note: You may wish to follow this with Mirror Circle, either before or after processing. Your choice may depend on how many volunteer to try paraphrasing.

Mirror circle might also be used later in the program. It can be used as a gathering or a closing as well as a go-around.

This was adapted from The Friendly Classroom for a Small Planet

PEOPLE'S PERCEPTIONS I

Purpose: To set the tone of the workshop, by letting people experience that no one person (or group) has a monopoly on the truth. To show that to get the "whole picture," we may need to look at things from someone else's perspective.

Time: 15 minutes

Materials: None

Procedure: **Set Up:**

1. Two facilitators A and B work together in this exercise.

2. A will stand in the center of the room, hands behind his/her back. A is to express feelings with face, hands and maybe other body language (e.g., the facial expression could be eager and happy, the hands, twisting and nervous).

3. B will divide the group in half (it doesn't need to be exact). One group stands in front of A, the other group stands behind A.

4. Ask the group to observe A for a minute or two and then discuss what they see with those in their group.

5. While remaining in place, ask each group to describe A from its point of view. There will probably be "facts" about clothes, etc., and "perceptions" about how A feels or what kind of person A is. Be alert to what each group sees that the others can't see and to different perceptions.

6. Ask if one group knows anything that the other doesn't. How do they realize that?

7. Allow the groups to talk with each other and ask questions if they wish. Maybe they would like to trade positions. Ask if we get a better idea of the whole picture when we look from more than one viewpoint. Have participants return to their seats in the full circle.

Processing:

- Has this any relation to real life?
- How can we find out about other people's point of view?
- How do we feel about other people who have points of view that are different from ours?
- Can we respect someone even if we disagree with their point of view? How?

PEOPLE'S PERCEPTIONS II

Purpose: To provide an opportunity for participants to discover that people's perceptions of others are not always accurate.

Time: 15 minutes

Materials: None

Procedure: **Set Up:**

1. In this exercise participants pair off consecutively with three different partners. In each pairing, they will try to decide something about their partner. They will each make that decision in silence, at the same time, in just a few seconds. Then they will share their decision with their partner.

2. Ask participants to find a partner, preferably someone they don't know well. When they are paired, they are to decide — at the same time and in silence, whether their partner is the type of person who likes Pepsi. Tell them to start and call time after about 5 seconds. Take ten seconds (total) to share their decision with their partner.

3. Next, ask them to find new partners, again, preferably someone they don't know well. Proceed as above with this question: Is your partner the type of person who likes mushrooms on pizza?

4. Find new partners and decide as above: Is your partner the type of person who listens to rap music?

5. Ask everyone to return to the circle after they have shared their decisions.

Processing:

- How did that go? Were there any surprises?
- Has this any relation to real life?
- Would it be more or less difficult to make decisions if the questions asked were about people's opinions (e.g. on gun control or abortion)?
- How do we feel about people who have opinions different from ours?
- Can we respect someone even if we disagree with their point of view? How?

Note: This was adapted from Playing with Fire; Creative Conflict Resolution for Young Adults.

PEOPLE'S PERCEPTIONS III

Purpose: To show that two people can look at the same thing and see it differently. To give us the experience of asking others to help us see their point of view. To encourage people to have the patience to show someone what they see. This is an attitude that sets the tone for respect and openness.

Time: 15 minutes

Materials: Copies of any picture that can be seen in more than one way (e.g., old woman/young woman picture which follows). It seems best to keep the picture simple and resist the urge to use a difficult picture. The value is in seeing and sharing what you see.

Procedure: **Set Up:**

1. Explain that you are going to pass out pictures to everyone and ask them not to talk until you give the signal. Pass out the pictures.

2. After a minute, ask someone to describe what he or she sees. Ask everyone who sees the same thing to go and stand by that person.

3. Ask if someone sees something else. Ask others who see the same thing to stand by this second person.

4. By this time people will be milling around, asking for help and showing each other what they see. That's fine; let it happen. Moving around is important, partly because it is active and partly because it's easier for participants to "show and tell" each other and ask for help.

5. Ask if anyone else sees something different.

6. After five or six minutes ask everyone to return to the full circle.

Processing:

- Has everyone been able to see both pictures?
- Ask what happened here. Does the same thing happen in real life?
- Consider what it would be like if we were talking about beliefs instead of views of a picture. Could we still ask for clarification and help each other see various viewpoints?

Note: An alternative method is: Step 1. Stand in the middle of the circle with two copies of the picture and with outstretched arms, rotate slowly 2 or 3 times around, asking participants to observe without speaking. Then do steps 2 and 3. Give copies of the picture to each group and continue from step 4. (This moves faster and there is less chance people will "figure it out" and see two images before Step 4.)

Picture designed by E.G.Boring.

PEOPLE'S PERCEPTIONS IV

Purpose: To see that two people can perceive or see things differently.

Time: About 15 minutes.

Materials: Copies of a picture that is seen differently from two different directions - enough for half the people in the group (see "Princess/Old Woman" picture which follows).

Procedure: Set Up:

1. Explain that this exercise involves looking at a picture and telling a partner what you see.
2. Count off by half the number of people in the group. Ask like numbers to arrange themselves on opposite sides of an imaginary line you indicate.
3. Ask them to leave about three feet between the lines so you can place a picture between them. Ask everyone to be silent until you give the signal to begin.
4. With the help of other facilitators, place pictures (all facing in the same direction) between each pair of people.
5. When all the pictures are in place ask everyone to tell their partner what they see.
6. After 2 or 3 minutes signal for silence and ask how it is going?
7. After several comments ask if they would like to change places to see the picture from the other person's viewpoint. Then return to the circle.

Processing:

- How did you find that?
- Were you surprised when you changed places?
- Has this anything to do with real life?

Note: Keeping the lines at least three feet apart is important.

Co-facilitators could take part in this; others could observe at various points along the line and report what they heard.

PEOPLE TREASURE HUNT

Purpose: To develop community building and cooperation.

Time: 15 - 20 minutes

Materials: "Find Someone Who" sheet (either the handout which follows or one of your own development).

Procedure: **Set Up:**

1. Pass out "Find Someone Who" sheets, and pencils. Ask everyone to mill around, talk to people and fill out the sheet as completely as possible, without using any name more than once.

2. End it when it seems appropriate. Ask everyone to return to their seats. Read the list, and all those to whom that category applies stand up for a moment.

Note: "Human Bingo" is a variation on this by using Bingo Cards with various categories.

This exercise is useful when the group is waiting for everyone to arrive at the first session.

Find Someone Who

INSTRUCTIONS: Get up and go around the room and ask different people if one of these categories fits them. Write that person's name on the line next to the category. Try to get as many as you can, but only use each person's name once.

Owns a pet____

Is left handed____

Is the oldest or youngest in the family_________________________

Is an aunt or uncle______________________________________

Plays three sports_______________________________________

Participates in a club at school______________________________

Gives good advice to friends________________________________

Got into an argument recently_______________________________

Has traveled to other countries______________________________

Speaks more than one language_____________________________

Thinks that racism can be eliminated__________________________

Has a big family____

Likes to cook____

Believes that what goes around comes around____________________

Goes to church____

Hates being teased_______________________________________

Can play a musical instrument______________________________

Is a night person____

PERSONAL SPACE

Purpose: To explore personal space in a nonverbal way.

Time: 5 minutes

Materials: None

Procedure: **Set Up**

1. Ask people to count off by half the number in the group and stand across from their partner on either side of an imaginary line that you designate. Have one line be about 10 feet from the other line.

2. When everyone is arranged, call one line the Signal Givers, and the other line the Signal Responders.

3. The Signal Givers stand still and give signals to their partners to either come forward or to stop as follows:

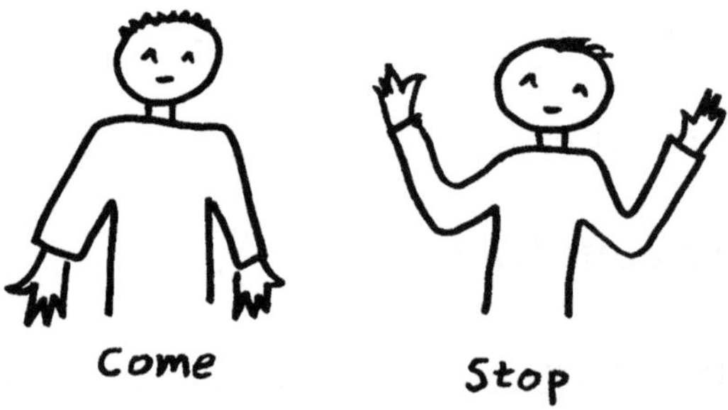

4. The Signal Responders will respond according to their partners' signals.

5. If there are no questions, ask everyone to keep a respectful silence during the exercise and then begin.

6. After all pairs have reached a comfortable space, ask them to freeze and look around and quietly compare the personal space of other pairs with their own.

7. Have people return to their original positions. Switch the roles of Signal Givers and Signal Responders and repeat as above.

Processing:

- How does personal space relate to violence?
- Does the comfort level of personal space vary in any ways?

Note: This might be used just before a Gathering. In this case there would be no need to process. The Gathering might be: My space is important to me because....

PICTURE SHARING

Purpose: To bring feelings to the surface. To acknowledge them, accept them and share them. It is particularly effective before Facts and Feelings in an Advanced Workshop

Time: About 10 - 20 minutes

Materials: A collection that includes many different types of pictures so a variety of feelings surface.

Procedure: **Set Up:**

1. Place the pictures on the floor in the middle of the circle.

2. Explain that after everyone has had a chance to look at the pictures, each person will speak about one picture, completing the following sentence: "When I see this picture I feel.......because......."

3. Have everyone walk around the pictures to look for one that speaks to them. Ask them not to pick up the picture, simply remember which it is. Each may sit down as soon as s/he has chosen a picture.

4. When all are seated model what everyone will do, that is, pick up a picture, hold it for all to see, and complete the sentence above. Replace the picture in case someone else wishes to use the same picture. Invite others to continue, going in pop corn style.

Processing:

- How did you find that?
- Is it easy or difficult to express feelings?
- Did people connect their feelings with their backgrounds, their "Point of View?"*

Note: *It is handy to place this exercise at the beginning of a session or after a break. This allows time for putting the pictures on the floor before starting the activity.*

Don't worry if there is some quiet time between speakers. Naturally if it goes on for too long you might ask if those that haven't spoken are exercising their "right-to-pass." If so, just process.

** See the exercise "Point of View" (which follows) for a fuller explanation of this phrase.*

POINT OF VIEW

Purpose: To consider the idea that people see situations from their own point of view. (In an Advanced this exercise can provide a reason for looking at our past to determine where our points of view originate.)

Time: About 20 minutes

Materials: 2 sheets of newsprint as follows:

POINT OF VIEW			
Experiences	Values	Beliefs	Goals
Needs	Expectations	Wants	Feelings

Procedure: Set Up:

1. Say to the group that we all look at everything from our own point of view. Our point of view influences how we respond to events, including conflict. What makes up our points of view? It could be a variety of things —(mention the words listed on the newsprint).
2. Choose a situation in which two people A and B have different points of view, e.g., parent/teen re curfew, recovering addict/dealer re using drugs, female/male re sex, money, or pregnancy.
3. Record "A" and "B" on the two sheets of newsprint. In the chosen situation what might A's point of view be? Record suggestions on A's sheet under appropriate categories (a couple of suggestions in each category would be sufficient).
4. What might B's point of view be? Record suggestions on B's sheet.
5. After doing both sheets, process.

Processing:

- Might people's points of view vary at different times?
- Do most people have a sort of general point of view about life?
- Might knowing where we're coming from in a general sense help us handle particular situations?

Note: Naturally different people may have different opinions concerning A and B's points of view. That's fine. This concrete situation is only used as an illustration.

Later in the workshop the same situation might be used in the exercise, Points of View.

POINTS OF VIEW

Purpose: To try taking two different points of view in a conflict - to see if we can identify with both points of view.

Time: About 30 minutes

Materials: "A" and "B" sheets from the exercise Point of View

Procedure: Set Up:

1. Explain that this exercise gives us a chance to try on two different points of view in a conflict, that of person A and person B as the group had suggested in the exercise Point of View. (Point out the sheets.)

2. Have the group count off by half the number of people. Ask them to find their like number and arrange themselves on opposite sides of an imaginary line.

3. Let those on one side of the line be the A's and those on the other side be the B's.

4. When you say "Begin," the A's will play out their point of view and the B's will play out their point of view until you call, "Freeze."

5. If there are no questions, have them begin.

6. Call freeze after 2 or 3 minutes. Have people exchange roles and proceed as in steps #4 and #5 above.

Processing:

- Was it easy or hard switching roles?
- Did switching roles give you any insights?
- How might you find out another person's point of view in a real conflict?

POWER TRIP

Purpose: To provide people with a concrete way to consider how they feel about power.

Time: 15 - 20 minutes, depending on the amount of discussion that occurs.

Materials: A sheet of old newsprint or newspaper for each group of four.

Procedure: **Set Up:**

1. Divide everyone into groups of four and assign each group a place to work.

2. Each group will be given a sheet of paper. That represents power.

3. When the groups receive their piece of paper, each person will hold onto a corner of it with only the thumb and forefinger of one hand. You <u>may</u> wish to have people put their other hand behind their back. Each will consider what that "paper of power" means to them.

4. Then, when you say that they may begin, each will try to get as much power as she or he wants.

5. After all the groups are finished, ask them all to come back to the circle, staying with the people in their group.

Processing: In each group, ask:

- What happened?
- Did you talk before acting? (Unless you prohibited talking)
- Did people get as much power as they wanted?
- Were there any surprises?
- How does this relate to power in our lives?
- What words does the word "power" bring to mind?

Note: You may wish to address the last question using a brainstorm. After the brainstorm you might ask: What's the difference between power <u>over</u> and power <u>for</u>? Thinking about this before talking about Transforming Power is helpful.

Power Trip *followed by* ***Ice Cream*** *provides a contrast between "grabbing" and consensus.*

QUICK DECISIONS

Purpose: To practice making quick decisions in stressful situations; to aid in creative thinking.

Time: 30 minutes

Materials: Suggested scenarios — or make up your own.

Procedure: Set Up:

Divide participants into groups of three, either standing or sitting. (This allows restless people a chance to move around). One at a time, read as many of the scenarios as will fit in your time schedule. For each scenario, allow:

-- 15 seconds for quiet individual thinking
-- 1 minute for small group discussion to reach agreement on best action to take.
-- 5 minutes or less for presentation of each team's solution and group discussion. Avoid getting bogged down in too much discussion — move on to the next scenario.

Processing:

- How did that go?
- Was it difficult to make a decision so quickly?
- Was it easier or more difficult to come up with a group decision or a personal one?
- Were you surprised at some of the other solutions suggested in your group?
- Are quick decisions always the best or right decisions?

Scenarios:

1) Four teenagers are walking down the street, talking and laughing. A patrol car pulls up and two police officers get out. They tell the boys to stand against a nearby fence and begin patting them down. Your group of three recognize one of them as Karim, who is in your gym class. He and his friends are vigorously protesting, and things are getting hot. What do you three do?

2) Your group of three is on the subway. You hear two guys making sexual remarks to a young woman who is trying — without success- to ignore them. She looks around, either to change her seat or find someone she knows, but the train is crowded and there seems to be nothing she can do. The guys get bolder. What do you three do?

3) Your group of three has gone home with a classmate to her home to work on a school project. You get right to work, but the girl forgets the chores she has promised to do right after school. Her mother comes home unexpectedly early. She gets upset at the mess the work project has created. They argue. It gets nasty. What do you three do?

4) A young mother and a toddler who looks about two years old are standing at a bus stop, next to your group of three. The little boy is beginning to cry and the mother has slapped him once without comment. She now says "Shut up!" and starts to slap him again. What do you three do?

RAINBOW LUNCH

Purpose: To provide a lively thought provoking activity towards the end of a Basic (see Note); to experience challenges that some people face every day.

Time: 30 minutes

Materials: Lunch (school lunches, bag lunches, or pizza and soda ordered specially - anything will do); 7 or 8 sets of symbols (each set contains 3 pieces of paper, one with an eye, one with a hand and one with a mouth; each paper is folded so its symbol does not show; the 3 papers in each set are paper clipped together); 7 or 8 blindfolds

Procedure: Set Up:

1. Before people get their lunches explain that "Rainbow Lunch" is a cooperative meal. People will eat in trios. Each trio will sit at the end of a table.

2. Each person in the trio will take one of three pieces of paper. The person who gets an "eye" will eat blindfolded; the one who gets a "hand" will eat sitting on her/his hands; the one who gets the mouth will eat without talking. The task for each trio is to cooperate and have a nice lunch.

3. Say that though it may sound "weird," people usually have fun and it's worth trying. (Naturally, people do have the right to pass.)

4. If there are no questions, divide the group into trios. Facilitators may have to participate to fill in a trio or two.

5. After trios are arranged at the ends of tables, give each trio a set of symbols and a blindfold. After they pick their symbols they may begin, first going and getting their lunches. They may end when they wish.

6. Processing might be done as the gathering for the next session e.g., "I found the "Rainbow Lunch was ....because...." Or it could be processed with questions just before or after the gathering or in place of the gathering.

Processing:

- What was it like to eat like that?
- What was it like to be a helper or be helped?
- Why do you suppose we did this as part of an AVP workshop?
- What connection does it have to life outside the workshop?

Note: It's good to explain the day before that everybody will be eating a special lunch together the next day. Naturally the meal could be a "dinner" instead of a lunch.

RED YELLOW GREEN

Purpose: To recall what it's like to be yelled at and to consider a process that might help us act wisely in such situations rather than reacting in kind.

Time: About 30 minutes

Materials: A chart:

RED	STOP	Breathe deeply, count to 10, etc.
YELLOW	THINK	What came before?
GREEN	ACT	Acknowledge other's "state"

(The design of a traffic light provides a good visual image.)

Procedure: Set Up:

1. Explain that two facilitators are going to do a skit that might happen to anyone. It's something that might happen at work or on the street.

2. Person A approaches an acquaintance B one morning and says, "Hey B, how's it going?" B turns away saying, "Get lost. Get out of my face!" (Run this twice.) (Practicing the skit helps it go smoothly.)

3. Ask the group if they've ever experienced something like this. What do they think A's usual reaction would be?

4. Some will probably say that A would react in kind. That's where the Red, Yellow, Green process might help. Read, or ask volunteers to read the chart.

5. After reading "YELLOW, THINK, What came before?", ask the group what might be on B's mind.

6. After some suggestions, have the two facilitators try the skit again trying to "ACT" on one of the suggestions. For example, if some think B had an unpleasant experience before A came along, A might acknowledge this by saying something like, "Hey, you seem upset. Would you like to talk or do you need some space"?

7. If time permits, you might ask for two volunteers to do the skit based on another suggestion, e.g., one in which A had insulted B the previous day.

Processing:

- Might you be able to use this process in real life?
- What does the expression, "Don't take it personally," mean?

Note: Using "Mind Bag AKA Baggage" as a gathering before this exercise is helpful.

REFLECTIVE LISTENING

Purpose: To practice Reflective Listening (AKA Paraphrasing) and experience affirmation.

Time 15 minutes for steps 1 thru 6; an additional 15 minutes for steps 7 thru 9.

Materials: The topic "Things I like about myself and/or Things I do well." on newsprint.

Procedure: Set Up:

1. Explain that people will try to be good listeners and use "Reflective Listening." paraphrasing what the others say.
2. First one person will speak for a minute about a given topic. When time is called, the listeners will reflect back what they heard. The speakers will then tell their "listeners" how they did.
3. If there are no questions, form pairs, decide who will speak first, and begin. The first topic might be, "My idea of a good friend is...." Say that the speakers will speak for about a minute and you'll raise your hand when time is up.
4. When time is up have the listeners reflect back what they heard. Then the speakers can remind the listeners if they've forgotten anything. Explain that you'll give them about a minute to do both of these things.
5. Now have the partners switch roles. The new topic might be, "Something I hope to do in the future is.......because..." (Time them as in steps #3 and #4.)
6. Next, have everyone join the circle and ask how it went. If you haven't brain stormed the Do's and Don'ts of Listening this would be a good time to do so. Or, if you have done this already, ask if they used the Do's and Dont's.
7. Now have everyone find new partners, preferably choosing someone they don't know too well. This time both people will take turns speaking about the same topic. It is this: "Things I like about myself, and/or Things I do well."
8. Explain that besides reflecting back what they heard to their partners, listeners will try to remember what they heard. Later people will introduce their partners to the group according to what they heard. Say that you will time both the speakers and the listeners' reflections as before. If there are no questions, begin. (Repeat the procedure of steps 3 through 5.)
9. People might introduce their partners when they return to the circle, or they might do this as a closing circle at the end of the session or the end of a day. (If you choose the latter, it would be good to explain that.) In introducing, mentioning a couple of affirming facts about one's partner would be sufficient.

Processing:

- How did you like being the listener?
- Are you usually listened to with care?
- How does listening relate to violence?
- How did you find the last topic?

Note: This exercise goes well soon after "Listening and Brainstorming Do's and Don'ts."

It would be possible to do this exercise in two parts, doing steps 1 - 6 and processing them, and later doing steps 7 - 9 and processing them.

If time is short it is also possible to use just one of these parts.

Having the participants brainstorm their own Do's and Don'ts works well.

RISKING CHANGE

Purpose: To present the possibility of making changes in our life and to consider what might happen in a relationship if one person chooses to change his/her behavior in some way. (relationship here might be parent/child, peer/peer, male/female, etc.)

Time: About 15 minutes

Materials: A poster showing the following:

red
orange
yellow

blue
green
yellow

Procedure: Set Up:

1. Point to the poster and mention that we all learned about mixing primary colors in school. Red and Yellow mixed together gives Orange. But if you change from Red to Blue and mix it with Yellow you get Green.

2. Does this happen in life - in relationships? That is, if you're "Red" and the person you have a relationship with is "Yellow," your relationship might be called "Orange." But if you decide to make some changes in your life and become "Blue," even if the other person doesn't change and stays "Yellow," will your relationship change to "Green"?

Processing:

- Can anyone give an example re sibling/sibling, student/teacher? etc.
- Is it a risk to change?
- Can you change someone else?
- Is or isn't it wise to change?

Note: Some younger people may be defensive about changing who they are. You can just acknowledge that—you might say that change might be as simple as avoiding put-downs. Even this might surprise some peers and change relationships.

You might want to have everyone consider one or two ways in which they might like to change. And/or, you might have a "go-around": One thing about myself I'd like to change is....

The following sheet can be used to make hand-out cards to serve as a reminder of any plan to change.

RISK CHANGING YOURSELF!
OURSELVES
CHANGE OUR RESPONSES
OURSELVES
SITUATION OR RELATIONSHIP
SITUATION OR RELATIONSHIP
OTHERS
OTHERS
OTHERS MAY NOT CHANGE

RISK CHANGING YOURSELF!
OURSELVES
CHANGE OUR RESPONSES
OURSELVES
SITUATION OR RELATIONSHIP
SITUATION OR RELATIONSHIP
OTHERS
OTHERS
OTHERS MAY NOT CHANGE

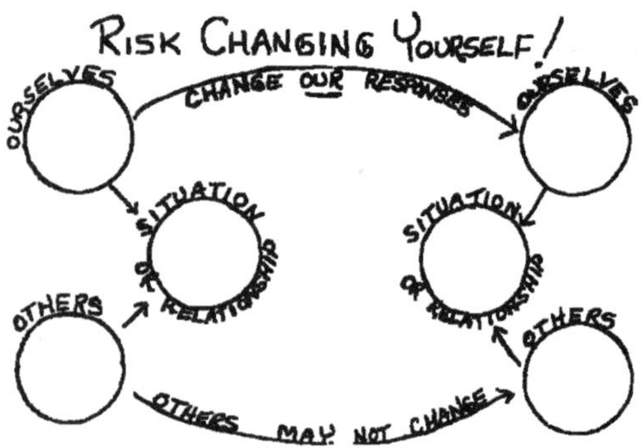
RISK CHANGING YOURSELF!
OURSELVES
CHANGE OUR RESPONSES
OURSELVES
SITUATION OR RELATIONSHIP
SITUATION OR RELATIONSHIP
OTHERS
OTHERS
OTHERS MAY NOT CHANGE

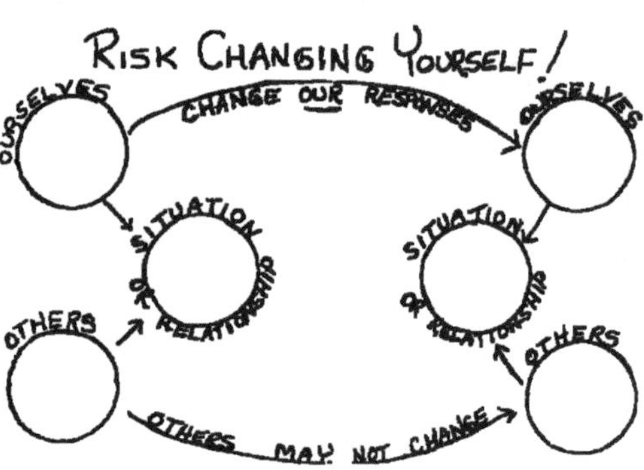
RISK CHANGING YOURSELF!
OURSELVES
CHANGE OUR RESPONSES
OURSELVES
SITUATION OR RELATIONSHIP
SITUATION OR RELATIONSHIP
OTHERS
OTHERS
OTHERS MAY NOT CHANGE

RISK CHANGING YOURSELF!
OURSELVES
CHANGE OUR RESPONSES
OURSELVES
SITUATION OR RELATIONSHIP
SITUATION OR RELATIONSHIP
OTHERS
OTHERS
OTHERS MAY NOT CHANGE

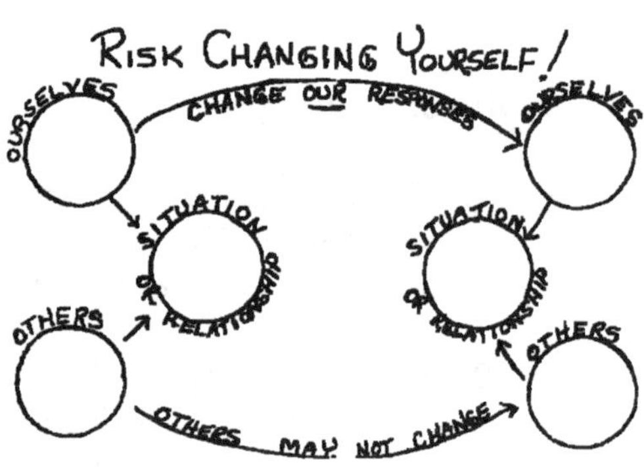
RISK CHANGING YOURSELF!
OURSELVES
CHANGE OUR RESPONSES
OURSELVES
SITUATION OR RELATIONSHIP
SITUATION OR RELATIONSHIP
OTHERS
OTHERS
OTHERS MAY NOT CHANGE

RISK CHANGING YOURSELF!
OURSELVES
CHANGE OUR RESPONSES
OURSELVES
SITUATION OR RELATIONSHIP
SITUATION OR RELATIONSHIP
OTHERS
OTHERS
OTHERS MAY NOT CHANGE

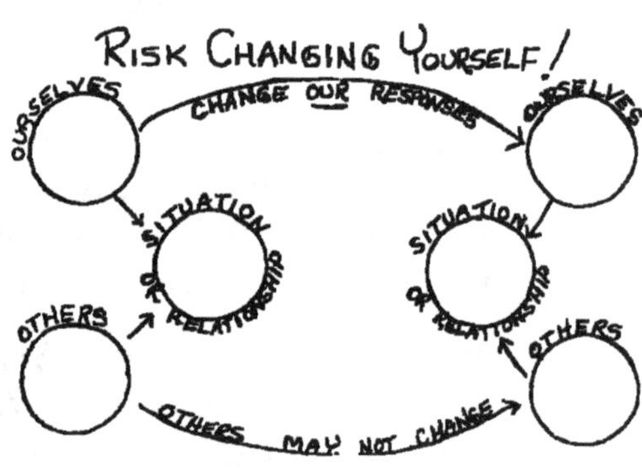
RISK CHANGING YOURSELF!
OURSELVES
CHANGE OUR RESPONSES
OURSELVES
SITUATION OR RELATIONSHIP
SITUATION OR RELATIONSHIP
OTHERS
OTHERS
OTHERS MAY NOT CHANGE

RISK CHANGING YOURSELF!
OURSELVES
CHANGE OUR RESPONSES
OURSELVES
SITUATION OR RELATIONSHIP
SITUATION OR RELATIONSHIP
OTHERS
OTHERS
OTHERS MAY NOT CHANGE

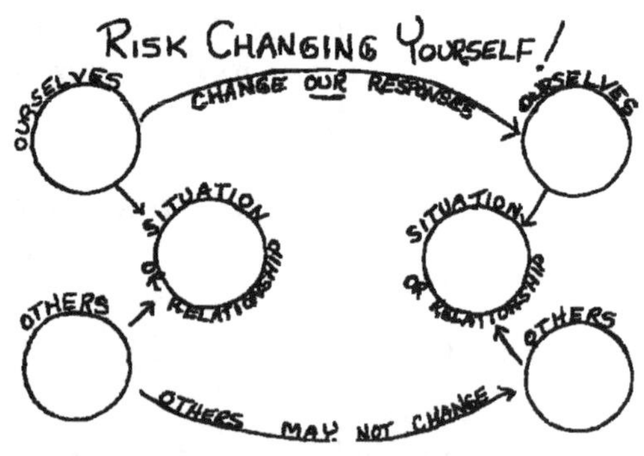
RISK CHANGING YOURSELF!
OURSELVES
CHANGE OUR RESPONSES
OURSELVES
SITUATION OR RELATIONSHIP
SITUATION OR RELATIONSHIP
OTHERS
OTHERS
OTHERS MAY NOT CHANGE

SECRET SPOT

Purpose: To practice cooperation.

Time: 15 minutes

Materials: None

Procedure: **Set Up:**

1. Divide participants into groups of four. The members of the group are to join hands in a circle. **No talking!**

2. Say:
   "Take 30 seconds to select a personal secret spot in the room which you would like to visit with your partners - without speaking or breaking hands.
   You have 5 minutes to visit your spots."

Processing:

- Did any group go to all "Secret Spots"? How was this idea communicated?
- How many people thought you were to go to only one spot?
- On what basis did you decide that you were successful as individuals and as a group?
- Was success "winning" or "cooperating"?
- How is this like real life?
- Do we know in real life what people are thinking?

SHARING: "A CONFLICT I RESOLVED NONVIOLENTLY"

Purpose: To have participants share experiences they have resolved nonviolently; to make the group aware that everyone has done this sometime.

Time: 30 - 40 minutes

Materials: Paper (pad) and pencil for each group

Procedure: **Set Up:**

1. Divide the group into smaller groups of 4 people. Ask for a volunteer from each group to act as a scribe.

2. Give instructions: "I am going to ask each person to share with the group an experience that s/he has had of resolving conflicts nonviolently. I will give each person a minute to think, and then each person will have three minutes to tell his/her story to the group. The scribe should take brief notes on the story. Then, after all members of the small group have shared, one story should be selected by the group for sharing with the larger group. (Anyone may report the story; the scribe, the person who told it, or someone else.)

3. Have each group report the story it has chosen. When all groups have reported, ask if there are any other stories that were not reported that anyone wants to share.

Processing:

- How do you feel about the stories?
- Does it feel good when you are able to come to a nonviolent solution?

Note: This can be an excellent lead in to the Transforming Power talk. As the stories are shared, a facilitator can listen for TP guidelines and, when they seem clear in a story, write the guidelines on newsprint. E.g., "It really made a difference when you listened respectfully to your friend" or "It sounds like the atmosphere changed when you found out you had something in common with your neighbor."

(This should not be forced. Not every story will fit into the guidelines.)
Later, during the discussion of TP guidelines, the facilitator can refer back to those examples listed on the newsprint. " So, in Joe's story, without his knowing it, Transforming Power was operating through him when he was willing to apologize for his mistake, rather than argue about it with his father."

SHARING STORIES

Purpose: To share personal stories about violence - real experiences, not made-up stories - to bring the issue of violence "home" and help participants realize it's not about "them," it's about "us."

Time: About 45 minutes

Materials: A poster as follows:

> **The story can be about:**
> a) violence that happened
> b) violence that could have been avoided and how
> c) potential violence that was avoided and how

Procedure: Set Up:

1. Explain that in this exercise people, working in small groups, will tell stories that involve violence or potential violence. Point out the poster and read it.
2. The stories will be personal. They might be about a time when the teller was or wasn't violent to someone else, or when someone else was or wasn't violent to her/him. Or the story might be about a time when they saw violence first hand. The violence doesn't have to be physical. It could be put-downs, ignoring, yelling, etc. (You might refer to the Violence Brainstorm for ideas.)
3. People may tell any story they feel comfortable sharing. People will have 3 or 4 minutes each to tell their story. When one person is finished, another may begin. After everyone in the small groups has had a chance to share, the group will choose one story to bring back to the large group.
4. The story that is chosen needn't be told by the person whose story it is. It can be told by someone else in the group and the person whose story it is need not be mentioned.
5. If there are no questions, form groups of four or five people. Have a facilitator with each small group.
6. Check with the groups every five minutes or so to see how everyone is getting on. As the small groups finish ask them to return to the circle as a group.
7. After everyone has returned to the circle, ask for volunteers to tell the story their group chose.

Processing:

- How did that go for you?
- Were there any surprises?

Note: Be sure that co-facilitators understand that you need their help. If the facilitator in each small group tells a personal story it will help the group open up. Also, the facilitators in each small group can keep things moving, encourage others to tell their stories, and be aware if some are deeply effected by this exercise.

This exercise works better with people who are thirteen or older. If it's a mixed group of older and younger participants, it might be beneficial to form groups of mixed ages.

To try the exercise with younger participants, you might ask participants to share "a form of violence I'm aware of in my community." If you choose to do this emphasize that they only speak about something with which they feel comfortable.

This exercise may bring up deep feelings. After processing, to give closure, you may wish to have a "go-around," "Right now I feel..." A group hug or a circle backrub are other possibilities.

SIX POINT PROBLEM SOLVING

Purpose: To develop problem solving/conflict resolution skills in relationships

Time: 45 minutes

Materials: Flip chart or handouts (see following page - Family Vacation)

Procedure: **Set Up:**

1. Divide participants into groups of 5 or 6. Post flip chart or pass out handouts. (See following page) Explain that each group is a family, and ask participants to divide the assigned roles among their group.

2. Working from the roles chosen, the group will decide on a solution to the problem which all family members are willing to accept.

3. As each group goes through the steps, they are to write their solutions on newsprint. A volunteer from each group will present how the group arrived at the solution.

Processing:

- How did that go?
- Was it difficult to arrive at a solution?
- If so, what was difficult about this? What was easy?
- Did all family members feel heard and taken into account?
- If so, how did that happen?

6 Point Problem Solving - Family Vacation

We are all problem solvers - we do it every day and each of us has a way to approach it in a way that frequently works. This is *another* approach to solve problems where:

- there is no easy solution and
- where we want to preserve our relationships with the others involved.

The Situation

Your family wants to take a vacation. Finances are very limited and each family member seems to have a different goal in mind. Think of this as an opportunity for all to build new relationships within the family.

Positions:

- **Father:** Prefers a hotel or motel with service. After a year of working he wants luxury - he doesn't care for camping.
- **Mother:** Wants a change of routine from cooking / housework. She enjoys the out-of-doors.
- **Teenage Son:** Is excited by the outdoors and the possibility of camping, hiking and fishing.
- **Teenage Girl:** Wants some social activity - would like to bring a friend along.
- **Younger child:** Just wants a "family vacation."
- **Grandma:** *(when 6 on team)* Enjoys visiting with the grandchildren but doesn't want to be stuck baby-sitting them while the adults go off by themselves. Would like some nice scenery and perhaps going to a summer stock theater production.

Your Task :

Using 6 Point Problem Solving, put steps 2 thru 5 on Newsprint and select someone to present how you arrived at your solution..

Steps

1. **Identify and define the Problem:** to identify the needs of each individual.

2. **Restate the Problem:** in a way which states the ***common need*** of all.

3. **Brainstorm Alternative Solutions:** Generate a variety of solutions. Do not evaluate, judge or belittle any solutions offered.

4. **Evaluate These Solutions:** Which looks best? Ask each person how s/he feels about each solution.

5. **Decide on the Best Solution Acceptable to All:** Keep testing until everyone feels satisfied. Does it meet the needs stated in step 2?

6. **Evaluate:** Periodically check with everyone to see how your agreement is working.

STEREOTYPING
(A variation on "Let's Go Swimming")

Purpose: To demonstrate and increase awareness of stereotyping.

Time: 60-90 minutes (see Note at end)

Materials: Pencil and paper

Procedure: **Set Up:**

1. Team decides in advance what ethnic or other groups they wish to have participants represent. This could be ethnic groups common to the area where participants live (e.g., Asians, Afro-Americans, whites etc.), or it may be perceived groups in their school or community (e.g., "geeks," "jocks," "Goths," etc.). More than four groups may be too complicated, unless absolutely necessary.

2. Participants count off by the number of groups decided upon. Each group is assigned an ethic or cultural identity as above. (e.g., "Ones, go to this corner, you are all Hispanics, Twos, go to this corner you are all Native Americans" etc.)

3, Once in their groups, say "You are now to roleplay your new identity. Answer the following questions in your group, and write down the answers on paper":
   A) How does your group describe the other groups?
   B) How does your group describe itself?

4. Ask each group to announce its answers to questions A & B above.

5. Have each group discuss among its members the descriptions heard. Were the descriptions accurate? biased? Might a group like to change its descriptions?

6. Have groups return to the circle and report on the discussion held in Step 5.

7. Process as a large group. It's very important to give people a chance first to ventilate any strong feelings. Perhaps have everyone take deep breaths — breathing in the positive and exhaling the negative.

Processing:

- How did you feel about hearing either stereotyping of the group you were part of here today, or your own ethnic group?
- Did you change any opinions when you heard what other groups had to say?
- Does sharing stereotypes out loud help to overcome them?
- What insights did you gain?

Note: Do not begin this exercise unless there will be sufficient time for processing!!! Be alert for signs of real frustration and anger.

TAKE THE BLAME OUT

Purpose: To explore the unproductive feelings that go with blaming and to illustrate how feeling statements can be used to avoid blaming.

Time: About 20 minutes

Materials: A poster with the Feeling Statement Formula

Procedure: **Set Up:**

1. In the large group do a brainstorm for blaming statements people have heard but <u>don't</u> write them down.

2. Break into groups of three or four for discussion. Ask each person to say a (powerful?) blaming statement that has been used against them (or that they have used or heard used by or against someone they cared about.) Discuss people's feelings about this. Ask the group to choose one blaming statement and alter it into a feeling statement.

3. Ask people to return to the circle, staying with their group. Have each group report what the blaming statement was, the feelings that resulted from it and how it was made into a feeling statement.

Processing:

- What's the effect on people when they get blamed?
- How would it be different if a feeling statement were used?
- Would it be possible to use any of these feeling statements in real life?

TALK IN THE DARK

Purpose: To provide an opportunity, toward the end of an Advanced Workshop, for people to talk to others with fewer distractions and hence in a deeper way.

Time: 15 - 20 minutes

Materials: A list of topics on which to speak (see suggestions below).

Procedure: **Set Up**

1. Explain that in this exercise people will be speaking in pairs, with their eyes closed, and the lights dimmed.
2. Facilitators will help people find partners. People may wish to hold their hands up in front of them to make contact with the person to whom they're speaking.
3. Have people push their chairs back as this exercise will be done standing.
4. Ask people to close their eyes. Have two or three facilitators (depending on the size of the group) arrange people as if they were going to do concentric circles. Be sure there is a good amount of space between pairs.
5. Explain that you will announce a topic. The pair can choose who will speak first. You will say when the second person should speak. Give each person about 2 minutes.
6. When both people have spoken, have facilitators gently move one of circles (outer or inner) one person to the right. Alternate the circle you move after each topic.
7. Possible topics are:
   a) Something I liked about this group is...
   b) One thing that was meaningful to me about this workshop was...
   c) A way in which I'm growing is...
   d) Something about AVP that I'd like to use in my life is...
   e) Something I'd like to do in the future is.. (after both partners have spoken on this topic, ask partners to encourage each other re their future hopes)

Processing:

- What did you think about speaking to someone with your eyes closed?

TERRITORY

Purpose: To provide an opportunity to experience various outcomes of conflict, namely, Lose/Lose; Win/Win; Win/Lose; Win/No-Lose; and Compromise

Time: About 15 minutes

Materials: None

Procedure: **Set Up:**

1. Explain that this exercise is done in pairs. Once they are in pairs you'll explain the task.
2. Have them count off by half the number in the group. Ask them to find their like number and stand with them, not too close to any other pair.
3. Have them call themselves A and B.
4. Ask each pair to visualize an imaginary line separating them.
5. Explain that the task for all the A's is to have their B come over to the A's side of the line. The task for all the B's is to have their A come over to the B's side of the line. The A's and the B's will be working on their tasks at the same time. (Repeat the task at least twice.)
6. Mention that they'll have about two minutes, and you'll call time. Then say that they may begin.
7. After two minutes or so, ask them to return to the circle and sit next to their partner.
8. When they're back in the circle ask for a pair to show what they did. Ask if others did something similar.
9. Repeat #8 until no pair has anything new to show.

Processing:

- Did any of the demos show a Win/Win? (that is, both A and B completed the task - both went on one side and then the other or just exchanged sides)
- Did any show a Lose/Lose?; a Win/Lose; a Win/No-Lose (one person didn't care about the task); a Compromise (they straddled the line in some way)
- Might another name for a compromise be a Fair/Fair, if both A and B feel good about the outcome?
- In real life is it wise to continually adopt a No-Lose attitude (i.e. to give in to another all the time)?
- If the directions had been, "Get your <u>opponent</u> to your side of the line" or "<u>Bring</u> your <u>partner</u> over to your side of the line" might the results have been different?
- Can the use of one word or another affect how we behave in real life? Might that give others control over our actions?

Note: It is also possible to have the pairs form a long line. In many rooms this places the pairs quite close to each other and one pair may influence another.

You might wish to have partners hold hands, or make it an optional thing to do. You might do this in #6, just before you say that they may begin.

It is good to ask co-facilitators to circulate around the room to observe how pairs are interacting.

Co-facilitators might take part in this to even numbers but they may bias the results unless they take quite a passive role.

THINGS I HEAR(D) OVER AND OVER

Purpose: To consider (in an Advanced Workshop) if the things we hear(d) over and over affect our lives.

Time: About 25 minutes

Materials: None

Procedure: **Set Up:**

1. Explain that in this exercise people will be recalling things they hear or heard from different authority figures (parents, teachers, etc.) in their lives. Two examples might be, "Big boys don't cry," and "You are so stupid."

2. People can either lie, preferably on blankets, like spokes in a wheel with their heads to the center or sit on chairs in a circle with their backs to the center. If it's a large group and they are to sit, you may wish to form 2 circles, an inner and an outer, both facing out. Whichever arrangement you choose, encourage people to close their eyes so they can hear the statements with less distractions.

3. Explain that after they are arranged, people may call out things they hear or heard in popcorn style, i.e., randomly, without being called on and without stating names.

4. If there are no questions, arrange the group as you think best and begin.

5. When the statements wind down, usually after 7 or 8 minutes, ask the group to get back in the large circle.

Processing:

- Did others call out things that you hear or heard?
- Did or do you believe or follow the things you hear(d)?
- Do any of your behaviors or attitudes today stem from the things you hear(d)?
- How did or do you respond to such sayings?
- Would you tell us how you might respond now knowing about Transforming Power?

Note: People may get deeply and emotionally involved in this exercise. Be prepared to give it extra time if needed.

This exercise is similar to Injunctions of Childhood. In this version things people hear(d) might include negative statements as well as directives.

An option is to split this exercise. Go as far as the first two processing questions in Things I Hear(d) Over Part I. Later consider the last three processing questions in small groups, calling this Things I Hear(d) Over and Over Part II.

TIC TAC CHALLENGE

Purpose: To reinforce the Win/Win concept, or to introduce it if you haven't done Territory or discussed competition vs. Win/Win.

Time 15 minutes

Materials: Five packages of TicTacs or some other tiny candy or sweet.

Procedure: **Set Up:**

1. Explain that people will work in pairs. Have two facilitators demonstrate that the people in each pair will put their right (or left) elbows on a chair seat or table (or even the floor)and clasp their hands together.

2. Have them count off by half the number in the group. Like numbers will form pairs.

3. When they're arranged, explain the challenge. When you say "begin" they will have only 15 seconds. Each person will get a tic tac for every time her or his partner's hand touches the chair or table. Each person will keep count.

4. Say "Begin" and start timing.

5. When time is up, several facilitators can distribute tic tacs.

Processing:

- Would some pairs like to tell what happened?
- How did you decide what to do?
- Does our past experience often influence how we act today?
- How wise is it to always act automatically?
- How might we avoid always acting automatically?

Note: This exercise may have different results depending upon whether it's done early or late in the workshop.

You may wish to have them try this without talking. If so, you might add this in #3 before you explain the challenge.

Someone may ask if this is arm wrestling. If so, simply say that it may look like it, but it isn't . Try not to mention this phrase yourself.

TRIANGLES FOR ADVANCED

Purpose: To experience the consensus process while making a design.

Time: 30 minutes

Materials: 3"x3"x3"posterboard triangles of six colors - enough for each person to have one set with each of the six colors (perhaps held together with a paper clip)

Procedure: **Set Up:**

1. Explain that this exercise has two parts. In the first part, each person will work as an individual without talking. In the second part, people will work in small groups and talking is allowed.

2. Form groups of 5 or 6. You might use the same groups as in Goal Setting I. The groups needn't have the same number. Assign the groups a workspace.

3. Explain that each person will receive a set of six different colored triangles. Without talking each person will use the triangles to make some kind of a design, in whatever fashion s/he wishes. If there are no questions, have them begin, reminding them to work in silence.

4. After two or three minutes, call time. Ask each group to have a "go-around" among its members. Each person will explain why s/he made the design that s/he did. Next the task of each group is this: Use all the triangles and come up with one design that represents the whole group.

5. Before coming back to the circle for processing, have everyone walk around to see all the designs. Ask them to return to the circle staying with their group.

Processing:

- How did each group come up with the one design?
- Was it easy to reach your decision?
- Would anyone have liked to have more of a say?
- Did anyone say, "Well it's not what I want, but I can live with it?"
- How might we use consensus with family and friends? in school or work?

Note:. There may be a variety of results: one group may like one person's design and have each person copy it; a second group may take parts of each person's design and incorporate into a whole in some fashion; a third make create something entirely new. All are fine. The result is not as critical as the process.

TWO CHAIRS

Purpose: To experience and consider the subject of volunteering when discussing or generating workshop Ground Rules/Agreements.

Time: 10 minutes

Materials: Two chairs

Procedure: **Set Up:**

1. Place two chairs facing each other in the middle of the circle.
2. Ask for two volunteers to sit in the chairs. Watch for dynamics in the group.
3. When two people have taken the chairs, ask "Why were you willing to sit there?" If you saw others about to get up, ask them what they were thinking/feeling.
4. Ask others why they chose not to get up. Affirm both the risk takers and those who were more cautious. It certainly isn't wise to volunteer in all situations!
5. Ask the two volunteers to rejoin the circle.

Processing:

- Was anyone "encouraged" or "volunteered" by someone else?
- Is there a difference between "encouraged" and "volunteered"?
- How do people feel about someone else "encouraging" or "volunteering" them?
- If Ground Rules/Agreements are being generated, ask if the group would like to add something about volunteering. Using participants' words is empowering.
- This is also a good time to add "right to pass" to the list. This is not something participants usually think of themselves, but it relates to volunteering.

Note: This exercise must move quickly and be upbeat!

TWO OR THREE QUESTION INTERVIEW

Purpose: To get to know each other and hence build community.

Time: 20 - 30 minutes

Materials: Pencil and paper for all (if you want people to write their questions)

Procedure: Set Up:

1. Ask everyone to think of two or three questions they would like to ask someone whom they would like to get to know as a friend. Suggest some questions, e.g., What kind of house would you like to live in? What sort of things really interest you? You might ask people to write their questions.

2. Have people pair off, preferably with someone they don't know too well. When everyone has a partner ask both people in the pair to ask each other their questions and chat for a few minutes.

3. After three or four minutes signal for silence and ask people to change partners. Repeat several times. Then return to the circle.

Processing:

- Did you find this easy or difficult?
- Did you have anything in common with your partners? (No one has to mention what the commonality is.)
- Were the differences interesting?

VIOLENCE BRAINSTORM (With Options)

Purpose: To provide a safe way to consider how different people see violence.

Time: 30 minutes.

Materials: Newsprint and magic markers

Procedure: Set Up:

1. Explain that in this "Brainstorm" people will call out what the word "Violence" means to them and two facilitators will write people's ideas on newsprint.
2. No one will discuss others' ideas during the brainstorm. After the brainstorm, people may ask questions and make comments about what's been written.
3. If there are no questions, ask, "What word or words come to mind when you think of violence"?
4. Encourage the group to just call out.
5. After about six or seven minutes, assuming that the sheet is quite full, admit that though there may be other words for "Violence" we'll now consider what's on the brainstorm thus far. Explain that other words can be added by anyone throughout the workshop.

Processing:

- Does anyone have any questions about anything that's been recorded?
- Does anything surprise anyone?
- How did it feel doing this?

Note: Strong differences of opinion may arise. If time is short for thorough discussion, you might put such differences on your "Unanswered Questions" sheet and explain that you'll consider them later.

Some facilitators like to arrange the brainstorm like a tree to consider the acts, the feelings, and the roots of violence. To do so, ask participants to first call-out "acts" of violence; Then ask them to call out "feelings" connected with violence; finally ask them to call out the "roots" of violence.

Even if a tree isn't formed, you could consider the roots of violence. Save a small part at the bottom of each sheet by drawing a line across about one foot up from the bottom.. As input slows, mention that all the words above the line relate to violence. Ask, "Might any of these words be considered causes or roots of violence"? Circle any suggestions. Ask if there are other causes. Write them below the line This may get at the idea that violence often breeds violence.

Going back to this brainstorm at other times during the workshop may be profitable. e.g., When discussing feelings you might refer to the sheet if "anger" is on it, asking: "Is anger itself violent? Need it always lead to violence"?

Option 1: *After brainstorming "What is Violence" you may wish to brainstorm "What is Nonviolence (the Opposite of Violence)" and then compare the two. Consider whether some words are found on both, e.g., music, religion etc.*

Option 2: *You may wish to brainstorm "What is Nonviolence" later in the workshop. It might be done before introducing Transforming Power.*

Option3: *"What is Nonviolence" might also be done as a Silent Brainstorm in Session 6. In such, people are asked to maintain a respectful silence throughout. Several markers are made available and people may go up and quietly record their idea of nonviolence on the newsprint. Each person may go up more than once. More than one may go up at a time. It would be a group reflection. It would not need processing.*

VOICES WITHIN

Purpose: To think about some of the voices we often hear, almost as if they were playing on a tape. To consider how they might influence us, and, to decide if we wish to work at changing them, perhaps playing new tapes.

Time: About 20 -30 minutes

Materials: Index cards or scrap paper and pencils for everyone; newsprint with the following questions: In what setting do these voices occur? Is it around certain people? How do you feel when they occur? What do you do? Are they useful? destructive? friendly?

Procedure: **Set Up:**

1. Explain the purpose of the exercise as stated above. Mention that we may have heard some of these voices in doing ***Things I Hear(d) Over and Over*** (if the group has done that exercise).

2. Hand out the paper and pencils and ask people to list 3-5 of these voices on their paper. These voices may be positive or negative. Have them list at least two that they would be willing to share. You might give an example.

3. After people have made their lists, form groups of three to five. Ask people to share two of their voices and consider the questions on the newsprint.

4. Come back to the big circle and ask people how that went. Were there any similarities in the voices shared? Do they influence a person's point of view? Might they lead to forming stereotypes or prejudices?

5. Ask people to go back to their small groups. Have them discuss ways of strengthening the positive voices, and lessening the impact of the negative ones. Might they invent new tapes?

6. Return to the circle and ask if there are any suggestions the groups would like to share.

Note: It would be helpful to have facilitators participate in this exercise, or at least to give some examples of their voices and how they deal with them.

Some of these voices might be used in Buttons, to see if a person can respond in a new way to negative voices.

WACKY WISHES
(AKA Goal-Wish Problem Solving)

Purpose: To share and work on individual problems in a safe setting. To become aware of the wisdom of the group, and the value of fantasy and imagination in solving problems. To get perspective and affirmation in handling problems. To increase awareness of the role of affirmation and safety in communications and problem solving.

Time: 30 - 40 minutes

Materials: Pad and pen for each group

Procedure: Set Up:

1. Divide into groups of 3 or 4. Try to avoid "best friends" in the same group. Ask for a volunteer from each group to act as a scribe.

2. Each person is to think of a problem they have that they feel would be safe to share in the small group. Give a minute to think about this.

3. Each person takes a turn to explain the problem, briefly.

4. The group then takes each problem in turn, going around the group twice on each:
   a) On the first round, each person should "make a wish" for the best thing he can think of that might happen concerning the problem. Encourage participants to be very imaginative in the wish solution, e.g., "I wish you could grow wings ten feet tall, fly to Massachusetts, and....."

   b) On the second round, each person should contribute whatever realistic suggestions s/he has to make about the problem.

5. The scribe should take down, on a separate sheet for each person, both the wishes and the realistic insights. The person who owns the problem then gets to keep the record.

Processing:
- How did you feel hearing fantastic solutions?
- Were there any suggestions you found helpful?

WHAT COLOR IS CONFLICT

Purpose: To see what the group thinks conflict is and to consider if there are any positive aspects about conflict (often used with eleven year-olds).

Time: 15 minutes

Materials: Many sheets of different colored paper.

Procedure: **Set Up:**

1. Lay the colored paper on the floor inside the circle of people. Say, "If conflict was a color, what color do you think it would be"? Ask people to pick up a sheet of paper that seems like the color of conflict to them.

2. When everyone has a sheet of paper, ask them to tell the group why they chose the color they did. Record, or have a teammate record, the answers (which will probably be brief) on newsprint. You might write "Conflict" in the center and radiate the ideas around it.

Processing:

- What does the newsprint tell us?
- If the ideas are mostly negative, why might that be so?
- What are some examples of conflict?
- Does conflict always lead to someone being hurt?
- Is there anything that might be good about conflict?
- Can we ever get rid of conflict in our lives?
- Can some conflicts be solved peacefully?

*Note: It's all right if the group doesn't come to any definite conclusions. After the **Intro to Win/Win** exercise, you might refer back to this discussion and see if people's ideas may have changed.*

WHO AM I BECOMING? (MODIFIED)

Purpose: This exercise gives us a chance to consider the value we place on our own characteristics, and to remember that we may choose to change.

Time: 30 minutes

Materials: Seven small slips of paper, a pencil, and a writing surface for everyone. Newsprint and markers for a brainstorm.

Procedure: Set Up

1. Explain that this activity will give everyone a chance to get a clearer picture of who we really are - and, of who we might become.
2. Say that all people have both good and bad characteristics or qualities. Brainstorm some characteristics such as being loyal, unreliable, caring, selfish, fun-loving, etc. Probably getting ten or twelve characteristics on the sheet would be plenty.
3. Next explain that everyone will be given five slips of paper. Everyone will put a different characteristic that describes themselves on each of the slips. Hence, each slip will answer the question, "Who am I?" No one besides themselves will see the slips, so there's no need to worry about spelling. Often we only focus on our negative characteristics; yet deep down we have many good qualities. We have to remember to put down our good characteristics.
4. Distribute five of the slips of paper and a pencil to everyone. Ask them to work in silence.
5. When everyone has finished, ask them to look over their slips and pick out the one that's most important to them. Ask them to put that one on the top. Next have everyone pick the next most important and put that second from the top. Have everyone put all five in the order of importance for them.
6. Now ask everyone to turn the stack of slips upside down so that the slip that is most important is on the bottom, and the one that is least important is on top.
7. Ask everyone to look at the slip that is now on top and say to themselves, "I am ...." and fill in what's written. Consider how it feels to be this kind of person. Now fold this slip and put it on the floor. Think how it would feel if you didn't have this characteristic.
8. Repeat #7 with their next two slips. Then ask everyone if they'd like to do the same with their last two slips. Everyone may do as they wish. They may pick up, or throw out anything they've put down.
9. Finally, give everyone two more slips of paper. Since we're always in the process of becoming, ask everyone to consider what kind of a person s/he'd like to become. Write two characteristics on the two new slips of paper. Now consider - how would it feel to be the person with these characteristics - the characteristics we've kept from before and these two new ones?

Processing:

- How did that go?
- Was it difficult? helpful?
- Have we any choice in who we are becoming?

Note: It is wise for the facilitator to actually do the steps of this exercise along with everyone else, that is, fill out the slips, order them, etc. It acts as a model and helps with the timing.

WHO, ME ?

Purpose: To gain some insight/understanding for the fact that we are role models, whether we like the idea or not, whether we consider ourselves good role models or not.

Time: 30 minutes

Materials: Paper and pencils; a poster with the questions listed below; newsprint with a list of possible qualities a person may have, e.g., leader, follower, creative, sports fanatic, kind, competitive, assertive, etc.

Procedure: **Set Up:**

1. Pass out paper/pencils. Ask participants to find a place in the room where they can have space around them and some privacy. This part of the exercise is done in silence.

2. Ask participants to answer the following three questions on paper. Tell them this will be private, and will not be shared, although they should be prepared to share their thoughts about it in small groups.

3. Ask the questions one at a time:
   (Allow two or three minutes for thinking and writing per question.)
   - How do I see myself?
   - What would young people get from taking me as a role model?
   - What would I want them to get?

4. Allow time in small groups for participants to share thoughts. Ask each person to mention one leadership quality s/he sees in each of the others in the group.

Processing:

- Was this hard? easy? intimidating? scary? energizing? believable?
- Have you considered this idea before?
- Any new thoughts or questions?

Note: This is most appropriate for an Advanced workshop when the group has shown the capacity and desire to speak in depth. It was developed from a more basic format used in youth workshops in which questions are:

- How do I see myself?
- How do I think others see me?
- How would I like others to see me?

WHO SAYS I AM?

Purpose: To explore feelings about being labeled and how people deal with those feelings.

Time: About 20 minutes

Materials: Newsprint and marker; a poster as follows:

> **Questions re. Labels Brainstorm**
> Have any of these labels been applied to you?
> What were your feelings about this?
> Did you think about doing something about it?
> How did you handle it?
> Choose one of these experiences to share in the circle.

Procedure: Set Up:

1. In the large group, do a brainstorm for labels which participants have heard applied to people - as individuals, or possibly as groups in school, in the community or world wide.

2. Split into groups of three or four to discuss the questions on the poster, Questions re Labels Brainstorm (see materials).

3. Return to the circle in groups to share the experiences they've chosen. (You may wish to write down strategies people have found successful.)

Processing:

- What did you think of what you heard?
- Was it a surprise to find how many of us get labeled?
- Why do people do this "labeling stuff"? What is its effect?

Note: You may wish to follow up this processing with the Go-around: When people are labeled, they feel...

Light & Livelies
Light & Livelies
Light & Livelies
Light & Livelies
Light & Livelies
Light & Livelies
Light & Livelies
Light & Livelies
Light & Livelies
Light & Livelies
Light & Livelies
Light & Livelies

SECTION H

LIGHT & LIVELIES

Introduction to Light and Livelies

List of Light and Livelies

Individual Descriptions
(in alphabetical order)

LIGHT AND LIVELIES
Introductory Material

The directions for the Light and Livelies that follow have been written in a step-by-step format similar to that of the Exercises. It is hoped that this will make them easier to explain. Curiously enough, though they are light activities, some are as difficult to explain as some exercises. No time frame is given since most L&L's usually take five to ten minutes. Materials are listed only when appropriate. Processing does not pertain.

As with the general Exercises, Light and Livelies are introduced at appropriate places in the Agendas. Generally speaking, they provide energizing activity and/or humor to balance sedentary activities and emotionally "heavy" exercises. With young people, they are especially important. They are the icebreakers and community builders. Frequently they pertain to the theme of a Session. For example, Elephant and the Palm Tree is often used in Session 2 of a Basic since Session 2 often involves cooperation.

Those Light and Livelies that involve touching, such as Crocodiles (Alligators) and Frogs and Human Pretzel are only introduced after a sense of community, support and trust has been established.

Having as many facilitators as possible participate in the Light and Livelies models the fact that physical, humorous activities can benefit everyone and may even be an alternative to violence.

Some Light and Livelies may be done either sitting or standing. Most will be more energizing if they are done standing.

Usually Light and Livelies are placed just before a Break. This makes it easier for everyone to have a more relaxed and refreshing break.

Light and Livelies are designed to be just that — Light and Lively. They are not meant to go on too long. Try to read the crowd. It is wise to stop before the group loses enthusiasm. One way to stop is to say that the activity will end, for instance, after two more turns. At the end thank everyone and explain that there will be a Break. Mention the time you would like everyone to gather after the break.

Light and Livelies are not usually processed! Sometimes, particularly in school settings, someone will ask, "What did we do that for?" IF this happens, ask the group if they have any idea why AVP might include Light and Livelies in each session, or if the particular Light and Lively related to any other activity done in that session. This may be done as soon as the question arises or put on the Unanswered Question sheet and discussed at a later time.

LIST OF LIGHT AND LIVELIES

A What? (Modified)
Back to Back(Modified)
Balloon Bounce
Ball Toss (AKA Pattern Ball)
Big Wind
Bonnie
Bump Tag
Crocodile (AKA Alligator) and Frogs
Earthquake
Elephant and Palm Trees
Fire on the Mountain
Hot and Cold (AKA Listen to the Universe)
Hula Hoops
I Love You Baby, But I Just Can't Smile
I'm Going on a Picnic
Jack and Jill
Jail Break
John Brown's Baby
Line Up 1 and 2
Mrs. Mumbly
Name That Tune
Noah's Ark
Pretzel
Pruee
Red Handed
Simon Says
Sing Fling (AKA Sing and Toss)
Touch Blue
Vegetable Cart (AKA Ethnic Food Cart, Fruit Cart, etc.)
Waking Up in the Jungle
Wha' Cha' Doin'?
Whass'up Whass'up (AKA Howdy, Howdy)
Who Are Your Neighbors?
Who's the Leader?
Zip Zap Boing

A WHAT? (MODIFIED)

Materials: Cut out "Happy Faces" and "Hearts" for everyone in the group, or any two different objects, such as a pen and a shoe.

Set Up:

1. Have the group sit or stand in a circle with two facilitators opposite each other, each supplied with half of the "Happy Faces" and "Hearts."
2. Pass a "Happy Face" to the person on your right, saying, "This is a Happy Face." Ask that person to say back to you, "A what?" You reply, "A Happy Face; pass it on." Let them pass it on using the same dialogue. Let the group pass it to three or four people. After people have the idea, ask that the "Happy Face" be returned to you.
3. Go to your left saying, "This is a Heart." Hopefully the person on your left will say, "A what?" and you'll say, "A Heart; pass it on."
4. Explain that your co-facilitator will also be passing out "Happy Faces" and "Hearts." Each facilitator will pass out "Happy Faces" and "Hearts" alternately. The challenge is to see if we can keep things straight.
5. If there are no questions, begin. Let the passing continue until everyone is receiving both "Happy Faces" and "Hearts" at the same time.
6. Used as a closing for a Middle School Mini-Program, the following ending would be appropriate: My wish for you is that you'll all receive and give many "Happy Faces" throughout your life, so that your heart, and the hearts of the people you meet will not be broken like "Heartbroken Pat's (Chris')."

Note: The facilitators should pass out the "Happy Faces" and "Hearts" at approximately the same rate. The rate should be fairly quick for the activity to be a challenge.

Other "things" can be passed out in the same way. For example, a pen and a shoe, two different tinker toys or even, a Handshake and a High Five, or a Handshake and a Hug (depending on the closeness of the group).

BACK TO BACK (MODIFIED)

Set Up:

1. Explain that this is a changing partners game. Everyone will start with a partner except you. Partners will stand either Back to Back or Face to Face.
2. When you call out either Back to Back or Face to Face everyone has to change partners and arrange themselves according to what was called. Of course you will try to find a partner, so someone else will become the leader.
3. Ask everyone to find a partner. Have co-facilitators be prepared to "even things up."
4. If there are no questions, begin.

Note: In an Advanced workshop, the caller can change the body parts, e.g., calling "hand to hand", "hand to knee", "elbow to ear." The exercise could be called "Body Parts."

BALLOON BOUNCE

Materials: Four balloons for each team of a particular color; a large triangle indicated on the floor with masking tape.

Set Up:

1. Have each team arrange themselves at the corner of a triangle.
2. Explain that the teams will have to move their four balloons to the side of the triangle opposite them, keeping the balloons in the air at all times.
3. If there are no questions, give the teams their balloons and have them begin.

Note: This L&L is fun for teams in a T4F.

BALL TOSS (AKA PATTERN BALL)

Materials: 6 to 8 Koosh balls, soft balls or small socks sewn in ball-like shapes.

Set Up:

1. Have the group stand in a circle. Say that we'll be gently tossing a ball around the circle to form a pattern. It is important to remember the person to whom you throw the ball, and the person from whom you receive the ball.
2. The first time the ball goes around, people will cross their arms over their chest to show that they have already received the ball.
3. If there are no questions, begin. You may have to remind people from time to time to cross their arms.
4. After the ball has come back to the beginning, send it through the same pattern one more time to be sure everyone has remembered the pattern. Then slowly add more balls (4 to 7 depending on the size of the group), all following the same pattern.
5. If the balls are falling all over the place, you may wish to call, "Freeze." Explain that it is a cooperative challenge to keep the balls in the air. Ask for suggestions that might help, e.g., before you toss a ball you might call out the person's name or adjective name to let him/her know it's coming.
6. After a while, call, "Freeze" and suggest reversing the pattern. That is, start passing the balls to the person who has been throwing the balls to you. Naturally, you'll start receiving balls from the person to whom you used to throw them. You might want to work with just one ball at first. Then you can have all the balls reverse, starting from where they were when you called, "Freeze."

Note: Other challenges:

1. *Have some balls go forward while others go in reverse.*
2. *You might have darker ones go forward and lighter ones go in reverse. You might want to save this challenge for an Advanced workshop.*
3. *Time how long it takes for the ball to move through the pattern. Then ask for suggestions to decrease this time. This would be appropriate for an Advanced or a T4F.*
4. *Hold onto one ball of a different color (e.g., red). When group is doing well, freeze and say* ***red means reverse****, Resume play, including red ball; the first three of four balls continue in the original pattern. Gradually reduce the number of balls in play until none are left.*

BIG WIND

Set Up:

1. Remove your chair and stand in the middle of the circle.
2. When in the center you'll say, "The big wind blows for everyone who....(and add your own description) e.g., likes to laugh." It can be anything as long as it's true of yourself.
3. Everyone who fits the description has to change seats. You will try to get a seat and, if you do, there will be a new leader in the center.
4. The new leader will say, "The big wind blows everyone who...(and s/he'll add something new that's true of her/himself.)"
5. If there are no questions, begin.

Note: This is an energizing activity in which we may learn a little bit more about some people in the group. In a Basic workshop participants often call out only physical descriptions. Facilitators can include more abstract descriptions as they see fit. Or you may wish to save "deeper" descriptions for a second use or for use in an Advanced Level workshop.

One group suggested that two chairs be removed from the circle and that two "leaders" call out something that is true of both of them. This adds an element of cooperation to the fun. Naturally, it would be possible to have one leader at first and then, at a later point in the workshop, play this L&L again with two "leaders."

BONNIE

(To the tune of "My Bonnie Lies Over the Ocean")

Set Up:

1. Everyone is standing in a circle. Make sure there is elbow room between people. Arms are raised.
2. As the song is sung, the group changes position with every word that starts with a "B." Move from arms raised to touching toes. Stay in that position until the next word that starts with "B." Move up and down with the song and end with arms up.
3. Be sure to invite everyone to sing along. You might go through it slowly at first, and then repeat at a faster pace.

Variation: Double Bonnie

1. Position everyone in two concentric circles facing each other. This makes an "inner circle" and an "outer circle," with people paired off.
2. Partners should stand with enough room between them to reach their arms forward and not touch.
3. One circle starts with arms up, the other circle starts with arms touching toes. Participants change position with the words that start with "B," ending up in the position where they started.

BUMP TAG

Set Up:

1. While still sitting, explain that in this game people will start out in pairs standing shoulder to shoulder, with their arms linked. Ask a pair of facilitators and a pair of volunteers to demonstrate this.
2. You will ask one of these pairs to break up to become the "runner" and the person who is "it." Point to the pair of facilitators to illustrate this.
3. To avoid being tagged, the "runner" can link arms with one person in another pair. When the "runner" links with one in a pair, the other person of that pair is "bumped" and becomes the "runner" who tries to escape "it."
4. Have the "runner" illustrate this with the pair of volunteers.
5. If the "runner" is tagged by "it," the "runner" becomes "it" and "it" becomes the "runner" (that is, they change roles).
6. If there are no questions, ask everyone to push back the chairs so no one runs into anything and to choose partners.
7. Ask for a pair of volunteers to be the "runner" and "it." Then begin.

Note: This game can get quite physical. A good amount of space is needed so that no one gets hurt. You may wish to remind people before beginning that they can affirm others by taking care not to hurt them.

Instead of having pairs, groups of four five or six can link arms. In this way everyone is involved. Sometimes with pairs, some people are left out of the action.

Sometimes it is hard for "it" to catch someone. You might allow "it" to call "help," if s/he wishes, and a volunteer could become "it."

CROCODILE (AKA ALLIGATOR) AND FROGS

Materials: a noisemaker or shaker for the "crocodile" and sheets of newspaper for lily pads

Set Up:

1. Ask everyone to imagine that the floor in the middle of the circle is a pond full of lily pads. Place "lily pads" around as you say this or have teammates do it. A dozen or so sheets placed randomly about the floor will do.
2. Explain that you or another facilitator will be a crocodile, while everyone else will be frogs. As an alternative, have a participant be the crocodile.
3. The goal of the crocodile is to catch the frogs; the goal of the frogs is to escape being caught.
4. When the crocodile is sleeping and snoring, as indicated by the noisemaker, the frogs are safe. They will swim around the pond without stepping on the lily pads.
5. When the noise stops and the crocodile is awake, the frogs must jump on a lily pad to be safe. They may share a pad with other frogs and help and support each other, but they must be sure that no part of them is in the pond. It is all right to have one foot on a lily pad and the other in the air.
6. If some part of a frog is in the pond, the crocodile can "catch" him/her. That person is then out of the game. The crocodile or a teammate may also remove lily pads. If there are no questions, begin.

Note: There's no need to "catch" people too quickly. Most people don't like to be eliminated, so picking up lily pads slowly at first seems wise. Also, ending while there are several frogs left would seem ecologically sound.
Having teammates help with lily pad removal is very handy. Sometimes it's hard to have the noisemaker be noisy enough if you're picking up papers at the same time as trying to make noise.

EARTHQUAKE

Set Up:

1. Explain that this L&L involves "houses" and "tenants." A house is made with two people facing each other with arms held high and palms touching. Have two co-facilitators show this. A tenant is a person who goes into a house, which means, stands under the arch made by the two house-people. Ask a volunteer to do this.
2. Ask everyone to form trios as demonstrated. This exercise works with a group which numbers one more than a multiple of three, e.g., 1 plus 18; 1 plus 21. Adjust numbers using team members.
3. If you call:
   a) "tenant," all tenants must move.
   b) "houses," all houses, staying together, must move over a new tenant. The tenants stay still. The leader can be considered a tenant.
   c) "earthquake," all houses break up and everyone forms new trios. Roles will probably change.
4. Mention that you, of course, will be looking for a spot. If you find one, the person without a spot will become the leader. If there are no questions, begin.

ELEPHANT AND PALM TREES

Set Up:

1. Ask everyone to stand in a circle.
2. Explain that, when you point to someone and say "elephant," the task of that person will be to put hands and arms together and point them at the floor to form the trunk of an elephant. Have your teammates illustrate or ask for volunteers.
3. The two people on either side will face the person forming the elephant's trunk, and will each create an elephant ear with their arms in the shape of a C or a backwards C. (demonstrate with your arms.)
4. Point to someone else, say, "elephant," and have the three of them form the elephant's trunk and ears.
5. Ask for another volunteer. When you point and say, "palm tree," that person will raise both arms above her/his head to form the trunk of a tree. The two people on either side of this person will wave their arms away from the person like the branches of a palm tree. Then point to someone else, say, "palm tree" and see if that threesome can make a proper palm tree.
6. If someone mimes the wrong action, that person takes the leader's place in the center and makes the next call. Answer any questions and begin.

Note: Depending on time and the size of the group, you may wish to introduce "skunk." When you point to someone and say "skunk," that person turns to face outward and forms the tail of a skunk with both hands. The people on both sides turn away and hold their noses.

When first introducing this game, you may wish to postpone adding "skunk" and wait for another time when an energizer seems appropriate. At that time, replay and add the "skunk" challenge.

FIRE ON THE MOUNTAIN

Set Up:

1. Ask the group to stand in a circle. Count off by twos starting with yourself. This L&L requires an odd number of people. Ask one co-facilitator to sit out if necessary.
2. Ask the "2's" to take two steps forward, continuing to face inward, to form a smaller circle within the circle of "1's." This circle shouldn't be too tight.
3. Ask those in the inner circle to raise their arms above their heads to form a "mountain." Explain that those in the outer circle will walk around the "mountain" until you call, "Fire on the mountain."
4. Then, to find protection, those in the outer circle will step inside the inner circle and stand in front of someone. That person will give protection by putting her/his hands on the shoulders of the person in front of them. Step inside the circle yourself and ask the person you stand in front of to do this.
5. Since the outer circle has one more person than the inner circle, someone will not find protection. That person becomes the new leader.
6. Those that were the "mountain" will step back a little and become the outer circle along with the new leader. They will walk around the new "mountain" until the new leader calls, "Fire on the mountain." Continue playing in this manner.

Note: After each call, the inner circle may have to enlarge a bit also to allow for people in the outer circle to come inside the inner circle. At first the inner circle may have to be reminded to raise arms.

HOT AND COLD (AKA LISTEN TO THE UNIVERSE)

Set Up:

1. Explain that in this L&L a volunteer will leave the room for a minute while the group chooses a spot in the room for the volunteer to find. The volunteer will find the spot by listening to everyone slap their thighs.
2. If the volunteer is going near the spot or "getting hot," everyone will slap loudly. If the volunteer is far away from the spot or "cold," the slapping will be soft. If there are no questions, ask for a volunteer and have her/him step out of the room.
3. Ask someone to pick a spot and then have the volunteer come back into the room.
4. After the first volunteer finds the spot, ask for another volunteer to step outside the room. Continue... .

Note: This can be made more challenging by having the volunteer do something when they find the spot. For example, you might have the volunteer go to a table <u>and</u> pick up a book.

HULA HOOPS

Materials: 2 hula hoops

Set Up:

1. Ask everyone to form a circle and join hands. Have a teammate stand opposite you in the circle.
2. For just a moment, break hands with the person on your right. Put a hula hoop over your arm and rejoin hands. Have your teammate do the same with the person to her/his left.
3. Explain that the goal is to have the group cooperate to pass the hula hoops all the way around the circle, back to the person who started it without breaking hands.
4. You and your teammate start, each passing the hoop over your own bodies. Since your hoop is to the right and your teammate's is to the left this should cause them to go in opposite directions, creating a challenge when they arrive at the same person.

I LOVE YOU BABY, BUT I JUST CAN'T SMILE

Set Up:

1. While the group is seated in a circle, a facilitator places a chair in the center and sits on it. The facilitator in the center then "role plays" with another facilitator as follows:

   The person in the center is looking sad. One by one, others, beginning with the second facilitator, try to make this person laugh. The center person responds to each one, "I love you, baby, but I just can't smile."
2. If the person in the center laughs, he or she is out of the center and whoever caused the laughter is in the center chair. Continue until all participants are laughing, or the energy winds down.

Alternative Inclusive Version

1. The person in the center (standing) tries to make someone in the circle laugh. The response is still, "I love you baby, but I just can't smile." Move around the circle and focus on different people.
2. Whoever laughs joins the center person and they both (or all) try to make someone else laugh. Game continues until everyone is inside the circle.

***Caution:** This may be uncomfortable for anyone who is really feeling low.*

I'M GOING ON A PICNIC

Set Up:

1. Group sits in a circle. First person says, "I am going on a picnic and I'm taking some...." (Say something that starts with the letter "A," for example, "**ants**").
2. Go around the circle. Next person says, "I'm going on a picnic and I am taking some **ants** and some...... (Says something that starts with the next letter of the alphabet, for example, **bananas**).
3. Continue around the circle; each person repeats what the person before said and adding something starting with the next letter of the alphabet. Some people may choose to take strange things on a picnic, like elephants!

JACK AND JILL

(based on the nursery rhyme)

Set Up:

1 Decide ahead of time on four hand motions, for example:
   a) snap fingers of left hand   c) clap hands
   b) snap fingers of right hand   d) slap thighs

2. Use the traditional nursery rhyme:
   JACK AND JILL WENT UP A HILL
   TO FETCH A PAIL OF WATER
   JACK FELL DOWN AND BROKE HIS CROWN
   AND JILL CAME TUMBLING AFTER.
3. Start the rhyme and go around the circle, with each person just saying one word in turn. Try this a few times to get the flow of it.
4. Now the whole group does the motions while each person says his/her word:
   JACK (snap left fingers) AND (snap right fingers)
   JILL (clap hands) WENT (slap thighs)
   UP (snap left fingers) THE (snap right fingers)
   HILL (clap hands) TO (slap thighs), etc.
5. It is a more unifying experience if people are not excluded for making a mistake. Just start at the beginning and go around again. Or start with someone different or go in the opposite direction.

JAIL BREAK

Set Up:

1. Explain that this game is a bit like "Musical Chairs" in pairs.
2. Put your chair in the middle of the circle and ask for a volunteer to be your partner. Have that person place her/his chair beside yours.
3. Go to two people in the circle, say that they will be partners and ask them to place their chairs together, facing one way. Have the next two people place their chairs together, facing another way.
4. Continue around the circle, having pairs place their chairs randomly around the room, facing in a variety of directions. Try to leave at least three feet of space around any pair of chairs.
5. When everyone is arranged, ask pairs to link arms. Say that pairs must move with their arms linked and they must keep the same arms linked.
6. Give each pair a number which will be kept for the whole game, with you and your partner having the last number.
7. Explain that the chairs in the center stand for jail. You and your partner want to get out of jail. You will call two or more numbers and the pairs with those numbers must find new seats. Or you might call, "Jailbreak," and everyone must find new seats. The pair that ends up in jail makes the next call.
8. Ask everyone to be careful so that no one gets hurt.
9. If there are no questions, discuss with your partner what to call and begin.

Note: This will only work with chairs without arms.

This L&L tends to generate a lot of energy. You may have to repeat the warning about being careful.

You may wish to ask a co-facilitator to serve as a referee in cases where two pairs try to sit in the same chairs.

JOHN BROWN'S BABY

(to the tune of "Battle Hymn of the Republic," (AKA "John Brown's Body")

Set Up:

1. Everyone stands in a circle. The group sings the song through once with all the words and then five more times. With every repetition actions are substituted for words. In the first repetition substitute for baby; in the second repetition substitute for baby and cold, etc.

JOHN BROWN'S BABY HAD A COLD UPON ITS CHEST (3X)
AND THEY RUBBED IT WITH CAMPHORATED OIL.

2. **For the word:** **substitute the action:**

For the word:	substitute the action:
baby	arms cradled in front, move arms side to side
cold	make sneezing sound
chest	hit chest with palm of hand
rubbed	rub circles on chest
camphorated oil	hold nose

3. The last time the song is sung, it will go like this: (with the actions)

JOHN BROWN'S [___] HAD A [___]
UPON ITS [___] (3X)
AND THEY [____] IT WITH [____]

LINE-UP 1

Set Up:

1. Explain that this L&L challenges everyone to cooperate in silence. They may, however, use gestures.
2. The group's task is to arrange themselves in order, according to the month and day of their births.
3. If there are no questions, they may begin. If they ask, "Where is the beginning of the line?" say that they'll have to figure that out in silence.
4. When movement ends, ask if they all feel comfortable with the arrangement. If not, they can continue. If they are comfortable, ask them to state the month and day of their births in order.

Note: Sometimes one or two people may end up slightly "out of order." Affirm the group nonetheless. It's not an easy task in silence. Sometimes even when we speak, we don't fully understand what another is saying.

LINE-UP 2

Set Up:

1. Explain that this L&L challenges everyone to cooperate without talking. Humming is allowed because people will have their eyes closed.
2. Females may wish to keep one arm across their chests.
3. Say that you and another facilitator or two (arrange this beforehand) will watch so that no one goes too far astray or walks into something.
4. Ask everyone to stand and push their chairs back so there's plenty of room.
5. Ask everyone to close their eyes so you can state the task. Then say, "Without talking and without peeking, arrange yourselves in order by height. Remember, you may hum."
6. When movement ends, ask if they all feel comfortable with the arrangement. If not, they can continue for a while. Finally, have them open their eyes and see how they've done.

Note: As in Line Up 1, total success is definitely not critical. The trust shown in doing this exercise is the important thing. You may wish to congratulate them on this.

MRS. MUMBLY

Set Up:

1. Have the group sit in a circle.
2. Explain that you have been looking for Mrs. Mumbly but you just can't find her. Say that you are going to ask your neighbor (either to your left or right), "Have you seen Mrs. Mumbly?"
3. Your neighbor may reply one of two things, "What?" or "No, but I'll ask my neighbor." Then that person asks her/his neighbor, "Have you seen Mrs. Mumbly?" and action continues around the circle.
4. The catch is that people are not allowed to laugh or show their teeth while speaking.
5. If there are no questions, begin. Go all around the circle.

NAME THAT TUNE

(also can be used to break into groups)

Materials: Have folded slips of paper ready on which you have written names of very familiar songs such as Old McDonald; Twinkle, Twinkle, Little Star; Row, Row, Row Your Boat; Happy Birthday; London Bridge. You will need one song for each group to be formed. There must be as many slips of paper for each song as the number of people you want in each group.

Set Up:

1 Put slips in a small container. Everyone draws a slip and reads without letting the others see. Without talking, have people stand and move around while humming their song until they find others with the same song. They will then remain standing together.

2. As the groups quiet down, ask each small group to hum its tune for everybody.

Note: *This is good for dividing into groups for Broken Squares. Be sure that songs are divided to match the count you want.*
Caution: *Be sensitive in choosing which songs to use. Participants not raised in the United States where these songs are common, might not be familiar with some of the songs.*

NOAH'S ARK

Materials: Slips of paper with names of different animals on them for half the group; a second set of slips with "mates" of the same animals for the other half of the group.

Set Up:

1. Ask the group to create room (push chairs back) or move to a large space.
2. Explain that we are in Noah's Ark, where all the animals have broken loose in the dark and are trying to find their mates by voice alone.
3. Divide into two groups. Have the groups go to opposite sides of the room. Give each person a slip of paper with the name of an animal. Be sure that each animal is represented in each group.
4. The task is for people to close their eyes and to mingle while calling for their mates with their animal sounds. Since eyes will be closed, it is important to be respectful. Females may wish to hold their hands up at chest level, palms facing out.
5. When mates find each other, they may open their eyes and stand silently together until all mates have found each other. If there are no questions, begin.

Note: It is helpful to have two or three facilitators act as protectors so participants don't walk into something that may hurt them. You may wish to assure the group that this precaution will be taken.

One variation is to have people pair off first. Each pair can choose its own animal. The pairs then separate to opposite sides of the room and continue with step #4.

Another variation is to have silent animals with eyes opened. Pairs mime animals such as fly, giraffe, slug, butterfly, amoeba, hippo, ape, rabbit, fish, hawk and dolphin.

PRETZEL

Set Up:

1. Ask the group members to stand and create or move to an open space.
2. Ask for two volunteers to leave the room until called back to perform a special task with this group. The task will be explained to them upon their return.
3. Ask the remaining group members to join hands in a circle with you. As facilitator, lead about 1/2 to 2/3 of the group under a pair of arms opposite you. Ask the group to continue forming a "pretzel" while holding hands and twisting themselves over, under and through each other.
4. Call in the two volunteers and describe their task, which is to untangle the "pretzel" without asking people to let go of each other's hands. The group cooperates with the volunteer's directions.
5. The task is complete when the group is untangled and again in a simple circle.

Variation:

An even number of people in a circle each join right hand to right hand across the circle, thus forming a pretzel. Do not take hand of person next to you; do not take both hands of one person. The group then works together to untangle their pretzel into a simple circle. This tends to be easier in smaller groups (8-12).

Note: *Because of the physical closeness required of those forming the pretzel, facilitators should include this only after the group shows signs of interpersonal comfort and cooperation. Without choosing a group member, the facilitator should be aware of those members who have shown sensitivity to close touch in previous exercises when stating the need for volunteers. Awareness of individual physical limitations might affect whether this exercise is used.*

PRUEE

Set Up:

1. Explain that in this exercise people will mill around with their eyes closed searching for "Pruee." You will pick "Pruee" from someone in the group after everyone has their eyes closed. After "Pruee" is picked, s/he may open her/his eyes but s/he may not say anything.

2. To find "Pruee," people will go around saying, "Pruee? Pruee?" If they run into someone else also saying "Pruee? Pruee?" that won't be "Pruee," because "Pruee" can't speak.

3. If people saying "Pruee? Pruee?" run into someone who is silent, they have found "Pruee!" Then they will join "Pruee" by holding hands. They may then open their eyes and be silent.

4. Eventually everyone should end up in a long line of "Pruee attachments."

5. Suggest that people hold their hands up at chest level with palms facing out as they go about searching for "Pruee."

6. Say that facilitators will be watching everyone to be sure that no one's safety is endangered. (Plan this with teammates before starting.)

RED HANDED

Materials: Two small bells that can be held in a tightly closed hand

Set Up:

1. Ask the group to stand in a circle. You and one person across the circle will each hold a bell concealed in one hand. Have everyone make fists in front of them, waist high.

2. Start passing one bell to your right or left without having anyone see the bell. Ask the other "bell person" to do the same as everyone else mimes passing bells. Practice for a minute.

3. Explain that in a minute you will go into the circle and close your eyes. The group will start passing or miming passing bells. When they tell you to open your eyes, they will continue passing or miming passing the bells. You will try to "catch someone red handed" with a bell.

4. If you catch someone "red handed," s/he will take your place and continue as in #3.

Note: This is often more difficult than it appears. If someone in the center becomes very frustrated, you might ask if s/he would like a friend to come into the center and help. When they catch someone, that person can try it either alone or with a friend.

A variation, probably more challenging, is to have people pass the bells behind their backs.

SIMON SAYS

Set Up:

1. Ask the group to stand in a wide circle with space between persons. A facilitator explains that the leader stands in the center of the circle and gives commands, either "Do......" or "Simon says, do..... ."
2. Everyone is to do only what "Simon says." Those who act on the leader's command ("Do this") are out and those who act on Simon's command continue actions in the circle.

Variation:

When someone is caught acting on the leader's command, ("Do this"), he or she could move to the center and become leader rather than be cut out of the game.

Note: *The familiarity of the game might make it usable early in the workshop. It does, however, seem competitive, which may lead some participants to feel left out. As with any active game, be aware of members' physical limitations.*

SING FLING (AKA SING & TOSS)

Materials: 1 or 2 koosh balls or small socks sewn in ball-like shapes

Set Up:

1. Have the group stand in a circle. Say that everyone but a "singer" will be gently tossing a ball around the circle.

2. The "singer" will stand outside the circle with her/his back to the circle. S/he'll sing or hum a song. When the song stops the ball stops. The person holding the ball when the song stops becomes the new "singer." The previous singer joins the circle and the game continues.

3. If there are no questions ask for a volunteer to be the "singer" and begin.

Note: A variation would be to use two balls and two "singers." This might make people feel safer when singing. The two would work cooperatively to choose a song and a signal for stopping.

TOUCH BLUE

Set Up:

1. Explain that this game involves touching a person on the shoulder who meets a particular description. For instance, if the leader calls, "Touch someone who's wearing something blue," everyone would look for someone wearing something blue and touch that person on the shoulder.
2. If there are no questions, begin. You can play even though you're leading the exercise. Other calls might be: "Touch someone who's wearing a watch"; "Touch someone who's taller than you"; "Touch someone who you think was born in the same season as you."
3. After about four fairly quick calls, invite others to call out.

VEGETABLE CART (AKA ETHNIC FOOD CART)

Set Up:

1. Ask the group to name four vegetables.
2. Explain that each person will be given the name of one vegetable and they'll keep that name for the whole game. Go around the circle, giving a vegetable name to each person.
3. Remove your chair from the circle. When you call out one vegetable name, everybody who has that name will have to switch seats. If you call out two vegetables, everybody who has either of those names will have to switch seats. If you say, "Vegetable Cart," everyone has to switch seats.
4. Of course, you'll be trying to get a seat. Since there is one less chair than there are people, a new person will become the leader. If there are no questions, begin.

Note: You can play with four "Fruits," four "Ethnic Foods" or four "Sneakers," too. Instead of "giving" each person the name of one of the four vegetables or sneakers etc., you might ask people to choose in their own minds one of the four vegetables. Ask them to keep their choice throughout the whole game. If people become overly enthusiastic about getting seats, you should suggest that everyone be careful so that no one is hurt, particularly if the chairs aren't too sturdy.

WAKING UP IN THE JUNGLE

Set-Up

1. Have everyone stand in a circle. Ask that everyone pick an animal noise. They don't have to tell others what they chose.
2. Explain that in a minute everyone will crouch down and start making their animal noise very softly as if they were just waking up in the jungle.
3. Then gradually everyone will rise up and as they do the noise they're making will become louder and louder, as loud as they like.
4. If there are no questions, ask everyone to crouch down and begin.

Note: This L&L is a good tension reliever, usually used in an Advanced Workshop.

WHA'CHA'DOIN?

Set Up:

1. Explain that in this L&L people will first work in pairs as you and a teammate will model.
2. You start miming some action, e.g., combing your hair. Your teammate asks, "Wha'cha'doin?" You say some action other than "combing my hair." You might say, "Tying my shoes." Your teammate then mimes "tying shoes." You ask, "Wha'cha'doin?" Your teammate might reply, "Jumping rope." You mime "jumping rope." etc.

3.Say that everyone will first practice in pairs and then action will be sent around the circle. If there are no questions, ask people to form partners and try it. You and some teammates may have to circulate and encourage people.

Note: If time is short, you might simply model the process and just send action around the circle.
This can be a good "waker upper." It might even be started as people are arriving and waiting for others to arrive. Once a few people learn the process they can show others.

WHASS'UP WHASS'UP (AKA HOWDY, HOWDY)

Set Up:

1. Have everyone stand in a fairly tight circle. Be sure there's enough room for people to walk around the outside of the circle.
2. Ask for a volunteer to walk around the circle. That person will tap someone in the circle on the shoulder and continue walking in the same direction that s/he started.
3. The person who was tapped starts walking in the opposite direction of the "tapper." When they meet, they shake hands and both say, "Whass'up? whass'up?"
4. Then, still walking, they both try to get back to the place of the person who had been tapped.
5. The person who gets back first rejoins the circle. The person who gets back second becomes the "tapper."
6. If there are no questions, ask for a volunteer to begin.

WHO ARE YOUR NEIGHBORS?

Set Up:

1. Remove your chair from the circle.
2. You will ask someone in the circle, "Who are your neighbors?"
3. That person has to give the adjective name of the two people beside her/him. If the person is not able to do this, you'll take that person's seat and s/he will be in the middle.
4. If the person does name the neighbors, you'll ask, "How are your neighbors?"
5. The response may be one of three things. If they say, "They're all right," everyone will move one chair to the right. If they say, "They're all left," everyone moves one chair to the left. If they say, "They're all mixed up," everyone switches seats any way they wish.
6. You'll try to get a seat. If you succeed, whoever doesn't get a seat asks the questions. If you don't get a seat, you'll ask someone else the questions.
7. If there are no questions, begin.

Note: This game is fun in an Advanced or a T4F, especially if at least some people know each other. It can help people learn each other's names and loosen up.

This L&L might be co-facilitated.

WHO'S THE LEADER?

Set Up

1. Explain that in a moment you'll ask for a volunteer to leave the room for a few moments.
2. When that volunteer leaves, you'll ask for a second volunteer to be the "leader." The leader will start doing some motion, e.g., tapping one hand on her/his thigh. Everyone will follow what the leader does. If the leader starts to rub her/his hands together, so will everyone else.
3. When the volunteer who has gone outside returns, s/he is to try to guess who the leader is.
4. If there are no questions, ask for a volunteer to be the "guesser" or "detective."
5. When the "guesser" leaves the room, ask for a volunteer to be the leader. Have the leader start some motion and invite the "guesser" to come in and start guessing.
6. When the "leader" is discovered, ask for two more volunteers and continue as above.

ZIP ZAP BOING

Set Up:

1. Have the group stand in a fairly tight circle. Say that you'll be passing two words around the circle, "Zip" and "Zap." Each word has its own direction. 'Zip' goes to the right; 'Zap' goes to the left.
2. Have a co-facilitator placed about five people to your right. Say, "Let's try sending 'Zip' to the right" and do so. Prearrange that your co-facilitator will call out, "Boing," when the action reaches her or him. At this point explain that "Boing" can be used to reverse the action. Ask the person fourth from your right to start "Zap" to the left.
3. It may get boring if several people over-use "Boing" and keep someone trapped. You may add a rule that keeps things moving around the circle. For example, no one may say "Boing" more than once until action has gone all the way around the circle or no one may say "Boing" more than twice in the whole game.
4. An alternative to limiting "Boings" is to introduce a fourth word, "Perfluey" or "Double Boing." Whichever word you choose passes the action across the circle to someone you name. For instance, call "Merry Mark, Double Boing!" Merry Mark must start either " Zip" to his right or "Zap" to his left!

Note: Having co-facilitators fairly equally spaced around the circle may help things move, particularly with the use of "Perfluey" or "Double Boing." A third facilitator might be the first to call out "Merry Mark, Double Boing."

Standard Agenda Components
Standard Agenda Components
Standard Agenda Components
Standard Agenda Components
Standard Agenda Components
Standard Agenda Components
Standard Agenda Components
Standard Agenda Components
Standard Agenda Components
Standard Agenda Components
Standard Agenda Components
Standard Agenda Components
Standard Agenda Components
Standard Agenda Components
Standard Agenda Components
Standard Agenda Components
Standard Agenda Components
Standard Agenda Components
Standard Agenda Components
Standard Agenda Components
Standard Agenda Components
Standard Agenda Components

SECTION I

STANDARD AGENDA COMPONENTS

Gatherings

Closings

Affirmation Pyramid
Head, Heart, Hand
Make A Difference
Namaste Circle
Rainstorm
Texas Hug
World Ball
Yarn Web

Dividing Into Groups

Affirmation Posters

Evaluations (general and written)

Certificates

What's Next?

GATHERINGS

Gatherings are used at the beginning of each session to "gather" the energy of the workshop back together after an extended break. They set the tone for each session, and, if possible, reflect the themes that will be explored during the session. As the workshop develops, they may become more in depth and provide an opportunity for participants to share at a deeper level. Of course, as with all planning, the gatherings are chosen for the level and depth of the workshop or the needs of the particular group. They may take a variety of forms.

Sentence Completion Gatherings
(Those with * might be used when pressed for time)

*My favorite positive word is....
My idea of a good friend is....
A place I really like is...because....
I feel good about myself when.....
*One of my favorite foods is....
Something I do well is.....
If I could be an animal I'd be a....because...
Someone I respect is...because...
One reason I like living here is...because...
Something most people don't know about me is....
Something I like about this group of people is....
My space is important to me because....
I think my goals are....
The best present I ever received is.... (it doesn't need to be tangible)
Something I have always wanted to do is...
My favorite hiding place is....
A relationship in my life I'd like to transform is....
What I'd like to tell my family about this workshop is....
(See also Concentric Circle topics as possible gatherings)

Exercise and L&L Gatherings

Mind Bag
Mirror Circle
Picture Sharing
L&L - Wha'Cha'Doin?

Go-arounds
(These are similar to gatherings, used to check on group energy at any time)

Right now I feel....because...
One word that says how I feel right now is...
What this says to me is...
(used after reading a short selection to the group, e.g., "The Nature of Conflict" on page J-8; answer popcorn style.

CLOSINGS

Closings, naturally, are used to bring closure to a session, to a day of perhaps several sessions or to the whole workshop. Closings may emphasize unity; they may affirm the group or the individuals in the group simply as good people; they may acknowledge a job well done or time well spent. They also provide a means to say a "group good-bye" until we meet again, or, at the end of the workshop, to say a "group good-bye" with hopes of meeting again and with wishes of peace for the future.

The Closings that follow are:

Affirmation Pyramid
Head, Heart, Hand
Make a Difference
Namaste Circle
Rainstorm
Texas Hug
World Ball
Yarn Web
A special closing, "Bonfire," is in the Exercise Section

AFFIRMATION PYRAMID

Set Up:

1. Have the group stand in a tight circle. Say that, "We are about to form a pyramid with hands."
2. Explain that you will start by stretching your hand into the middle of the circle. Then others will place a hand on top of others' hands.
3. As people put out their hands, they'll complete a positive phrase such as, "Something I liked about today (this session, this group, etc.) was......" Naturally, people may choose to pass.
4. After everyone who wishes to go has done so, ask the group to bring their hands down a little, and then raise them up with a "Whoop!"

Note: Though some pass, affirming feelings come about nevertheless.

HEAD, HEART, HAND

Set Up:

1. Instead of doing a regular evaluation, try this as a combo evaluation/closing.
2. Draw a large "person" on newsprint. Have three different color post-its, say, blue, yellow and pink.
3. Say that the blue post-its will contain thoughts and will be placed near the person's head; the yellow ones will contain feelings and be posted by the persons heart; the pink ones will contain tools and will be placed near the person's hands. As you say this, write "thought," "feeling" and "tool" on their respective colors and place them in their respective spots.
4. Give each participant one of each color post-it. Ask them to write a thought they have about AVP on their blue post-it, a feeling they've had during the day on their yellow post-it, and a tool they might try to use on their pink post-its.
5. As they finish writing have them place their post-its by the head, heart and hands of the "person."
6. When everybody is finished read the results aloud and thank everyone for their input. You might everyone to read his/her own post-its.

MAKE A DIFFERENCE

Set Up:

1. Give each person an index card and a pencil. Ask everybody to write something on the card that they could do that would really make a positive difference, at school, in their home or in the community.
2. Explain that they will be the only ones to see what they've written. When they've finished writing, have tape available so they can fold their cards and tape them closed.
3. Have them write their names and class number on the outside of their cards. Explain that in a week or two someone will bring the cards to their classes and hand them out.
4. Then they can check on themselves to see if they've tried their own idea.

NAMASTE CIRCLE

Set Up:

1. Have the group stand in a circle. Mention briefly a couple of ways people greet each other, e.g., shaking hands or giving a "High 5."
2. Explain that the Hindu people from India greet each other saying the word "Namaste." First one person holds her/his hands palms together and says, "Namaste," bowing slightly. Then the other does the same.
3. The greeting "Namaste" means the following: The good which is in the deepest part of me greets the good which is in the deepest part of you.
4. This closing circle will give everyone a chance to first return this greeting and then to initiate this greeting.
5. Explain that you will start going around the circle to your left, giving this greeting to everyone in turn. As you move on to the fourth person to your left, the second person will start going around giving the greeting to the first person to her/his left. You might want to have a teammate be the first person to your left so s/he can model this.
6. If there are no questions begin. The circle will turn in on itself and then open again after you get back to place.

Note: *This closing would be fitting for an Advanced Workshop's 6th Session. If you have done "A What?" with Handshake and High 5, this closing is a nice follow-up.*

RAINSTORM

Set Up:

1. Have the group stand in a fairly tight circle with you in the middle of it.
2. Explain that this closing doesn't involve talking but it does involve making some sounds using our hands and feet. Ask everyone to mimic what you do as soon as you make eye contact with them and continue to do it until you come around to them again.
3. Start with one person and go around the circle eight times doing the following: Circle 1: Rub hands together; Circle 2: Snap fingers; Circle 3: Pat thighs; Circle 4: Pat thighs and stamp feet; Circle 5: Just pat thighs; Circle 6: Snap fingers; Circle 7: Rub hands together; Circle 8: hold both hands palms down indicating quiet.
4. Lastly, step back into the circle and say something like, "My wish for you is that all the storms in your life will pass as quickly."

Note: *Don't mention the name of this closing either verbally or on the agenda sheet.*

TEXAS HUG (AKA [Name of School] CRUNCH)

Set Up:

1. Have the group stand in a circle holding hands or with arms around others' waists. Say that this closing is called a Texas Hug. (Though some call it a Tennessee Squeeze.)
2. Say something like, "In my life, though I've always wanted to move forward, sometimes I have taken steps backwards. If this is true of you perhaps you could take a couple of steps backward to show this." (Do it.)
3. "So far in this workshop, I think we've all been trying to take steps forward. Who knows where we'll get." (Take several steps forward. Others will probably follow.)
4. Hopefully the Hug will make people laugh. Thank them for coming and say that you look forward to seeing them in the next session.

Note: *This is a good fast closing when pressed for time. You may simply say "Take one step back." When this is done, say, "Take two steps forward."*

WORLD BALL

Materials: A "world ball," is a soft cloth globe, or an inflatable one, about 12" - 14" in diameter.

Set Up:

1. Show the world ball and mention that it has the countries of the world on it.
2. Explain that you'll be passing the world ball around. When people get it, they can point to some country that "speaks to them." Perhaps their ancestors came from this country. Perhaps it's a country they've visited or a country they'd like to visit. All will tell why they've chosen the country they have.
3. If there are no questions, begin, modeling the length of time you hope most will take.

YARN WEB

Materials: A good sized, brightly colored ball of yarn (multicolored is even more symbolic)

Set Up:

1. Form a circle. Explain that the group is going to form a web by tossing the yarn from one to another.
2. Just before each person tosses the yarn, they'll complete a sentence, e.g., "Something I want to remember as I leave this room is........" Also, before people toss the ball of yarn, they'll hold onto the yarn so a web will be formed. If there are no questions, begin by modeling both the sentence and the toss.
3. After everyone has received the yarn and spoken, ask that the ball of yarn be tossed back to you. You might ask if this web brings anything to mind (e.g., the idea of community; no man is an island; importance of support).
4. You might wish to raise the web above your heads or "pluck" it to feel interconnectedness.
5. Finally, ask everyone to put the web on the floor and face outwards. As you collect the yarn, probably in a wad, mention that "though we're leaving the web we can all try to bring the spirit of the workshop with us." Also remind everyone that the people they'll be meeting have not had the same experience. "Others may not feel as positive as probably most of us feel just now. Try not to take any negativism personally." End by thanking everyone for coming.

Note: This is often used as a closing for a Basic School Workshop.

DIVIDING INTO GROUPS

When dividing into groups by counting off, you count by the NUMBER of GROUPS you wish to form, not the number of people in each group. For variety, ask participants to choose their favorite season, time of day or one of five colors, or say "Count off by apple, orange, lemon, pear, apple, orange, lemon, pear, apple..." or horse, goat, duck, cow, horse, goat..." or any other crazy group. If necessary to adjust, ask for volunteers to move to a different group to balance the numbers.

People like change. Don't always do things the same way. New ways of dividing up may catch them by surprise. Some variations are:

"**Name That Tune**" [located in Light and Lively section]

"**Barnyard**" [similar to "Name That Tune"]

Written on slips of paper are the names of farm animals, as many of each animal as you want in each group.
Participants draw one slip from container and read it without anyone else seeing.
Invite everyone to stand, make the sound of the animal named on the slip and walk around until they find their groups. Remain standing together.

"**Handshakes**"

Ask participants to think of a number from 1 to 5 (i.e., the number of groups needed). Walk around without talking, shaking hands the number of times that is their own number. The other person shakes back with his/her number. Keep shaking until they find their groups. If groups are uneven and need adjusting, ask volunteers to move.

"**Match Up**" [located in Exercise section]

Good for forming pairs. This can be done more seriously as an exercise or as a Light and Lively.

"**Partners**"

Buy several sets of educational card games that have matching pairs (e.g., "Go Fish"). Distribute to the group and invite everyone to find his/her partner. Good for any paired activity or, if using "Go Fish" or "Old Maid," for groups of four.

"Cards"

Preselect a set from a regular deck of cards. If you want groups larger than four, select cards of the same suit. For example, 6 hearts, 6 clubs and 5 diamonds. Shuffle the cards, pass them out and ask all the hearts to stand together, all the clubs to be in one group, etc. If you want groups with four or fewer, select cards with the same number, for example, 3 fours, 3 fives, 3 sixes, 3 sevens, 3 eights will yield five groups of three.
You can also use red and black; ask for people with either fives and sixes to form a group. You might also have deuces wild. There are countless creative ways to form groups with this method. People also tend to go to their correct group because they have evidence in their hand of where they are supposed to be.

AFFIRMATION POSTERS

Affirmation Posters are great self-esteem boosters. This is true when first received and when read at a later date, perhaps at a time when you're feeling discouraged. They also provide a tangible way for people to remember AVP workshops.

Sometimes facilitators start the posters, putting people's Adjective Name in large letters on sheets of colorful construction paper, one name per sheet. Then people write short affirming messages on everyone else's posters. They also sign them. The message might be as short as one positive word that describes the person whose poster it is or it can be a sentence or two. One or two facilitators might write affirming messages on everyone's sheets as an example.

If you choose to have facilitators start the posters as just described, you might use one or two of the posters as a model. As you are explaining what the posters are for, you could show one or two and read an affirming message on each.

It's also possible to simply provide colorful construction paper and markers and pens and have people write their own Adjective Names on the poster. People may wish to decorate their posters with drawings or even colorful stickers if they're available. In this case, before the posters are introduced, a facilitator or two could start their own poster as a model. You could ask the group what some affirming messages might be.

Different groups use Affirmation Posters differently. Some use them for every workshop. Others only use them in Advanced Workshops. Time might be a deciding factor.

Sometimes the subject of Affirmation Posters is brought up around the 3rd Session of a workshop. Then people will have time during breaks and mealtimes to complete them. It might be necessary to leave a bit of time in Session 6 for the posters to be completed.

Usually the posters are handed out at the end of Session 6. Sometimes this is done at the same time that certificates are given out.

EVALUATIONS

Just as with any AVP workshop it's important to have evaluations in Youth Workshops to see if the workshop is meeting the needs of the participants. Usually a verbal evaluation is done at the end of each session. It works well if one facilitator leads the evaluation and another "scribes" or records the comments.

You might start by explaining that AVP continues to change and grow because of comments made in evaluations. Mention that you're interested in hearing both positive and negative comments that any participant might have regarding any of the activities done. You'd also like to hear any suggestions anyone has that might have made the session better.

Naturally some people may like something that some other people dislike. Point out that that's perfectly fine. It's not wise for facilitators to try to defend an activity or how things went. Just take down the comments, using participants wording if possible. The team can consider the comments at team planning time.

Considering each item on an agenda separately can become tedious. You might quickly review the entire agenda and then ask participants for comments on what speaks to them.

Frequently young people don't evaluate at great length. Usually recording comments directly on the Agenda sheet suffices. Sometimes after comments like "cool" or "that was hard," you may wish to ask a question such as "Can you say why you found it cool?" or "Can you say what you found hard about it?" Probably you won't want to prolong the discussion too long. By the end of a session, almost everyone needs a break.

Try to consider the evaluations when planning subsequent sessions. For instance, someone may say that they wish they could have spoken with the people in their own circle when doing Concentric Circles. You might try to address this remark when forming groups for a later activity. In Creative Construction, which usually involves four groups with four or five people in each group, you might form two of the groups from those in the outer circle and two of the groups from those in the inner circle of Concentric Circles.

At the end of the workshop, it's valuable to have participants complete a written evaluation. Several samples follow. You may wish to use one form for Basic Workshops and a different one for Advanced Workshops. In case you have some participants who are not fond of writing, you may wish to introduce a "smiling face" and a "frowning face" for positive and negative feelings about activities, respectively.

WRITTEN EVALUATION
Suggested for Basic Workshops

Please give us your comments (positive or negative) and any suggestions you have to make things better:

ACTIVITIES (Exercises & L&L's)

DISCUSSIONS

GROUP

FACILITATORS

WRITTEN EVALUATION
Suggested for Basic Workshops

Please give us your comments (positive or negative) and any suggestions you have to make things better:

ACTIVITIES (Exercises and L&L's)

DISCUSSIONS

GROUP

FACILITATORS

WRITTEN EVALUATION
Suggested for Advanced Workshop

Would you help us learn by telling us about your experience in this AVP workshop?

1. Please tell us about something you learned about yourself during this workshop.

   What did you learn in general?

2. What were some of the most valuable aspects of this experience?

3. How do you think anything from AVP will affect your life?

4. What suggestions would you have to improve the workshop?

5. Any additional comments (facilitation [team], exercises, pace, structure, group, arrangements)?

6. For future AVP workshops, what would make it easier to participate (sign up)?

7. Anything else you'd like to say?

CERTIFICATES

Youth programs often lack the usual eighteen hours suggested for community workshops. Because of this, official AVP certificates usually are not distributed at the end of the workshop. In many places, however, facilitators make their own certificates and distribute them at the end of the last session. Some programs also create "Appreciation Certificates" for apprentice youth facilitators who have facilitated at the workshop.

WHAT'S NEXT?

Bringing up the question, "What's next?" also occurs in the last session. Naturally, the answer will depend on the level of the particular workshop in progress. If another workshop is to be offered, it would be wise to have a sign-up sheet available at the time the question is posed. Some programs offer support meetings. Having flyers with "place and time" of such meetings would be helpful. Participants themselves may have their own ideas concerning "what's next," including trying to use the spirit and skills of AVP in their lives.

References References
References References
References References
References References
References References
References References
References References
References References
References References
References References
References References
References References
References References
References References
References References
References References
References References
References References

SECTION J

RESOURCES

Bibliography

AVP, CCRC and HIP

Bibliography

Brown, L. (1999) Raising Their Voices: The Politics of Girls' Anger. Harvard University Press

Carlsson-Paige, N. & Let, D. (1998) Before Push Comes To Shove: Building Conflict Resolution Skills With Children. Redleaf Press.

Crum, T. & Warner, J. (2000) The New Conflict Cookbook: Parent/Teacher Guide for Helping Young People Deal With Anger and *Conflict*. At Works

Garbarino, J. (1999) Lost Boys: Why Our Sons Turn Violent and What We Can Do To Help Them The Free Press

Ciuerra, N. & Slaby, R. & Morre, A. (1995) Viewpoints: A Guide to Conflict Resolution and Decision Making for Adolescents. Research Press

Hersch, P. (1998) A Tribe Apart: A Journey Into the Heart Of American Adolescence Ballantine Books, NY

Kriedler, W. J. (1984) Creative Conflict Resolution: More Than 200 Activities for Keeping Peace in the Classroom. Addison Wesley Co.

Kreidler, W. J. (1997) Conflict Resolution in the Middle School: A Curriculum and Teacher's Guide. Kendall Hunt Publishing Co.

Kreidler, W.J. & Furlong, L. (1996) Adventures in Peacemaking: A Conflict Resolution Activity Guide for School Age Programs. Kendall Hunt Publishing Co.

Kreidler, W.J. & Hale, J.G. (1995) Teaching Conflict Resolution Through Children's Literature. Scholastic, Inc.

Kreidler, W.J. & Whittall, S.T. (1999) Early Childhood Adventures in Peacemaking, 2nd Edition, Educators for Social Responsibility.

Lieber, C.M. (1998) Conflict Resolution in the High School: 36 Lessons. Educators for Social Responsibility.

MacBeth, F. & Fine, N. (1995) Playing With Fire: Creative Conflict Resolution for Young Adults. New Society Publishers.

Porro, B. & Todd, P. (1996) Talk It Out: Conflict Resolution in the Elementary Classroom. Association for Supervision and Curriculum Development.

Pollard, B.K. (2000) We Can Work It Out: Conflict Resolution for Children. Tricycle Press.

Pransky, J. & Carpenos, L. (2000) Healthy Thinking/Feeling/Doing From the Inside Out: A Middle School Curriculum Guide for the Prevention of Violence. Abuse and Other Problem Behaviors. Safer Society Press, Brandon, VT.

Prutzman, P. & CCRC & Stern, L. & Burger, M. & Bodenhamer, 0. (1992) The Friendly Classroom for a Small Planet: A Handbook on Creative Approaches to Living and Problem-Solving for Children. New Society Publishers

AVP, CCRC and HIP

AVP and two related Conflict Resolution Programs for Youth

A Common History:

Children's Creative Response to Conflict (CCRC) was developed in 1972 for a public school system in New York City, by Quakers who drew upon their experience in providing training in nonviolent methods to many civil rights demonstrators and activists in the 1960s.

In 1974, the CCRC workshop was adapted for adults, specifically for use with prison inmates, and the new program was called *Alternatives to Violence Project*, or AVP.

In 1990 AVP facilitators Erik Wissa and Lisa Mundy, who worked for the American Friends Service Committee (AFSC) in Syracuse, NY, adapted the AVP workshops for the Syracuse schools. They called it the *Help Increase the Peace Program* (HIPP or HIP). Similar AVP programs were started in high schools in Buffalo, Walton, Albany, and Rochester, NY. During the 1990s, the HIP, AVP and CCRC programs were started in high schools throughout the US, Canada, and Central America. In Canada the youth program is known as Alternatives to Violence Educational Program for Youth (AVEPY).

AFSC built a HIP Nationwide Network of youth programs in over 26 cities. Many of these programs work cooperatively with local AVP facilitators, for many have found the facilitation skills to be interchangeable. A close look at the three programs, HIP, AVP and CCRC, shows they have so much in common it is not difficult for a person trained in one program to work in the others as well. A facilitator trained in one, might find a single T-for-F workshop to be quite adequate preparation for another.

Things in Common:

The three programs, HIP, AVP and CCRC, all offer experiential workshops designed around the themes of Affirmation, Self Esteem, Cooperation, Group Decision-Making, Communication, Active Listening, Community Building, Conflict Resolution, Bias Awareness, and Trust. Each program offers a series of three workshops of similar duration, which lead to a qualification as an apprentice facilitator. Workshop agendas are similar and draw upon a long list of games and creative exercises. Facilitator techniques are the same – calling for consensus decision making, role-modeling, empowering of participants, processing of exercises by group discussion like a Socratic dialog, periodic evaluation by participants. The HIP program has made an important contribution of a new component on Recognizing and Challenging Injustice.

Some of the terminology is different in the HIP Manual, so we offer these few equivalencies to help CCRC and AVP facilitators understand HIP agendas:

HIP Connection	means	a Gathering exercise
HIP Lift	means	a Light & Lively exercise
Think HIP	means	a Transforming Power discussion

References:

Today, CCRC workshops are offered through thirty regional centers in the US and Central America, under the guidance of Creative Response to Conflict, Inc (CRC, Inc.), Box 271, 521 North Broadway, Nyack, New York 10960. Phone: (914) 353-1796, Fax: (914) 358-4924 e-mail: CCRCNYACK@aol.com. Some AVP facilitators from various cities offer CCRC workshops to help school teachers incorporate the experiential methods into their classrooms, which is particularly effective for the elementary grades.

See The Friendly Classroom for a Small Planet, New Society Publishers (code #046), 1988. See also http://www.wcasd.k12.pa.us/PW/CCRC.html for an example where CCRC trained teachers transformed the culture of an entire system of elementary schools. See www.planet-rockland.org/conflict/.

For more information about the HIP Program, see www.afsc.org and search for HIP. The Help Increase the Peace Program Manual can be ordered from AFSC/MAR, 4806 York Road, Baltimore, MD 21212 (tel: 410-323-7200).

There are ninety local AVP councils in the US, which offer over six hundred workshops per year. A national organization of AVP volunteers, called Alternative to Violence Project, USA, Inc.(AVP/USA) provides support of local councils and sponsors an annual conference for facilitators. See www.avpusa.org, where links to other AVP websites can be found. See www.avpi.org.uk for AVP International information.

Social and Emotional Learning (SEL):

The valuable work of the early CCRC program has been emulated by many others. Research has been undertaken at various universities to evaluate the non-cognitive, or affective, learning style which is so powerful in CCRC, AVP and HIP workshops. Some educators have adopted the acronym SEL (Social and Emotional Learning) as a general term for this kind of experiential learning. For an excellent book for helping school leaders to plan for and justify a new program in conflict resolution, see Promoting Social and Emotional Learning: Guidelines for Educators, 1997, by Maurice Elias, Joseph Zins and others (available from casel.org and amazon.com). One of the experiential programs cited is RCCP (Resolving Conflict Creatively Program www.esrnational.org), which grew out of the CCRC program. The nine authors formed a group called the *Collaborative for the Advancement of Social and Emotional Learning*, or CASEL. See www.casel.org for a rich listing of relevant research papers and books, which may be purchased online, on the topic of SEL. Interested educators may also join a listserv called MCASEL through the casel.org website to stay informed about activities and developments in the SEL field.

Some other similar materials and programs for schools and parents include:

Emotionally Intelligent Parenting, by M. Elias, S. Tobias, B. Friedlander, www.casel.org
Tribes, by Jeanne Gibbs, from Center Source Systems, www.tribes.com
Cooperative Learning, by Dr. Spencer Kangan, www.kaganonline.com
Teaching with Love and Logic, by Jim Fay and David Funk, Love & Logic Press
Creative Conflict Resolution, by William J. Kreidler,
Educators for Social Responsibility, www.esrnational.org

INDEX

Listings in Italics Are Exercises, Light & Livelies or Closings

THE NATURE OF CONFLICT

1. Conflict is natural: neither positive nor negative, it just is.

2. Conflict is just an interference pattern of energies.

3. Nature uses conflict as its primary motivator for change, creating beautiful beaches, canyons, mountains and pearls.

4. It's not whether you have conflict in your life, it's what you do with that conflict that makes a difference.

CONFLICT IS NOT A CONTEST

1. Winning and losing are goals for games, not for conflicts.

2. Learning, growing and cooperating are goals for resolving conflict.

3. Conflict can be seen as a gift of energy, in which neither side loses and a new dance is created.

4. Resolving conflict is rarely about who is right. It is about acknowledgment and appreciation of differences.

5. Conflict begins within. As we unhitch the burden of belief systems and heighten our perceptions, we love more fully and freely.

Source:
The Magic of Conflict
By Thomas Crum